THE UNHEARD SCREAM

The Unheard Scream

Reproductive Health and Women's Lives in India

Edited by
MOHAN RAO

zubaan
An imprint of Kali for Women

The Unheard Scream:
Reproductive Health and Women's Lives in India

published by
Zubaan,
An Associate of Kali for Women,
K-92, First Floor, Hauz Khas Enclave,
New Delhi - 110016
zubaanwbooks@vsnl.net / www.kalibooks.com/zubaan

and

Panos Institute, India
49, First Floor,
Defence Colony Main Market,
New Delhi - 110024
panos@panosindia.org / www.panos.org.np

ISBN 978 81 89884 53 6

Text editors: Mitu Varma, T.V. Padma

Typeset at Print Services, B-17, Lajpat Nagar, Part II,
New Delhi - 110024
Printed at Raj Press, R-3, Inderpuri, New Delhi - 110012

THE PANOS INSTITUTE

THE PANOS INSTITUTE INDIA, is an independent nonprofit organization that works with the media to help stimulate public debate on key development issues so that ordinary women and men, especially the poor and marginalized, can voice their concerns in crucial decision-making processes and make informed choices about their lives.

The Panos Institute, India forms part of the global Panos family and acts as a country office for the Kathmandu-based Panos South Asia (PSA) that was set up in 1997. PSA works in India, Nepal, Pakistan, Bangladesh, Sri Lanka, Bhutan and the Maldives in the areas of Public Health, Environment, Conflict and Peace Building and Media Pluralism. Though programmes have been ongoing in India for several years, a country office was formally set up in Delhi only in 2000 to coordinate the growing number of Indian activities.

The Panos Reproductive Health Media Fellowships – from which the essays included in this book have been drawn – launched in 1997, initially by Panos London's Reproductive Health and Gender programme, were supported by the Ford Foundation. The management of the programme slowly shifted to Panos South Asia and in 2000, the programme received fresh support from the MacArthur Foundation. A key aspect of the programme has been journalist training, provided by Panos chiefly through an advisory panel of regional experts in health, reproductive health and rights, and the media.

Under the programme, 29 Indian journalists were selected after a rigorous application, screening and interview procedure, to investigate neglected, controversial or poorly understood reproductive health and gender issues and trace linkages with other crucial development concerns such as environmental degradation, poverty, social justice, gender inequalities and women's rights. Their findings have been published as lead stories, news features and editorials in English and Indian language newspapers all over India. Each Fellow produced five short 1000-word reports and a long 5000-word report on his/her chosen topic. A selection of the best of the long essays has been put together here, as a collaborative publication by Panos Institute, India and Zubaan. The overall editorial and management coordination of the Panos Reproductive Health Media Fellowships project has been the responsibility of the Panos India country director Mitu Varma, and project coordinator and editor, T.V.Padma.

ACKNOWLEDGEMENTS

THIS BOOK would not have been possible without the unstinting support and guidance of the Advisory Panel who took time off from their busy schedules to guide the Fellows in framing their project proposals, suggesting officials and Non-governmental Organization (NGO) activists to meet, areas to visit and advising on the final outputs, whether in the form of short pieces, or long essays. The panel includes Dr Imrana Qadeer and Dr Mohan Rao from the Centre for Social Medicine and Community Health, Jawaharlal Nehru University in New Delhi, Ms Kalpana Sharma, deputy editor of *The Hindu*, Mumbai, Ms Urvashi Butalia, founder, Zubaan Books and co-founder, Kali for Women, New Delhi, Dr Padma Prakash, associate editor, *Economic and Political Weekly*, Mumbai and Ms Bishaka Datta, founder-director, Point of View, Mumbai.

We are also grateful to Dr Vimala Ramachandran, then Associate Professor, Indian Institute of Health Management Research, Jaipur, who was a member of the Advisory Panel for the first two cycles of the fellowship programme and provided valuable guidance.

A special word of thanks to Ms Martha Radlett, ex-director of the Panos London Reproductive Health and Gender Programme, who initiated the programme, supervised it in its initial stages and was actively involved in the first two cycles. Thanks are also due to her colleague, Judith Mirsky for her support.

We also wish to acknowledge the support of Ms Geeta Mishra, who was with the Ford Foundation during the first two cycles of the programme as well as Ms Poonam Muttreja and Ms Deepa Nag Chowdhury from the MacArthur Foundation.

We are especially grateful to the individuals and NGOs who shared their experiences and views with the Panos Fellows and provided valuable insights. It is not possible to list them all here, but we are grateful for their contribution in making the narratives rich and multi-layered.

Panos Institute, India

Contents

Cairo and After
Flip Flops on Population Policy

Mohan Rao

Introduction

The last two decades of the twentieth century resonated with intense debates about reproductive health and rights, and indeed wrongs. These debates embraced women's rights activists, public health workers, policy makers, donors and academics. One stream of argument sees all reference to reproductive rights—which it resolutely fights—as undermining the family and the community, and is associated with the position of the Vatican, some Islamic countries and, more importantly, the Protestant fundamentalists increasingly setting the agenda in the USA. Another stream, at the opposite end of the ideological spectrum, argues that reproductive rights may perhaps represent population control by other means, and that issues of reproduction must necessarily be linked with wider socioeconomic concerns. Between the two are a range of institutions at the international level that have brought the agenda of reproductive rights centre stage, not least among them the World Bank and the Population Council. Placing reproductive rights squarely on the world agenda was the International Conference on Population and Development (ICPD) held at Cairo in 1994.

There was a coming together of seemingly opposed groups in crafting the "Cairo consensus". On the one hand there was the population control establishment, composed of a wide array of actors ranging from the World Bank and the Population Council to a number of NGOs, nation states, health personnel and academics (Bandarage 1997).[1] This extremely influential group apparently realized that the demographic goal of reducing fertility could not be attained without taking into account women's ability to make decisions regarding reproduction and fertility. In other words, even for purely instrumental reasons, there had to be a change in approach to the population issue. On the other hand were the women's rights activists, feminist academics and some health activists. Many of them undoubtedly brought to the fore First World feminist concerns—in particular the right to abortion, increasingly threatened since the religious Right came to influence policy under the Reagan and the two Bush presidencies. Others had indeed campaigned against coercive population control programmes and policies in the Third World. They were united in opposition to fundamentalist groups from the USA and from conservative Islamic countries and the Vatican (Petchesky and Judd 1998).[2] It is important however to remember, as Ravindran points out, that demands for reproductive rights and health did not originate in Cairo, and were not an idea formulated by the population control agencies or other international agencies that supported them (Ravindran 1998).[3] Nevertheless it is as the Cairo consensus that they cast their influential shadow.

The Cairo consensus has been described as a landmark accord, a turning point in the history of the population field, a sea change in the way population and reproductive health are conceptualized (Haberland and Measham 2002).[4] More fre-

---

[1]Bandarage, A (1997), *Women, Population and Global Crisis: A Political Economic Analysis*, London, Zed Books.

[2]Petchesky, Rosalind P. and Karen Judd (1998), "Introduction" in Petchesky R.P. and K. Judd, (Eds), *Negotiating Reproductive Rights: Women's Perspectives Across Countries and Cultures*, London, Zed Books.

[3]Ravindran, Sundari (1998), "Reclaiming the Reproductive Rights Agenda: A Feminist Perspective", in Mohan Rao (Ed), *The Place of Reproductive Health in India's Primary Health Care*, New Delhi, CSMCH.

[4] Haberland, Nicole and Diana, Measham (Eds) (2002), *Responding to Cairo: Case Studies of Changing Practice in Reproductive Health and Family Planning*, New York, Population Council.

quently it has been described as a paradigm shift in the way population and development are understood. Indeed it has been described as revolutionary (Cornwall and Welbourn 2002).[5]

The Cairo consensus was a significant, if somewhat modest, step forward. It meant a break from the past in various ways. It signalled a move away from demographically driven population policies that "attribute poverty and environmental degradation to women's high fertility, and, in turn, women's high fertility to an absence of information and methods" (Petchesky, R 1998: 2).[6] It also challenged the "moral arsenal" of Christian, Hindu or Islamic fundamentalists to curtail the rights of women in the name of tradition or culture, often fraudulent and concocted. It meant, further, a redefining of the population field that had neglected sexuality and gender roles, focusing instead largely on outcomes such as contraceptive efficacy or declines in birth rates, or, more recently, reproductive infections (Dixon-Mueller 1993).[7] Above all, it provided a fillip—and sanction from international covenant—to health and women's groups fighting coercive population programmes (while fighting for women's rights) in a number of countries. It was now possible for these groups to argue that these programmes violated international covenants that their governments were signatory to.

But was the Cairo consensus merely a "semantic revolution" (Correa 2000: 7)?[8] Was feminist rhetoric being used by international population agencies to legitimize and gloss over

---

[5]Cornwall, Andrea and A. Welbourn (2002), "Introduction" in Cornwall A. and A. Welbourn (Eds), *Realizing Rights: Transforming Approaches to Sexual and Reproductive Well-Being*, London, Zed Books.

[6]Petchesky, Rosalind P. (1998), "Introduction" in Petchesky, R.P. and K. Judd, (Eds), *op cit.*

[7]Dixon-Mueller, R. (1993), "The Sexuality Connection in Reproductive Health", *Studies in Family Planning*, Vol.24, No.5.

[8]Correa, Sonia (2000), *Weighing Up Cairo: Evidence from Women in the South*, DAWN, Fiji.

narrow instrumentalist concerns (Correa and Petchesky 1994)?[9] Was it merely a "Western" concept, lent credence by the undoubted economic and political power of the West—and therefore to be rejected? For as Hartmann, for instance, notes, the "new consensus" is nothing but a new strategy to obscure class, gender and race inequalities in a grand consensus in which everyone's interests are simultaneously apparently served. "Women, population and the environment have become formally linked, a holy trinity in the consensus cosmology" (Hartmann 1993: 1).[10]

There was, of course, no original sin committed at Cairo when liberal feminists, predominantly from the West, went into alliance with the neo-Malthusian population control establishment. Indeed it was precisely this relationship that had spawned the global population control movement in the nineteen fifties. However, during the intervening years, there had been a critical distancing. The fact that a section of feminists, referred to by Hodgson and Watkins as reproductive health feminists, were now willing to be fellow travellers with the World Bank, along with the population control establishment, was entirely new (Hodgson and Watkins 1997).[11] Was this a marriage of multinational-feminisms with international debt? It has been argued by other feminists that there can be no such thing as a "feminist population policy", that the Cairo consensus merely replaced population control with "population stabilization", that it paid little attention to neo-liberal macro-economic forces profoundly shaping the health of women worldwide, and par-

---

[9]Correa, Sonia and Rosalind, Petchesky (1994), "Reproductive and Sexual Rights: A Feminist Perspective" in Sen, G, A, Germain, and L.C. Chen, *Population Policies Reconsidered op cit.*

[10]Hartmann, Betsy (1993), "Old Maps and New Terrain: The Politics of Women, Population and Environment in the 1990s", Paper presented at the International Conference "Reinforcing Reproductive Rights", Women's Global Network for Reproductive Rights, 23rd February, Chennai.

[11]Hodgson, Dennis and Susan, Cots Watkins(1997), "Feminists and Neo-Malthusians: Past and Present Alliances", *Population and Development Review*, Vol. 23 (3).

ticularly in the developing countries and, finally, that the price paid for the consensus was too high (WGNRR, forthcoming).[12]

Critics also argued that in the agenda of rights of the ICPD, reproductive choice refers to the plethora of contraceptive devices that a "free" woman is supposed to be "empowered" to choose from. In other words, what is being attempted is to create a "rational", utility-maximizing consumer in the contraceptive market place, produced by the reproductive technology industry of the West. It has been noted that, in the era of reproductive technologies, the concept of choice is reduced to consumption that fosters a private enterprise in women's bodies (Raymond 1996)). [13] Was this, then, what all the storm and thunder of reproductive rights was about? Making contraceptives more acceptable? For of course there was a new generation of contraceptives—injectables, implants and so on, waiting for the cornucopia of the markets of Third World women's bodies.

Thus, as feminist discourse was co-opted by development jargon, did reproductive rights become divested of rights to food, employment, water, health care and the security of children's lives?

It is therefore not surprising that expressions of disquiet, dismay and indeed anger were soon forthcoming. In response to the Indian government's country paper at the Fourth World Conference of Women at Beijing in 1995, seven all-India women's organizations prepared an alternative document where the ICPD came in for stringent, devastating, criticism.

> The slogan of sisterhood needs to be placed in the contemporary international situation when the so-called developed First

[12]Women's Global Network for Reproductive Rights, "The ICPD and After", Amsterdam (forthcoming).

[13]Raymond, J.G (1996), "Connecting Reproductive and Sexual Liberalism" in Bell, D. and R. Klein, (Eds), *Radically Speaking: Feminism Reclaimed*, London, Zed Books, cited in Rupsa Mallik (1999), "Pre-Natal Victimization of the Female Life World", unpublished MA Dissertation, Institute of Social Studies, The Hague.

> World, led by the USA, wants to impose its agenda on the rest of the world in the name of globalization...the direct impact was seen in the recent Conference at Cairo...where the agendas of the G-7 group were pushed through and issues concerning Third World women were left unaddressed. For instance in Cairo the issue of abortion dominated the proceedings. The representatives of millions of Third World women in Cairo hoped, while supporting the struggles of Western women for their right to abortion, at least some attention would be paid to their experience. Instead they did not get the support of women representing the First World.
>
> We strongly believe that where the inequality of nations is increasing, where the development of the First World is in direct proportion to the underdevelopment and exploitation of the Third World, the slogan of sisterhood would mean to protect the interests of poor women in the Third World and to strengthen the global struggle against new forms of colonialism (*Towards Beijing: Crucial Issues of Concern*: 1995:36)[14].

Arguing that issues of development of poor countries in the new global order received short shrift at the ICPD, it was also said that the ICPD did not take adequate note of processes that governed health in Third World countries, which, in the current global scenario, were working fundamentally against the interests of the people of the Third World in general and women and children in particular. The alternative document notes that: "women's health should not be subordinated to population goals nor restricted to reproductive matters" (*Towards Beijing: Crucial Issues of Concern*: 1995:33).[15]

At the ICPD itself, the government of Eritrea, recovering from a bloody civil war, but nevertheless full of the painful hope that marks newly emergent countries—and which had in fact characterized the position of a number of Third World countries in the heady days of the sixties recalling their anti-imperialist past—issued a statement that was astonishing in

---

[14]"Towards Beijing: Crucial Issues of Concern"(1995), reprinted in *Lokayan Bulletin*, Vol.12, Nos.1-2, 1995.
[15]*Ibid.*

scope. This statement revealed a vision that is rare for neo-colonial times, throwing the gauntlet back at the West and indeed those rallying for reproductive rights. It was not arguing that reproductive rights were not important goals, nor was it arguing that these goals were neither desirable, nor unattainable. Nevertheless its position was that given existing conditions, there were prior claims to justice, to equity, and to rights that obtained moral and political precedence. It thus warrants quoting at some length.

> In the case of Africa in particular, it is debatable whether reduced population growth will mitigate its marginalization in the world economic order and accelerate its development. Africa enjoys, on the whole, considerable comparative advantages in terms of territorial expanse and natural endowments. Its population density—even taking into account current rates of fertility—is and will remain low in relative terms for the foreseeable future. The appalling poverty and deprivation that stalk the continent are not certainly due to overpopulation and they will not be eradicated if family planning were to be introduced through attractive palliatives and public education programmes. The scourge of ethnic conflicts, massive internal and external population displacement and widespread deprivation will not be healed by the most prudent and comprehensive demographic policy.
>
> In the event, what is required is a much bolder and holistic approach that addresses and tackles the real causes of underdevelopment. Existing imbalances in the terms of international trade must be adjusted to promote rapid and sustainable development in the countries that are lagging behind and in which the economic gap is widening...Furthermore, it is a matter of historical reality that population stabilization is likely to be achieved as a byproduct of, rather than an antecedent to, overall development. The various programmes associated with family planning, and especially the social safety nets for the elderly, public education programmes for adolescents, empowerment of women, etc., cannot be implemented on a sustainable basis from external funding. Internal development would be essential and indeed a prerequisite for an undertaking of this scale. In brief, the answer does not lie in a compartmentalized and piecemeal approach but in a comprehensive and innovative approach to the crucial issue

of development in the Third World. (Government of Eritrea: 1994 cited in Hartmann 1995:152)[16]

But these cries of course fell on deaf ears, for over this period, the rallying cry of Health For All (HFA) through Primary Health Care (PHC), the slogan that took all countries of the world to the Alma Ata declaration in 1978, was given a quiet burial. Did the ICPD contribute to this demise?

The Alma Ata declaration of HFA had a complex heritage. It was partly related to the failures of health development and of technology determined programmes that had characterized it. It was also related to the distribution of power globally, as post-colonial nations made their claim to a place in the sun. Above all, it marked *Zeitgeist*: the defeat of the US in the Vietnam war and the entry of China into the WHO both portended some new and exciting possibilities in health sector development.

PHC promised something revolutionary for health in Third World countries as the goal of HFA, it was evident, could only be achieved through overall and equitable development. There were other singular features of the Alma Ata declaration. For the first time, at the global level, a policy was envisaged that saw health as an outcome not just of interventions in the health sector, but more a matter of the socio-economic development that it would synergistically bring about. Second, that the issue of health sector intervention could not be compartmentalized; in other words, that the whole was greater than the sum of its parts. Hitherto piecemeal approaches had therefore failed to pay dividends—all too often simply because they were neither universal nor comprehensive. Third, that technical intervention without overall development had its limits; further that technology itself must emanate from local and national resources and be tied to the overall patterns of diseases and deaths. These priorities had to be determined nationally, and health sector development must therefore be a function of these epidemiological priorities and technical choices. Finally, that

[16]Hartmann, Betsy (1995), *op cit*.

these were not unattainable goals, indeed their attainability was less a function of resources than of political will. In other words, the Alma Ata Declaration drew attention to the need to address the underlying social, economic and political causes of ill-health and diseases (Werner and Sanders 1997).[17] Indeed, there was such a sense of hope and optimism accompanying those rallying for "Health For All" that there was talk of a new international economic order to arrest the continuing drain on resources from developing countries.

But it was also this period that saw a substantial shift in global power, as what was to echo across borders was not '*liberté, egalité* and *fraternité*', but privatization, liberalization and globalization. What defeated the hope and optimism of PHC was the onset of the "decade of despair"(UNICEF 1989:2).[18] It was marked by the rise of right-wing monetarist regimes in the USA and the UK, along with the domination of the mantras of what Hobsbawm describes as "ultra-liberal economic theologians", whereby "the ideological zeal of the old champions of individualism was now reinforced by the apparent failure of conventional economic policies" (Hobsbawm 1994: 409).[19] As the Keynesian world came increasingly under attack, that of actually existing socialism turned upside down. The collapse of the Berlin wall and the Soviet empire both provided more than a metaphorical setting for a new phase of global capitalism, a phase that saw the shrinking of spaces that had opened up with the post-Second World War welfarist state—to labour, to Third World countries and the marginalized in general.

The World Bank was now increasingly setting the agenda for health. World Bank lending in the health sector is thus larger than the entire budget of the WHO. Within the health sector, and especially following the publication of the influential 1993

[17]Werner, David and David Sanders (1997), *Questioning the Solutions: The Politics of Primary Health Care and Child Survival*, , California, Healthwrights.
[18]UNICEF (1989), *The State of the World's Children, 1989*, OUP, New York.
[19]Hobsbawm, E.J. (1994), *Age of Extremes*, Delhi,Viking.

Report *Investing in Health* (World Bank 1993),[20] the Bank's policies on health sector reforms have meant redefining public spending in health to an essential package of clinical services, and phasing out public subsidies especially for tertiary care. The bank also urges governments to foster competition and diversity in supply of health services. One hallmark of these reforms has been the concept of a fee for public services. Critics have argued that these policies have essentially been a clarion call for privatization and a more "cost-effective" version of selective PHC. In the process, public health is dismembered, diseases are divorced from their socio-economic contexts, and the concentration on specific technology dependent programmes sounds the death knell to concepts of PHC (Qadeer 1999).[21] In other words, as the prospects for HFA receded, we saw again the dominance of the magic bullet approach to public health, accompanying what Renaud resonantly described as eliminating society from disease, whereby disease occurrence is ascribed to individual proclivities and failures (Renaud:1975).[22] As we witness increasing privatization of health care, along with cuts in State spending on health, we see the reversal to technologically-driven vertical programmes. While a holistic vision of public health has been eclipsed, the chicken of technological determinism and methodological individualism has come home to roost with a vengeance. Thus while ICPD did not kill PHC, it singularly failed in not bringing it back on the agenda and, instead, helped bring to the fore an approach to health which was diametrically opposite.

Implementing this approach assumes that macro-economic policies that have eroded the previous gains in health some-

[20]World Bank (1993), *World Development Report 1993: Investing in Health*, Washington D.C., World Bank

[21]Qadeer, Imrana (1999), "The World Development Report 1993: The Brave New World of Primary Health Care" in Mohan Rao (ed), *Disinvesting in Health: The World Bank's Prescriptions for Health*, New Delhi, Sage.

[22]Renaud, M. (1975), "On the Structural Constraints to State Intervention in Health", *International Journal of Health Services*, Vol.5, No.4.

how cease to matter. In other words, what was now, again, brought centre stage was an increasingly biological notion of the determinants of ill health and disease in populations, turning public health on its head. Given the overwhelming influence of the Bank on health and population policies of borrowing countries, it is not surprising that when the Bank made a "paradigm shift" to reproductive health, borrowing countries were quick to follow. Thus while the onslaught of the Right provided the impetus for feminists in the West to highlight the critical importance of reproductive rights at the ICPD, it was also brought to prominence by the concerns of the population control lobby and the World Bank to infuse a new lease of life into faltering family planning programmes.

That macro-economic policies pursued uniformly across the globe at the instance of international financial institutions have been deleterious to health in general, and women's health in particular, is indisputable. But what is so striking, and surprising, is that the commitment to the RCH approach has made little difference. While the experience of Latin America and Africa is well known, that of China and Russia is particularly apposite, since they reveal a more significant retrogression in the health of women than would have been anticipated. The example provided by China is striking: reforms in China have meant an annual real increase in GNP by 9 per cent, quadrupling the size of the economy in merely 20 years.[23] Yet this has been accompanied by increasing income and health inequalities between and within regions and rural-urban areas, and between the sexes. In 1994, the prosperous coastal province of Zhejiang, for instance, had a Maternal Mortality Rate of 23.74 per 100,000 live births while the poorer inland province of Quinhai had a figure of 215.37. Infant Mortality Rates stagnated, and in some rural areas, increased. Data on the growth of Chi-

[23]Yuanli Liu,Keqin Rao, Timothy Evans, Yude Chen, and William C.Hsiao (2001), "China: Increasing Health Gaps in a Transitional Economy" in Timothy Evans et al (Eds), *Challenging Inequalities in Health: From Ethics to Action*, New York, Oxford University Press.

nese children also indicate increasing disparities in height between rural and urban areas. Despite the Chinese government's commitment to gender equity, the reforms have led to an increase in gender differentials in child survival along with increases in morbidity rates among females. The economic changes, along with the "one child per family" norm (now *officially* abandoned), have accentuated the problem of "missing girls". Poignantly, as in our country, medical expenditure is emerging as a leading cause of the impoverishment of families as the health system collapses, again particularly affecting women and girls.

With the collapse of the Soviet Union, the world turned upside down for the common people of Russia.[24] Levels of unemployment and poverty rose sharply with a two-fold drop in real income and a staggering increase in income inequalities, even as the social security system and health system, perhaps already ailing, died under the shock treatment prescribed by the World Bank and the IMF. Between 1991 and 1994, life expectancy among men decreased by close to seven years, from 63.6 to 57.5 years; among women it declined by close to three years from 74.4 to 71.1 years. Such a decline in life expectations in populations not at war or suffering the onslaught of the other horse of the apocalypse, famine, is historically unprecedented. Unlike China, where rural areas bore the brunt of the reforms, in Russia, the cities largely paid the price. At the same time, infectious and communicable diseases including the innocuous childhood disease, measles, that had disappeared, rode on poverty and hunger, extracting a toll. Tuberculosis and AIDS assumed epidemic proportions. A multivariate analysis revealed that labour force turnover explained a large part of the increase in death rates. Of the proximate causes, injuries and violence accounted for a third of the overall decline in life expectation while cardiovascular diseases

[24]Vladimir M.Shkolnikov, Mark G.Field, and Evgueniy M. Andreev (2001), "Russia: Socioeconomic Dimensions of the Gender Gap in Mortality" in Timothy Evans et al. (Eds), *ibid.*

accounted for a further quarter. The third largest category was alcohol-related, accounting for approximately 15 per cent of the decline. An interesting finding from Russia is that while the gender gap in mortality is considerable in all demographic and socio-economic groups, it is consistently smaller for men and women in higher socio-economic positions. In all populations, socio-economic disadvantage increases gender gaps in mortality. This is to say, issues of poverty, of class, took precedence over gender. Significantly, the Russian government, concerned with its declining population, has sharply curtailed access to abortions, making them much more difficult to obtain. At the same time, in another pro-natal move, the legal age at marriage for females has been reduced.[25]

The situation in India remains ambiguous, indeed deeply troubling. While officially the National Population Policy has partially reflected the shift in thinking at Cairo, at the grassroots however, the more things change, the more they remain the same. One important reason is that structural adjustment policies have further reduced India's commitment to primary health care. While health sector spending has shown a secular decline—about the only thing secular in these dark days—that for family planning has proportionately increased. Even while the Centre was committed to the Cairo Declaration and committed itself to a non-target oriented programme, several state governments announced population policies of their own, some at the behest of an American consultancy firm, Futures Group, whose function in the past has been to create fears of a "population explosion". These state population policies are deeply violative of the commitments made at Cairo, and include a plethora of incentives and disincentives, and a "two-child norm' eligibility to contest Panchayati Raj elections.

The irony, of course, is that PRIs (Panchayati Raj Institutions) are seen as a vehicle of democratization and a space for

[25]To an unbelievable 14 years—with permission from the local agencies, and to 16 years without.

the Dalits, the adivasis and women to find a political voice. Indeed a third of seats are to be reserved for women precisely to help empower them politically. But one hand of population policy takes away what the other hand of women's empowerment gives.

Health and women's groups approached the National Human Rights Commission (NHRC) last year with a memorandum that the two-child norm was discriminatory, anti-democratic and violative of commitments made by the Government of India in several international covenants. The state population policies were, the memorandum said, profoundly anti-women, anti-dalit, anti-adivasi and indeed anti-children (Rao 2002).[26] The NHRC, in response, issued orders to the concerned state governments, and a Declaration was issued at a National Colloquium in January 2003, which was attended by representatives of these state governments.

The NHRC declaration, "notes with concern that population policies framed by some State Governments reflect in certain respects a coercive approach through use of incentives and disincentives, which in some cases are violative of human rights. This is not consistent with the spirit of the National Population Policy. The violation of human rights affects, in particular the marginalized and vulnerable sections of society, including women"(NHRC 2003:1).[27] The declaration also noted: "further that the propagation of a two-child norm and coercion or manipulation of individual fertility decisions through the use of incentives and disincentives violate the principle of voluntary informed choice and the human rights of the people, particularly the rights of the child" (Ibid).

Yet, on the 30th of July 2003, the Supreme Court of India upheld the Haryana government law mandating the two-child norm for contestants to panchayat elections. Interestingly, while the Supreme Court spoke about the "torrential increase of

---

[26]Rao, Mohan (2002), "Population Policies: From Bad to Worse", *Economic and Political Weekly*, Vol.XXXVII, No.22, June.

[27]National Human Rights Commision (2003), *Declaration*: National Colloquium on Population Policies, New Delhi.

population", earlier the Rajasthan High Court judges, hearing a similar set of petitions, argued: "These provisions have been enacted by the legislature to *control the menace of population explosion...*. The government is spending large sums of money propagating family planning. One of the agencies to which the project of family planning has been entrusted for implementation is the gram panchayat. The panches and sarpanches are to set the example and maintain the norm of two children. Otherwise what examples can they set before the public?" (Sarkar and Ramanathan 2002:42)[28] Not surprisingly, this ruling has met with widespread middle class support in the country, for one area where the media has been truly successful is in communicating that the cause of all social problems in our country is related to "overpopulation".

But this is, of course, a red-herring. Despite population growth (which is declining substantially in almost all parts of the world), per capita food production increased by nearly 25 per cent between 1990 and 1997. The per capita daily supply of calories rose from less than 2,500 to 2,750 and that of proteins, from 71 to 76 grams. In other words, not one person in the world needs to go to sleep hungry. Yet given the fact that the overall consumption of the richest fifth of the world's population is 160 times that of the poorest fifth, 840 million people, 160 million of them children, are undernourished. Close to 340 million women are not expected to survive to age 40.

The over-population argument also elides the fact that there occurs a net transfer of close to 80 billion dollars annually from the countries of the South to those of the North. Indeed this figure has increased substantially over the last three decades. During this period, when a number of countries have implemented structural adjustment programmes, inequalities within and between countries have risen sharply: the income gap between the world's richest and poorest has more than doubled. In 1960, 20 per cent of the world's people in the richest

[28]Sarkar, Lotika and Usha Ramanathan (2002), "Collateral Concerns", *Seminar*, 511.

countries had 30 times the income of the poorest 20 per cent; today they command 74 times more. The same richest 20 per cent of the population command 86 per cent of the world GDP while the poorest 20 per cent have merely 1 per cent. More than 80 countries have per capita incomes lower than they were a decade or more ago.

Despite their obvious importance and gravity, these issues find little reflection in the media today. It could be argued that this has always been the case, that issues of common people, of hunger and deprivation, have never found a place in the media sun. While this is true enough, it is also important that we note a major change that has taken place in the media in the last ten or fifteen years. With the onset of liberalization, Indian newspapers have undergone a remarkable transformation. It has become increasingly difficult to find good, in-depth coverage of development issues as they affect the lives of ordinary people. Instead, what we have is endless froth, food, fashions and "life style" stories as newspapers garishly and insensitively, reflect the tastes and aspirations of the upper classes alone. Not only does this mean that readers are deprived of understanding the real issues, but also that whatever little space there was for such issues is now further reduced, or has altogether disappeared. As a result, young journalists not only do not have the opportunity to develop the skills that are required to cover development issues but they are in danger of losing what skills they have. The media response to this is to say that this is what people want, although no media person I know would agree with me that we get the media we deserve just as much as we get the politicians we deserve.

The new "life style" type of writing is mainly superficial, and made up of "bytes"—small, short catchy phrases that are meant to sound good, but that usually do not carry much meaning. This kind of writing also imposes its own pressures on young journalists who are, unfortunately, starved for time, and are not encouraged to read and reflect. Since they are often required to deal with the "here and now", their editors do not encourage them to be analytical, or to cultivate a sense of history. These are apparently subjects reserved for another level of the newspaper hierarchy.

The media's coverage of health issues provides a telling example. Much of the time health is equated with medicine—expensive medicine at that—or we have people on the AIDS or population control circuit repeating what they heard at the latest international conference supported by the drug industry or the population control lobby. Recently, we have had a newspaper, day after day, borrowing columns from a foreign newspaper on the genetic determination of diseases, and even of behaviours. This may perhaps be merely absurd in the First World context, but is utterly distasteful in the Indian, or any Third World context. It nevertheless serves a very useful function: to blame the victims of hunger and deprivation for the diseases and deaths that haunt their lives. Newspapers would be aghast if it was suggested that just anyone could write about economic affairs or defence, but not only do they make no investment in training journalists to write on major issues such as health or population, they do not even feel the need to do so. Thus the perspectives of common people are missing from any coverage of these issues, as indeed they are from coverage of other important issues.

Not only is it becoming increasingly difficult for young journalists to write with any depth on key issues, but most media organizations are no longer willing to invest in providing training or other opportunities for journalists to learn. Instead, a number of independent organizations, some related to the media and others not, have come forward in the last few years, and it is through these that young and middle level journalists have mostly been able to take out time to explore issues in depth. This is not always the best arrangement, for often employers are not willing to give employees time off for issues they do not consider important, or indeed to make space to publish the results of their research.

Panos South Asia, originally a part of the British charity, The Panos Institute, and now an autonomous South Asian organization, has for long been involved with work in and on the media. Among the organization's many activities have been the provision of information on issues of ecology, environment, HIV-AIDS, sustainable development, gender, to media organizations and media persons in countries of the North and the South. Awarding fellowships to journalists to do intensive work on particular issues is also a key activity. The Panos Reproductive Health Media Fellowships, which form the base of this book, have been in existence for some three years now and each year, a number of journalists have been able to focus on issues related to reproductive health, and to publish the results of their research in their newspapers or magazines. Apart from the articles they write, the Panos fellows are also required to write a longish essay on a subject of their choice within the broad frame of their fellowship, and a selection of these essays appears in this book.

During the 1990s, a number of influential academics, primarily of the Diasporic, neo-Orientalist variety, spoke of the peculiar culture of silence among Indian women. And yet, as Rupa Chinai shows in her essay on the north-east of India, the problem is not that women are silent, but that there is no one to listen. "Even if we shout," a north-eastern woman told Chinai, "there is no one to listen." Her essay, and indeed several others, demonstrate how women's health issues go far beyond the reproductive health paradigm, and are located in their living and working conditions.

In the name of reproductive choice, we have had the quinacrine sterilization scandal, tracked here by Rajashri Dasgupta, and the assisted reproduction rip-off, covered by Sandhya Srinivasan. While we hear of the boom in garment exports we know little of what this means to women working in export processing zones, and more specifically what effect this backbreaking work has on their health, an issue probed here by T.K. Rajalakshmi. And while AIDS occupies the headlines, at the expense of all other health issues in India, we have little understanding of how policies related to AIDS have impacted on sex workers. Both Geetanjali Gangoli and Vasant Bhosale turn their attention to this.

India's weak and under-funded public health system has virtually collapsed under the impact of structural adjustment policies. The irony, of course, is that even the RCH programme cannot be implemented under such circumstances. As a "grass widow" in Dhirendra Jha's essay remarks, "We get polio drops but no treatment for diarrhoea." Although officially there are no targets in the family planning programme now, Sreelatha Menon discovers that, under a USAID-funded programme in U.P.—barely a few hours from Delhi—doctors have not only never heard of Cairo and its resolutions, but are under so much pressure to meet targets that they use bicycle pumps to insufflate women's abdomens in order to carry out laparoscopic sterilizations! And this in appalling, unhygenic, camp conditions. This story, which Menon found difficult to place in her own newspaper, gave rise to a question in Parliament. Uttar Pradesh is not alone in this: Annu Anand's work in Madhya Pradesh and Uttaranchal uncovers similar collapsing health structures and the same obsession with targets.

Alongside the growth in consumerism—reflected in the new patterns of anti-female biases—the last decade has also seen a rise in violence on women, not only within the home but also outside. Identity politics, and its ally, the politics of communalism, have at times particularly targeted minority women—as Gujarat in 2001 so painfully showed—and this lethal mixture has resulted in pushing women back into their homes. K.P.S. Basheer tracks the phenomenon of the increasing curbs on the freedom of young Muslim women and declining age of marriage among them in Malapuram district in Kerala, an area flush with funds from the Gulf.

But what does the focus on reproductive health include ? Beholden to a medical technology industry, we continue to witness its negative side in the masculinization of births and in the phenomenon of sex-selective abortions. Does this represent reproductive choice, as is sometimes argued ? Manisha Bhalla, the youngest of the Panos Fellows, explores the issue of sex selective abortions in Punjab, where new practices are often upheld in the name of tradition. In a related essay, though with a different emphasis, Lyla Bavadam looks at how the medical establishment is "mid-wifing" a spurious concern with menopause, as an unwitting handmaiden to the medical technology industry. Even the focus on adolescent health, as Swati Bhattacharya discovers, has more to do with a concern for AIDS and less with sexuality and power, as these can threaten to undermine traditional family structures.

The Panos Reproductive Health Media Fellowships were a modest attempt to give young journalists the space to develop their skills, do in-depth research on the issue of their choice, and to get stories such as the ones above back into the media. Those awarded the fellowships were required to defend their proposals in interviews with the selection committee, and were then required to go through a brief orientation workshop. At the workshops, passionate and intense discussions on issues of gender, health, population and the media, were followed by detailed discussions of project proposals. The work done by one group of fellows was presented to the next, as well as to senior people within the media, for their feedback, both positive and negative. Each journalist was required to place at least five stories from his/her work in the newspapers they worked with, or wrote for if they were freelancers.

The project was exciting not only for its content, but also because it had the enthusiastic and warm support of the participants, and also of the Panos team (George Joseph, T.V.Padma and Mitu Varma) and of its Advisory Panel (Urvashi Butalia, Bishakha Datta, Padma Prakash, Imrana Qadeer, Kalpana Sharma and Mohan Rao). While the workshops were edifying, they were also fun. Panos cannot be held responsible that no damagingly serious affairs of the heart followed this project, but (merely !) wonderful friendships.

State-of-the-Art Cycle Pumps

SREELATHA MENON

It was a lazy Sunday morning in November 2001. All was quiet in Usayini, a small village amidst golden yellow mustard fields in Ferozabad district in India's most populous state, Uttar Pradesh. The day after, the health centre in the village was to hold its fortnightly health camp.

That camp, and countless others held before it—and no doubt many to be held after it—across Uttar Pradesh, tell a story of all that is going wrong in India's efforts to implement the Reproductive and Child Health (RCH) programme initiated in 1997.

Take the two districts of Ferozabad and Mainpuri in Uttar Pradesh. In the nine blocks of Ferozabad district the RCH programme is being implemented by a USAID-funded project called SIFPSA (State Interventions in Family Planning Services). USAID and India signed an agreement in September 1992, under which USAID was to provide US$ 325 million to reorient and revitalize family planning services in Uttar Pradesh. The objective was to bring down the Total Fertility Rate (TFR) from 5.4 to 4 at the end of the 10-year project, to increase the Couple Protection Rate (CPR) through use of contraceptives from 35 per cent to 50 per cent, to increase the percentage of births receiving ante-natal care from 30 to 40, and to increase the percentage of deliveries assisted by a doctor or nurse/midwife from 17 to 30.

There is no SIFPSA aid for the RCH programme in Mainpuri. Does it make a difference to the lives of the women in the two districts? Here are their stories.

Not a soul in Usayini village in Ferozabad district seemed to be aware of the SIFPSA camp, though its main objective is apparently to make health care accessible to women and children under the government's Reproductive and Child Health Care Programme. The village situated in Usayini block has the "privilege" of having SIFPSA camps at its doorstep every fortnight. But ironically, the villagers are blissfully unaware of the "privilege" they enjoy. Or of the fact that the camp is meant to provide a range of health services for women and children.

The reason becomes clear soon enough.

The camp has nothing to do with health services and its only agenda is to offer sterilizations. And for this, each Auxiliary Nurse Midwife (ANM) attached to the centre has been asked to get three cases per camp. Or lose her pay or even her job. That is the threat from above and the threat has been carried out in Usayini. Further, since none of them actually lives in Usayini, the ANMs did not feel the need to tell women of the village about the camp unless of course they knew of a possible "case" there.

An RCH Camp in Usayini

On Monday, the camp is late in starting. Even at noon there is hardly anyone at the centre. Dr M L Mishra sits in the sun and orders junior workers to spread a carpet outside for patients.

The first patient finally arrives at around 1 p.m. This is Guddi from Dariyar village. She comes accompanied by "her" ANM, Radha. Guddi is a 27-year-old mother of six children. Her face half covered by her sari, she says she has come for sterilization.

Soon the second patient arrives. She is Gayatri, a 26-year-old mother of four, from Kadkauli village. She is accompanied by "her" ANM, Geeta. She has also come for sterilization. In all 18 patients arrive, and all of them come for the same purpose, each brought there by an ANM. The RCH camp turns out to be a full-fledged sterilization camp.

These women are referred to as "cases" by the ANMs who bring them. It is a bad day for the Centre and for the 28 ANMs attached to it. Each ANM is expected to get at least three cases per camp. If not three, at least one. But to come empty handed to the SIFPSA camp is to attract the combined wrath of both the centre-in-charge and SIFPSA district-in-charge, and to risk a possible cut in salary or even the loss of a job.

ANMs who have not managed to bring in a case cower as Mishra showers abuses on them. "Why don't you come just to collect your salaries?" he asks sarcastically. His tirade goes on for some time, while the ANMs remain painfully mute. Mishra defends the stern measures against ANMs. There are orders from above asking every ANM to get three cases per camp. It is not too much to ask. Even one case is acceptable, he says. Till September these six ANMs brought just one case. So if their salaries were stopped they deserved it.

Soon a van arrives from the district hospital with a gynaecological surgeon, a woman gynaecologist, a paediatrician and an anaesthetist. The SIFPSA district-in-charge C K Mishra is also there. He, too, does not spare the ANMs for being "inefficient" and getting only 18 cases. The "cases" have had an average of five to six children besides having had an unknown number of abortions. But none of them has ever seen a doctor during pregnancy or been immunized. They are not aware of iron or vitamin pills either.

The 28 ANMs at the Usayini centre are a tense lot. All of them admit that they are obsessed with getting a case for the next camp. "That is all we think of day and night," they say. They also admit that they do not press women to go for other birth control options like Copper T or the pill. "If we promote Copper T, how would we get enough women for sterilizations?" asks Radha.

"The village women hate us. When we advise them to get sterilized they think that we have vested interests in promoting sterilization," say the ANMs. From the anxious ANMs to the stern SIFPSA district chief, the Target Free Approach (TFA) explicitly stated in the government's policy on family planning means nothing.

From the beginning, India's population policy has been guided by demographic goals, with the main objective being a reduction in the rate of population growth. There was an excessive focus on sterilizations as a means to curb the population growth rate. Coercion was always part of the family planning programme, with the use of incentives and harsh measures or disincentives. During the Emergency period, 1975–77, coercion reached new heights, with poor people, mostly men, rounded up for sterilizations. In 1976–77, sterilization figures reached an all-time high of 8.26 million according to official records, 1,774 people died due to family planning measures alone. But the "excesses" also brought the government down, bringing in their wake a shift from vasectomies to female sterilizations and targets for the number of women sterilized.

Since 1997, India has been implementing a Reproductive and Child Health (RCH) programme that has shifted the focus from achieving demographic targets to a Target Free Approach (TFA) and addressing client needs. But surveys by health Non Government Organizations (NGOs) such as Health Watch as early as 1997 indicated that service providers of the RCH programme, such as ANMs and Primary Health Centre (PHC) doctors, who have been trained for four decades to work for targets, cannot make a quick transition to a different approach without proper training. The major obstacle to training, according to Saroj Pachauri, former director of the Population Council, is the mindset that has, over decades, built all arguments to promote demographic goals for dealing with human issues. Therefore the RCH programme too has ended up targeting women in the reproductive age group and those who have not adopted family planning methods. It thus completely ignores the fact that reproductive health cannot be achieved in the absence of total health care.

The Failures

That sterilization is the primary agenda in the minds of RCH camp organizers is evident throughout. Take the case of Vimla who comes from a far-off village with her month-old infant for a laparoscopic surgery. She is given a local anaesthetic. When the surgeon discovers that she had a Caesarian delivery and hence cannot be sterilized through laparoscopy, he asks the attendant to take her to the adjoining room. She remains semi-conscious till evening along with other sterilized women. The ANMs take turns to look after her baby.

Her ANM Rajabeti is worried and frustrated. She says she is jinxed as this is her second "failure" this month. In the last camp she brought a case who was given local anaesthesia. The surgeon even cut her abdomen only to discover that he could not find the fallopian tube. The abdomen was stitched up again and she stayed at the centre for the whole day, and then went home, cursing the ANM. Rajabeti is in tears and she says that with such a history of "failures" it will become more difficult for her to persuade women to undergo sterilization.

Another ANM, Susheela Chauhan, had a similar experience in the last camp. The tube could not be located and the doctor had to sew up the abdomen without performing sterilization. The workers at the Centre are yet to forgive the SIFPSA official and the centre-in-charge for denying the women antibiotics after the failed surgeries.

A worker at the Centre shows a file with Mishra's signature scored off underneath the entries of the two women whose operations failed last fortnight. "Will anyone ever know what happened to them? The doctor has scored off his signature to cancel the entries. They were even refused antibiotics by Mishra saying that medicines were only for cases and not non-cases," the worker recalls bitterly. "But the wounds are the same, aren't they?" they ask.

All the women barring two, Guddi and Geeta, are from the Jatav community, a socially and economically disadvantaged caste. Women from other castes rarely come forward for these long trips say the ANMs. But all of them, without exception, were married at an early age (between 14 to 16 years) and have at least five living children. Gayatri from Kadkauli village, for instance, is a mother of four and has already had two abortions. She attributes her willingness to attend the camp for sterilization to her husband's support. Vimla who returned, a failed case, has six children and has had no abortions. She too has the support of her husband's family.

All the women are wives of small farmers who own about four to five bighas of land and are not well off. The district is synonymous with glass making and holds a monopoly in the manufacture of glass bangles for women. Bangle making, and its related activities like polishing and joining, provide home-based work for women in the towns. While women in villages have no share in this industry, glass factories in the town are an employment option for their men. However in rural areas the women are engaged in other work in addition to housework and childcare, as well as in working in the fields which grow wheat, mustard and potatoes. They also assist in dairy farming.

Women's Self-Help Groups under the Central Government scheme of Swarna Jayanti Swarojgar Yojna are sprouting in many villages, generating a new energy and confidence. Though they are still at a very nascent stage, and struggling to survive, these groups have the potential to become platforms for raising awareness about literacy and women's health rights. The district's literacy rate stands at 46.30 per cent, and the female literacy rate at 29.85 per cent. The literacy rate in rural areas is 42.13 per cent with the rural female literacy rate lower still at 23.13 per cent.

But as of now, these women rarely go to doctors for their medical needs. All their children were born at home and abortions, when needed, were conducted by traditional birth attendants or *dais* using crude methods. The sterilization service offered by the Primary Health Centre (PHC) with an ANM calling for them at their doorstep, has definitely been a motivation. But almost all the women say that services like immunization and pre-natal care are never provided to them and no ANM has ever approached them for that.

Take the case of Mumtaz, 30 years old, from Lalpur village. She is a Muslim woman, who, like many of the women mentioned earlier, really has no access to health care. While the private sector is out of bounds due to the cost, government hospitals and PHCs are hostile. Mumtaz has nine children living and has had about four abortions. She is a walking corpse.

Mumtaz the Non-case

Mumtaz is the only patient who attends the November 26 camp for reasons other than sterilization. She found her way to the camp thanks to the advice of ANM Chauhan. Mumtaz has been suffering from severe stomach cramps ever since she had a miscarriage a month ago. She never went to a doctor to get herself examined. "Since there is a gynaecologist at the camp I asked her to come along," Chauhan says.

But it is a futile mission. No one examines her and the ANM does not have the courage to demand an examination for her. A male physician merely prescribes some antibiotics and anti-fungal medicines without an examination. The gynaecologist is never referred to as she is busy operating on the "cases".

Chauhan advises Mumtaz to go to the district hospital but Mumtaz says she has no money to go anywhere now. "They charge six rupees," she says, having already shelled out that much to come to Usayini. Her husband is an alcoholic and does not earn anything. "All the money that I get is earned by two of my children," she says. The eldest is a daughter who is 14 years old, and the next is a son who is 10. "They join bangles for the factories and earn about Rs 50 every day," she says. Two more of Mumtaz's children, five and three years old, are yet to start walking. "I am helpless. Who do I tell this to?" she says in a low voice, a resigned look on her pain-scarred face.

Mumtaz says the ANM had advised her to go for sterilization several times but she could not agree, though for a strange reason. "One has to abstain after the operation. That is not possible for me," she says, meaning it is her husband who dictates the terms. Although Mumtaz does not want more children, there is nothing the PHC system can offer her, other than sterilization. This, her husband will not allow. Caught between the dictates of her husband and the priorities of the health care system, she bears children she doesn't want.

State-of-the-Art Cycle Pumps

A "case" is given an injection of local anaesthesia. A ward boy then brings a cycle pump with a wire fixed to it close to the laparoscope. The nozzle is fixed to the laparoscope and the ward boy pumps in air into the woman's abdomen. This is done to inflate the interiors for better visibility through the laparoscope. The nozzle is then removed and the surgeon operates on the woman. In minutes the task is done and the semi-conscious woman, wearing an underskirt and blouse, is carried by the attendant to the adjoining room. She is placed alongside other unconscious women, all lying on mattresses on the floor. Their respective ANMs cover them with red blankets. Later in the evening the ANMs collect Rs 25 for each case. They take the women in a van belonging to the Centre to their homes. The use of cycle pumps for insufflation is flagrantly against the safety norms of the health ministry. Dr Anjali Gule, a gynaecological surgeon with the district hospital, however, says they have to make do with what is available.

The other alternative available is the hand-held pump which also pumps in air, not carbon dioxide which is the prescribed gas. The hand-held pump is too tiring especially if you have 30 cases, says Gule.

So who does the pumping of the cycle pumps?

"The ward boy," says another surgeon, confirming the general prevalence of the practice witnessed in camps in Usayini, Tundla and Kotla blocks.

The use of cycle pumps is forbidden as it can kill women, says the head of the gynaecology department at the All India Institute of Medical Sciences, New Delhi. Hand-held insufflators should be used and the gas should be carbon dioxide as it dissolves in blood, unlike oxygen, she says.

The surgeons of Ferozabad recount a case where the patient collapsed and they struggled to revive her. "*Sar pe kafan bandh ke chalte hai,"* (they step out carrying their shrouds with them) say the doctors, fully aware of the danger to the women. Doctors also say patients are never given sedation even when necessary as they do not have emergency equipment like oxygen cylinders and respirators.

Bimla's Story

A month later on a chilly morning of December 29, Bimla who has been to the camp in Usayini arrives at the district hospital. Bimla is from Kailash Nagar, not far from the town of Ferozabad. She too is accompanied by Chauhan. Chauhan is attached to the Usayini centre and had taken Bimla to a camp there in October. She was sterilized by Gule but; a month later, found herself pregnant. So Chauhan has brought her to the district hospital, this time for a Medical Termination of Pregnancy (MTP) combined with sterilization.

But this failed operation is the least of Bimla's worries. What she is yet to recover from are the side-effects of the earlier operation. As she recounts her experience her eyes fill with tears.

As soon as she regained consciousness she felt as if her body was bloated with air. *"Jab hosh aya to dono taraf gubbare jaise phool gaya. Saans nahi le pa rahe the."* (When I came to, I found both my sides swollen like a balloon. I could not breathe.) She and her husband together earn about Rs 60 a day joining bangles, so her labour is essential for her family's survival. "I was in deep pain after the operation. I thought I would die. If I have survived, it is because of the ANM," (Chauhan) she says.

"I have four little children and I was helpless," she recalls. The ANM took her to a doctor and then stayed with her for two nights giving her medicines on time. "I finally felt better only after 20 days," she says. Unlike the other village-bound women, she has more access to the private clinics in town. But she says they are expensive and she would visit them only in an emergency. She says her sister-in-law was admitted to a hospital when she started bleeding after an abortion done at home. Bimla has never had immunization and has had two abortions at home. These were carried out by the local Traditional Birth Attendant (TBA). For Bimla, abortion was a birth control option.

The story of Pooran Devi, a dai in village Usayini, is quite similar. Her body became bloated after the operation. "I also felt giddy all the time," she says. The doctors told her she would get better with good food. But she says she is still having gastric problems and she has taken it upon herself to dissuade women from getting sterilized.

Target-Free Makes No Sense

Aradhana Johri, the then director of the SIFPSA project, defended targeted sterilizations. Andhra Pradesh, she said, had half the population of Uttar Pradesh and more than double the number of sterilizations per year. Hence SIFPSA was justified in striving for a three case per ANM target for every RCH camp.

This is also the reason for her to dismiss the country's commitment to a target-free approach to birth control and to giving people a choice of birth control measures. In this country, zero target is zero work, according to Johri. She further defended her case saying that SIFPSA wanted to promote sterilizations just as other NGOs were promoting other forms of birth control.

Johri's views are, however, diametrically opposite to the commitment the Government of India made at Cairo and in the National Population Policy. The International Conference on Population and Development held in Cairo in 1994 had endorsed a target-free approach to birth control, an approach which respected women's rights to make reproductive decisions free from pressure or coercion. The UN conference in which 180 countries, including India, took part, recommended a strategy that focused on meeting the needs of individual men and women rather than having demographic targets. Endorsing this, the NPP was also committed to a target-free approach, emphasizing first meeting the unmet needs for health and family planning.

Cycle pumps used for laparoscopies, Johri said, was a technical matter she was not aware of. She then blamed the government for not pointing out the need for insufflators prescribed under the norms of the health ministry. She equated targets with accountability. Three cases per ANM per camp was not such a big target, she said. One in four women needs sterilization. And if there are 30,000 women in the child-bearing age group in a block, 7,000 need a laparoscopy and are unable to access it. Nor are the ANMs overburdened, according to Johri. "There are 20 ANMs in every block and each has 375 women under her. Is it such a big task to find three of them for every camp?" she asked. Responding to complaints that ANMs were unable to offer spacing methods for fear of losing "cases" she said these were lies. "The ANM is a bloody lazy female who doesn't go to her area," was her opinion. If tetanus shots and immunizations for children were neglected, she said it was because of inefficient government machinery.

While SIFPSA denies overburdening the health system with targets, Johri admitted that few doctors were available for basic health services. There is only one surgeon in Chitrakoot, while Itawa and Auraiyya share a surgeon. The camps are being conducted despite this, she argued.

A USAID spokesman for the SIFPSA project, in New Delhi, Randy Kolstad, denies that a targeted approach is being pursued. He says he is constantly talking to SIFPSA on these issues and denies that such coercive methods are being used. "UP is larger than many countries," is Kolstad's weak explanation when asked why his department was not aware of these violations of human rights.

The Story of Kanti

Sterilization apart, no other service is available for the hapless women or their babies, contrary to the official RCH policy. Kanti from village Rampur is 19 and is pregnant for the third time. She has already had two deliveries. Both children died soon after they were born, first a boy who died a month after birth and then, a girl, who survived just five days. Her 22-year-old husband, Joginder, says they took the child to a doctor in a private clinic soon after birth and spent around Rs 10,000. But the child could not be saved. "We still do not know why the children died," he says.

Kanti is two months pregnant again, barely five months after her second baby. She has pain in her stomach, feels nauseous and sick all the time. And for the first time in three pregnancies, the couple decided to see a doctor. They arrive on a bicycle at the PHC in Usayini. It is deserted but for the clerical staff inside and the doctor-in-charge, M L Mishra, chewing paan masala and sunning himself outside. He is apparently on leave. The couple goes in, talks to the pharmacist and leaves quietly. They are not even taken to the doctor. They have been asked to come on Saturday when the ANM is present.

When the story is narrated to the doctor, Mishra grudgingly calls Joginder and talks to him. He asks them to see the lady doctor at the district hospital. He expresses shock that Kanti has never received tetanus injections but feels relieved when he learns that they are from the village of Ramnagar: it does not come under his area, the Usayini PHC.

"No ANM ever came to our house," says Kanti. She does not want such frequent childbirths. "It is my mother-in-law who insists that we have children. When the first one died she wanted another one", she says. "I am helpless", she adds, her face still that of a child. Joginder says it is a serious matter for them. If she does not have children, people will start talking. "They may even say that I am now trying my luck elsewhere," he says. They leave with this correspondent for the Tundla

PHC to see the lady doctor. Joginder is not very enthusiastic saying that doctors do not see patients in government centres.

The PHC is empty. Neither of the two medical officers is there. While the male doctor has gone to Agra for training, the lady doctor's on leave for four days. The ANM there is asked who sees patients on such days. "The pharmacist," she replies nonchalantly.

The ANM feels Kanti's belly over. She says Kanti may be having trouble because of her blood group. She suggests that she should visit again when the lady doctor comes back or, better still, go to the district hospital. Ramnagar, she says, does not come under Tundla PHC. It comes under Narkhi PHC and there is a sub-centre in Ramnagar.

Joginder offers to come along to Narkhi after taking Kanti home. Dr Sanjeev Gupta, the doctor-in-charge, is not present. He left at 1 p.m., the pharmacist says. He has no idea where the ANM looking after Ramnagar could be.

Close to Ramnagar are villages Shiv Shersinghpur, Narkhi and Nirbhayi Gadhi. They are far off from the main road and hidden from one another by long stretches of mustard fields. The ANM has to cover these four villages as well as four others on her own, walking through the fields which, the villagers say, are not safe.

The Story of Sharda

Kanti's story provides only one example of conditions on the ground—women just do not receive attention when they most need it despite the health programmes of the state and central governments. While 97 per cent of women in villages give birth at home, only 33 per cent are receiving any sort of medical check up despite the high rate of infant mortality.

In Uttar Pradesh the infant mortality rate is a whopping 86.7 per 1000 live births and the under-five mortality rate is 122.5 per thousand live births according to the second National Family Health Survey released in November 2000. This is the highest in the country, with the rural areas having figures worse than these state averages. The national averages, which are bad enough, are 67.6 and 94.9 respectively.

The story of Sharda from village Gadhi Nirbhayi, close to Ramnagar, is similar to Kanti's. She is another mother of dead babies. Another mother who never saw a doctor during pregnancy, never took tetanus injections, or received any counselling on nutrition. Sharda is 16 years old and has already had two babies. Both have died. Now she is under pressure to have a third. She says the babies died of jaundice, though no one took her to a doctor when she was pregnant and no one gave her tetanus shots either. But she hardly speaks as she is surrounded by her husband's relatives who make fun of her. *"Pagli hai. Yeh baat nahi karti hai."* ("She is mad. She does not talk.") Later when taken to an isolated part of the house, she is in tears. "I have no choice. There is pressure on me to have another child immediately. My mother-in-law wants it. Otherwise they will continue to make fun of me," she says.

The Arithmetic of an RCH Camp

So, is all the USAID money being used only for sterilizations? On paper at least, $225 out of the total of $325 are to be spent in Uttar Pradesh for specific activities and $100 on equipment, services and training for the project.

The wall leading to every PHC carries the SIFPSA budget for an RCH camp in bold letters.

While a single camp costs Rs 10,000 to the exchequer, the contribution of SIFPSA is Rs 3,700. Of this amount, while the Chief Medical Officer receives Rs 2,350 for "medicines and bandages" for each camp, Rs 1,350 is given to the PHC. The latter is meant for items like client cards, tents, dhurries, tea and conveyance. A day at a camp in the Eka Primary Health Centre was revealing. There was no evidence of money spent in the ways mentioned on the wall.

Seven hundred and fifty rupees are earmarked for client cards. But with just six women attending the camp on February 25, 2003, where did the money go?

Doctors admit that it is an excuse to use funds. While Rs 300 is allocated for a tent and a dhurrie, Eka had a tent with a gaping hole and edges that refuse to be tied down. No Centre bothered to rent a tent and dhurrie for a weekly event. Two hundred and fifty rupees is meant for tea but nobody was served tea.

Again, an amount of Rs 500 is set aside for conveyance for beneficiaries. But the women are simply abandoned after the camp. The Centre did not have a vehicle to take them home.

The ANMs were given Rs 25 per case and asked to take the women home. There was no record of how the Rs 300 kept aside for 'other expenses' was spent.

The PHC has about 50 staff members. In addition a team of three doctors from the district hospital is engaged for a day. A day's salary for all of them plus the expense on fuel to ferry doctors, SIFPSA officials, and district health officials to each camp takes the bill beyond Rs 10,000.

Six Cases, 50 Staff and Sterilization at 50

Six women are operated at a camp in Eka block in Ferozabad on February 25, 2003. The camp uses the service of three doctors (who are required to drive all the way from the sparsely-staffed district hospital), as well as the duty hours of 50 staff members of the Centre.

The cost is Rs 10,000 and this does not include the day's wages for the work.

The beneficiaries include Rama Devi, estimated to be 50 years old, but who claims to be 36. She has six children, and has had seven abortions. She can't be rejected as she claims to be 36, says the doctor who operates on her. Another "case" Malti, has had three abortions, all done by a local dai. She has five children. Three more women have histories of two to three abortions each.

Eka centre offers no MTP. Muneesh Kumari, an ANM, says the women go to local dais who use the *batti* or a medicinal stick that is inserted into the cervix to induce an abortion. The nearest facility for MTP is in Eta, 20 kilometres away.

"What good is it?" asks Dr AB, a surgeon at the district hospital, talking about the project. AB is bitter and has no hope of the government health services ever improving with projects like SIFPSA. It is all about some people making money out of health projects. Call it SIFPSA or RCH or any other name, he says. "It is an eyewash. These projects help neither the doctors who carry out the operations nor the women who are targeted for welfare," say the surgeons in the district who travel up and down every day to perform these operations.

The anger at SIFPSA is widespread among doctors who are carrying out the programme. The SIFPSA chief in Ferozabad pays a house rent of Rs 15,000 a month and earns nearly Rs 100,000. Does she do a single operation? they ask bitterly. The medical officer who does the actual work earns a mere Rs 25,000 after 24 years of service.

Coupled with the unending thankless work, are poor working conditions. The doctors' residential quarters tell a story of neglect. Located amidst a cesspool of drain water, the houses have not received a coat of paint in ten years. "Where does all the government money go?" ask doctors.

After SIFPSA and RCH, the hospital has an additional building for sterilizations and abortions, another one for eye surgeries as well as instruments worth lakhs, all of which lie unused. These are just excuses to spend funds, say doctors. There is only one gynaecological surgeon in the hospital on any given day. There are three buildings and he or she is expected to be available to all three to perform different functions. It is a farce in the name of women's health, they add.

The fungus-ridden walls of the Eka centre, the bad floors, the use of cycle pumps. . . doctors say these are proof of the futility of such projects. Spend the money to upgrade rural centres, spend more on consumables, pay the doctors, provide them accessibility to towns and the story of the village and women's health would be different. These are the things to do, the doctors add.

Deserted PHCs, Punishment Postings

For doctors and ANMs the PHC at Eka block in Ferozabad is a punishment posting. Eka is the remotest part of the district and the villages are totally inaccessible by road. Unlike other villages, tempos from the town don't ply to Eka for fear of being robbed. And the villagers are too poor to organize vehicles. Of the 30 ANMs posted at the Eka centre, except for a couple who belong to the area, all others are new transfers from other districts. There is even one from Delhi who has joined recently. Doctors point this out and say that no ANM goes there willingly. It is the unsuspecting new postings or transfers from other districts and punishment transfers who land up in Eka. The ANM who came from Delhi is already pulling strings to get out.

On February 25, 2003, the PHC is deserted though an RCH camp is to be held on that day. Eka may have a staff strength of 50, but only six ANMs turn up. Medical officer Virendra Bharti comes at about noon, much after the surgery team from the district hospital has arrived. And he leaves before they do.

"But can Bharti be blamed?" asks a doctor in the team. Considering that whenever he stays at the house attached to the Centre, he has to lock himself in for fear of being attacked. Doctors are on the hit list of local gangs here, he says. In a place this poor, Rs 25,000 is a great deal of money, more than enough incentive for crime. There is a canal nearby where abductors leave chained victims. An ANM was murdered last year in a village and another was kidnapped and raped. She left thereafter, says Bharti. Other ANMs confirm this. Bharti keeps his family, his wife and a child, in the safety of a house in town. The child has to go to school and the doctor posted in the village has no vehicle to get to the town 30 kilometres away. Every rural posting is a punishment as far as doctors are concerned. For, there is no incentive to make them work there: the work they do is not challenging, they are unappreciated and their conditions of work are abysmal.

The same day, February 25, 2003, the Centre at another block, Kotla, wears a deserted look. There is no camp and not one among its staff of 80 members can be seen. Doctors defend the absentee staff. "How do children of doctors posted in Eka and Kotla go to school?" ask the doctors from the district hospital. Look at the school gates in the town, they say. All other government officials, the police and the administration, have vehicles waiting to pick up children and to drop them home. Do you see any health department vehicle? Why should doctors not be at par with other officials, they ask.

It is said that doctors are being denied promotions all over Uttar Pradesh. Dr Virendra Bharti of Eka for instance has had no promotion in ten years. But he has used his rural postings to make his way into post-graduate studies. "I will be quitting now and doing my MS. After that it is private practice for me," says the doctor who was once a Resident in Delhi's government-run Safdarjung Hospital. Older doctors are not so lucky. They have spent 25 years in the service, are gynaecologists and moving towards retirement, and are doing surgeries for SIFPSA without any monetary benefits.

Dr AB is a Medical Officer with 25 years of service. He joined as MO and continues to be one. He has just seven years left for retirement. AB has worked in many rural centres before he finally bribed his way to a town posting. As for the doctors in rural centres, he says, they pay *powwa* or a bribe to higher officials and stay away from work unless an emergency like a camp requires them to come in. "No one questions us as we have paid the charges," he and his colleagues say. "There is no enthusiasm to work as we get the same deal whether we work or whether we don't work," says AB.

The work is unending in the district hospital where AB works with two other surgeons. "We are like camels, going where we are led. We do as little as possible on our own," AB says in bitterness. In the last one year not a single caesarian operation was performed in the hospital. "We send away all surgery cases. It is not possible to do anything here," he says.

Dr Meena, the ANM

Doctors have no incentives to work. So ANMs are replacing them.

The house of ANM Meena Roy (name changed) bears a board, which announces, in gold letters: Dr Meena Roy. Inside, a patient in labour can be heard, crying out in pain.

Roy, an ANM with Usayini PHC, is known as *docterni* (a "lady" doctor) in the neighbourhood. The patient has been there overnight. She was in labour and had come after a fluid discharge. Roy says she has told the woman that the delivery is a bit risky. "I have told them that I cannot guarantee the baby's safety," she says.

The top floor is always used for deliveries and abortions. It's not clear how much the "doctor" charges but she is the one-stop solution for all gynaecological problems in the area. The next day onwards the entire week is devoted to the polio campaign. Roy goes from house to house giving polio drops. She gets a few requests for abortions. Some women shyly ask for an abortion pill. Shanti, 28, a mother of six, is two months pregnant. She wants a pill too. Roy asks her to come to her house for an MTP. She turns down all such requests for pills and advises them to come for an abortion. She says she will charge Rs 350. Some women take her aside and ask for contraceptives. Roy sternly tells them: Only operations. No other way.

Roy meets at least a dozen women who have delivered just a week ago. Not in a single case does she suggest that they should come for immunizations. No women in the village have received tetanus injections either. Roy explains, "If they come to the Sub-Centre where I sit twice a week, I will offer them vaccines. There is no question of offering anything at their doorstep. Except polio drops."

Susheela Chauhan, the ANM from Usayini PHC, takes her job seriously. Around 45, she is a widow and has a daughter and a son. Behind her success is her cousin who stays and works with her. In fact, she helps him get assignments in the field during campaigns such as the polio drive, which enable him to make some money too. Otherwise he takes her to various villages where she is known as a *docterni* for offering services like abortion for a fee. But she is helpful even where there is no money involved as in Mumtaz's case. "I offer help to anyone who approaches me," she says.

Mainpuri – A non-SIFPSA district

In the adjoining district of Mainpuri SIFPSA has not stepped in yet and sterilization camps are conducted only at the district hospital. However, there are moves to upgrade the PHCs with funds from the World Bank to incorporate services like MTP and sterilization. But for the present the women in the villages are left to the mercy of nature and the traditional dais. But ANMs with no pressure to collect cases for camps are active in providing immunization services to women and children. Compared to Ferozabad, Mainpuri district has a literacy rate of 50.2 with rural areas slightly less at 47.87 per cent. Rural women have just 29.52 per cent literacy but this is still higher than Ferozabad.

The widespread receptiveness to immunization in the villages could be attributed to the higher literacy rates. Rural men have 62 per cent literacy while the corresponding figure for Ferozabad is 57 per cent. Agriculture, mainly of wheat, paddy, potatoes and mustard is the main occupation other than some dairy farming. The absence of land reforms and increasing desertification have left the villagers, mainly the socially and economically disadvantaged Dalits, reeling under poverty. The politics of caste has also led to inequities in the matter of receiving benefits meant for Below Poverty Line families. While there is a ray of hope in the growing number of women self-help groups, poverty and lack of access to health services have ensured that women remain where they always were.

Kiratpur: Mainpuri's Good Village with a Bad Scar

Kiratpur is barely 10 kilometres from Mainpuri town. To get there one has to depend on an improvised tractor, called *jugad gadi* (make-do vehicle). It rocks you vigorously as it moves slowly up the bad road. Buses are infrequent. Yet people prefer to go to the district hospital rather than the PHC. But most women have received tetanus injections during their pregnancy and children have been inoculated. The women know the two days the ANM visits the local sub centre every week. Dominated by the Jatav community, Kiratpur has been included in the Ambedkar Gav Yojna of the state government thanks to the efforts of its former Jatav *pradhan* (headman). The village has been the focus of activities for housing schemes of the Central Government and there are scores of Indira Awas Yojna houses with latrines in the village. The people are fairly well-to-do as excess land of about 650 bighas has been distributed. Each farmer has a minimum of one acre or three bighas of land in Kiratpur. Most girls go to school. But here the going gets rough. Education for almost all the girls stops at class eight as the secondary school is in town. Girls get married at 14 years. Abortions are rampant, some merely to end pregnancies and many to get rid of female foetuses.

Aneesa, 25, of Kiratpur died a month ago in January 2003. She had six children. She had a five-month old baby aborted after an ultrasound test revealed she was carrying a female. The bleeding didn't stop and she died. Her dai, Tara Devi, says she died of malaria. Almost every woman one talks to has a history of abortions, many of which are sex-selective. Vimla has three sons. She has had three abortions—all females babies. The abortions were done after ultrasound tests. Other villagers and her dai confirm this but Vimla herself is not willing to speak about it.

Abortion is the routine method adopted by women here to limit the number of children. Another woman, also called Vimla, has five children. She says she had an abortion recently because she did not want another child.

Manju Devi has four children and she had an abortion done a year ago. The dai did it. Now she is using a herbal mixture to stop birth. It has worked for a year. "I am hoping it lasts," she says. Contraceptives are not popular among the villagers and they also complain of non-availability. "We either go for the herbal contraceptive which is also hard to find or go for abortions which are the easiest option," say women in the Jatav village. Sex selective abortions are not exclusive to the Scheduled Castes. They are even more rampant among upper castes, particularly the Thakurs and the Brahmins.

In neighbouring Jhanjhai village, a predominantly Thakur-dominated village, sex selective abortions are common. Madhu, an ANM who works in Barnhal block but stays in Jhanjhai, reports that two women died in the village recently after they underwent abortions. While they were sex selective, they were done by crude methods. There was a woman who died after aborting a four-month old foetus. She bled to death in a private hospital, says Madhu.

The *Safai Ki Batti*

Whether they are sex selective abortions or otherwise, the method used is uniform and life threatening all over Mainpuri. The women invariably approach a dai whose job is confined to introducing a "herbal tent" or batti into the cervix. This is supposed to lead to contractions and expulsion of the foetus. The dai is not around when the baby is expelled and she does not take responsibility for sepsis either. The batti is used every where, whether it is village Kiratpur and Jhanjhai in Mainpuri block or in villages in Barnhal and Karhel blocks. It is there in the neighbouring districts of Ferozabad and Itawa as well, doctors say. In fact, a dai in Mainpuri said she had patients coming for the batti from neighbouring districts like Eta.

"It is very painful," says Vimla of Kiratpur who has had a batti for abortions twice. The abortion in the hospital is painless some of her friends have told her. Vimla says she decided to use the batti as it was cheaper to go to the dai. She may charge as little as Rs 100 or Rs 150. But go to the town for an MTP and you pay at least Rs 500, she says. Dai Tara Devi gives addresses of some of the shops where the batti can be bought. The most famous one is Raghuvar *ki dukan*. These shops are known to all dais in Mainpuri, Tara Devi adds.

This shop and several others in Mainpuri's main market sell boxes containing ten sticks each. A box costs Rs 50 and one of the shops agreed to part with a single stick for Rs 5. The packets of "female tangle tents" are either from an unnamed company in Kanpur or from Bhan Chemicals, Bareilly. The label merely says "female tangle tents." Two to three packets get sold every month, says Raghuvar's son. The other shops also give the same number.

Dr Arun Kumar Chauhan, a qualified Ayurvedic physician who practises in the market area close to the district hospital, says he just discovered that a pregnant girl he had referred to hospital has died. "She had come bleeding as a dai had inserted a batti in her", says Chauhan. "I sent her to the hospital. Later I enquired about her and found that she had died." She was 15-years-old and unmarried.

In many cases women develop infections. Often the dais insert battis even when the woman is not pregnant. She may have stopped menstruating, and the dai mistaking this for pregnancy inserts the stick. A mere pregnancy test would help in such cases, he says. But the dais don't bother to do all that. A batti, according to him, induces menstrual bleeding. He also says dais use it even in advanced stage pregnancies and this leads to complications.

Dr Ashok Gupta is a gynaecologist in Ferozabad district hospital but belongs to Barnhal block in Mainpuri. Gupta says the story of abortions is the same in both districts. Women go to dais and the herbal stick is used everywhere. He says the problem is not so much with the herbal stick as with the way it is used by ignorant dais. It is uncovered and exposed and hence unhygienic. Dr Gupta also wondered if the stick was in fact less unsafe than the hundreds of abortions performed illegally in the area by other unqualified persons. The only solution is to remove the stigma from abortions and make them available in health centres, he says. But abortions in health centres, are mostly linked to sterilization.

Poverty + Illiteracy = Population-Development

The stories of rural women in these two districts are pointers to the struggle of women in Uttar Pradesh to survive despite poverty—thanks to zero land reforms, early marriage (47 per cent) and endless childbirths (crude birth rate of 5 as compared to the national rate of 3.5 and 1.8 in Kerala). Coupled with these are government interventions which take the shape of targeted sterilizations in one district and absolute lack of any holistic health care in both places.

The poverty and lack of development in the rural areas is evident not only in the widespread use of safai ki battis in both districts but in the fact that only 21.89 per cent of households in the entire state have electricity as per the 1991 census.

While the Cairo Conference on Population and Development (ICPD) put equal emphasis on both, India, a signatory, has chosen to put population control before development. In Uttar Pradesh, the SIFPSA project funded by the US has been pushing targeted sterilizations, junking the ICPD declaration that advocated a target-free approach.

The failure to link women's education with the health policy has led to women not only living in poverty with no income but also remaining helplessly ignorant of their own health needs. That they allow ward boys to pump in air using cycle pumps, let dais thrust herbal sticks into them for abortions, often leading to fatal consequences, point to the pitfalls in having reproductive health policies rather than a policy for women's overall well being.

Selling the Parenthood Dream

SANDHYA SRINIVASAN

"Ovidac for the pleasure of parenthood" says an attractive poster illustrated by a photograph of a chubby baby boy outside Room 121, of the infertility Out-Patient Department (OPD) at a well-known private hospital in New Delhi. Private (paid) and free clinics are lined up next to each other in a hall packed with anxious women and men. There is another notice in the same hall: *"For information on IVF* (In-Vitro Fertilization) *please contact the Gynaecology OPD between 2 and 4 p.m."*

The patients await admission into a bare room, where two resident doctors at a table scan their papers and ask a few quick questions before sending the women behind a screen for a physical examination. A doctor explains that the hospital offers a "package deal" for IVF: if the first try, costing Rs 50,000 doesn't work, the next try could cost just Rs 20,000. The average annual income of an Indian is far below this.

Nearby, a bewildered young couple look for someone to help them out. Jaswant Singh (all names of patients have been changed) makes about Rs 3,000 a month in his shop selling cosmetics, hosiery and odds and ends. The couple has spent many times that amount on various doctors, trying to conceive a child after seven years of marriage. They've just been told they're too late for the test they were to undergo, and must come back the following week. "The hospital refuses to accept the results of outside tests, but we can't make their timings," says his wife, Amerjeet Kaur. "And it costs money that we can ill afford to come here each time."

Mushrooming of Infertility Clinics

Infertility treatments of all types have been widely publicized in the press since the first IVF baby in India received extraordinary publicity in 1986. Hoardings advertising infertility clinics have since proliferated in many public spaces such as bus stops and railway stations. These, and the crowded clinics themselves, testify to the widespread availability, and use, of infertility treatments in the country. They are provided by traditional healers, general practitioners and specialists through free-standing clinics and infertility departments in hospitals. An expanding—and unregulated—private sector fosters the proliferation of infertility-related technologies throughout the country, targeting urban slum dwellers, the middle class and the wealthiest of the wealthy, in small towns and big cities. The question is: have people really benefited? How many have? And, at what cost?

Conversations with providers, patients, and the other players in the system suggest that many desperate couples are taken for a ride.

Many infertility specialists are guilty of blatantly unethical practices, selling inappropriate and potentially hazardous treatments to desperate women. There is also the larger injustice of a society which breeds diseases like Reproductive Tract Infections (RTIs), Sexually Transmitted Diseases (STDs) and tuberculosis (TB) that lead to infertility in the first place. Many of these are preventable and even treatable, but a vast majority of Indians have no help for them.

Infertility: Incidence and Causes in India

"Up to 15 per cent of couples suffer from infertility at some time in their lives," says a senior infertility specialist. Actually, infertility is probably not that common in India. In an article, health researcher Shireen Jeejeebhoy quotes the 1981 National Census estimates that between four and six per cent of currently married women over 40 are childless.[1] Demographer Malini Karkal argues that infertility is relatively less common

[1]Jeejeebhoy, Shireen (1998), "Infertility in India: Levels, Patterns and Consequences for Social Science Research", *The Journal of Family Welfare*, 44, (2).

in India; the 1992–93 National Family Health Survey[2] estimates that only 2.4 per cent of currently married women aged between 45-49 (and 3.7 per cent of all women of the same age) have *never* given birth to a child. Yet, the prevalence of infertility is constantly over-estimated since over-estimates of infertility help justify the industry's existence.

A couple's inability to bear a child can be traced to a physical problem with one or both partners (with responsibility evenly divided between the sexes), if it can be traced at all—at least one-third of couples seeking treatment have "unexplained infertility". Among those for whom a problem *can* be identified, a "core group" has anatomical, genetic, or endocrinological problems that may be treatable, but are not preventable. However, a large proportion of infertility, particularly in developing countries, is caused by untreated infections affecting the reproductive system.

In men, the damage is usually caused by STDs, but also by TB, filaria, leprosy and mumps. In women, such infection is usually caused by damage to the fallopian tubes from pelvic inflammatory disease (PID), a possible consequence of untreated reproductive tract infections (RTIs) and STDs.[3] RTIs can be acquired through lack of access to clean water, unsterile procedures during childbirth or abortion, and they can be exacerbated by bad medical practices. "The current guidelines for 'clean delivery' don't prevent post-partum infection," says Dr Sharad Iyengar of ARTH, a voluntary organization near Udaipur in Rajasthan. Likewise, only 10 per cent of the estimated five to six million abortions performed each year in India are done in registered clinics.[4] Most abortions are done

[2]International Institute for Population Studies (IIPS) (1995), *National Family Health Survey (MCH and Family Planning), India 1992–49*, Bombay.

[3]Population Reports (1983), "Infertility and Sexually Transmitted Disease: A Public Health Challenge, *Issues in World Health Series L*, No.4, July; WHO Task Force on the Prevention and Management of Infertility (1995), "Tubal Infertility: Serological Relationship to Past Chlamydial and Gonococcal Infection", *Sexually Transmitted Diseases*, 22 (2): March–April.

[4]Indian Council of Medical Research (1989), *Illegal Abortions in Rural Areas: A Task Force Study*, New Delhi.

with inadequate equipment and poorly trained personnel.[5] Finally, though Intra Uterine Devices (IUDs) can aid the transfer of existing infections from the lower into the upper reproductive tract, it is an open secret that government services put in IUDs without checking for infections, says Dr Mira Shiva of the Voluntary Health Association of India (VHAI). "And how many primary health centres sterilize their equipment? They don't even have a budget for gentian violet."

Efforts to "educate" women about menstrual hygiene to prevent RTIs are meaningless when "they don't have privacy and access to clean water," notes Dr Shiva. Nor do they have the power to negotiate "safer" sex with a possibly infected spouse to protect themselves from STDs. If they do contract an infection, they may not develop symptoms, but even if they suffer discomfort, they are not likely to get treatment. This is because a woman's health comes way down in the list of priorities in any average Indian household.

Services for STDs and other RTIs—currently the single additional "reproductive health" component to the government's contraceptive-focussed family "welfare" programme—are available only at district and sub-district hospitals and some community health centres, which are even less accessible than the primary health centres and sub-centres. In rural India, this effectively rules out treatment for most women who cannot afford the transportation costs or the loss of working time to seek treatment. Published reports have recorded the appalling quality of government health services, particularly in the rural areas.[6] They are understaffed (or the staff are absent), drugs are unavailable, and equipment is broken down. Women's access to care is minimal even in better-off states, says Dr Shyamala Nataraj of the Chennai-based South India AIDS Action Programme. Instead, most women with infections will

[5]Barge, Sandhya, Manjunath Kini and Sunita Nair (1994), *Situation Analysis of MTP Facilities in Gujarat*, Ahmedabad Centre for Operations Research and Training.

[6]Mukhopadhyay, Alok (ed) (1997), *Report of the Independent Commission on Health in India*, New Delhi, Voluntary Health Association of India.

tolerate distressing symptoms. Most women at STD clinics have been referred only after they first sought treatment for infertility.

Tuberculosis is the third leading cause of death from infectious diseases in India.[7] It is also the leading cause of death among women in the reproductive age group. It is estimated to be responsible for between 10 per cent and 30 per cent[8] of female infertility. Although up to 80 per cent of the Indian population is infected with the tuberculosis bacterium, it is only in a small proportion that the infection develops into full-blown disease. It can travel to other parts of the body, including the genital tract, where a silent infection causes irreversible damage.

Limited funding has made research on pelvic TB a low priority, according to Dr Prabha Jagota, director of the once world-famous National Tuberculosis Institute in Bangalore. In any case, she argues, the incidence of pelvic TB depends on the incidence of pulmonary TB. So the TB control programme must concentrate on cutting transmission of TB by identifying and treating smear-positive TB. Low priority for public health, the concentration on vertical programmes, the obsession with the family planning programme and the consequent disarray in the public health system, irrational practices in the private sector and the financial burden on the patient—all these combine to render the TB control programme ineffective.[9]

There are other, less direct, causes of infertility that are very common in India: infections such as malaria, malnutrition, and exposure to toxic chemicals can reduce the chances of con-

---

[7] Murray C.H.L. and A.D. Lopez (1996), *The Global Burden of Disease and Injury. Volume I: A Comprehensive Assessment of Mortality and Disability from Diseases, Injuries and Risk Factors in 1990 and up to 2020*, Cambridge, Harvard University Press.

[8] Parikh, F.R., et al. (1997), "Genital Tuberculosis: A Major Pelvic Factor Causing Infertility in Indian Women", *International Journal of Gynaecology and Obstetrics*, 57(3).

[9] Uplekar, M. and Rangan, S. (1996), *Tackling Tuberculosis: The Search for Solutions*, Mumbai FRCH.

ception, or provoke spontaneous abortion. Dr Karkal points out, "Fertility is affected by so many deprivations, which should be addressed in the larger public interest."

And this is the point: infertility is a possible consequence of various illnesses with much more physically debilitating endpoints. These preventable illnesses are acquired in circumstances beyond the victims' control, from deprivation, and from infections contracted in poverty, within inequitable socio-economic relations that prevent even knowledgeable individuals from protecting themselves, or from getting proper treatment. The damage caused by such infections is rarely reversible. "The tragedy of infertility is that so much of it is preventable," says Dr Shiva.

Women Bear the Brunt

Though the problem which causes infertility can lie with the man, the woman or both, it is the woman who most keenly feels the consequences of childlessness. When a woman's worth is measured by her reproductive functions, the childless woman faces humiliation and even abandonment. "The woman needs to bear children for her own security as a wife, for acceptability in the household, and for status in the community," says Dr M Prakasamma, director of the Academy for Nursing Studies in Hyderabad, Andhra Pradesh, who has conducted focus group discussions with childless women and couples. And it is the woman who is blamed if she remains childless after more than four or five years of marriage. The woman labelled infertile is often described in derogatory language. Among the upper castes, especially, she is considered inauspicious at religious ceremonies. Indeed in some communities it is considered bad luck to see her face the first thing in the morning.

In a study of married, childless women in rural Andhra Pradesh, almost 30 per cent of them reported that their husbands had a second wife, spoke of taking one, or asked for a divorce. Almost 70 per cent of the women experienced "mild" to "very severe" violence, though only a few of them felt this violence was related to their childlessness.[10] Such pressures can drive women to seek treatment for infertility even when they might otherwise ignore serious health problems.

"So a girl gets married at 17, and if she's not pregnant in two years, her mother-in-law drags her to the doctor," says Dr Daisy Dharmaraj, director of Prepare, a voluntary organization working in Tamil Nadu, Orissa and Andhra Pradesh. "But there's no question of taking the husband along."

In a society where, among substantial sections of the population, children are additional household labour in the present and social insurance for the future, childlessness, particularly for the poor, signals a destitute old age. Those lucky to have children before infection destroys their reproductive systems must contend with the high infant mortality rate. The tragedy of a child's death can be compounded by a future without the prospect of another child. Adoption is not usually seen as an option.

The social pressure to have male children adds another dimension to women's predicament. Though it is the male who determines the sex of the child, women's status in the household, and financial security, can depend on whether they have sons.

Treatment Protocol and Guidelines

Any treatment for suspected infertility should be preceded by a clinical examination of both partners, a medical history, and diagnostic tests ruling out infection, hormonal disorders and other health problems. This includes tests of sperm quality for the man and to establish that a woman experiences regular ovulation and that her fallopian tubes are functional. The World Health Organisation (WHO) has developed an algorithm for the rational diagnosis and management of infertility.[11]

---

[10] Unisa, S. (1999), "Childlessness in Andhra Pradesh, India: Treatment Seeking and Consequences", *Reproductive Health Matters*,7(13), May.

[11] Rowe, P.J. et al (1993), *WHO Manual for the Standardized Investigation and Diagnosis of the Infertile Couple*, Cambridge, Cambridge University Press.

Once the problem is identified, treatment can include elementary advice (such as on how to time sex with ovulation), drug therapy—to induce ovulation, stimulate sperm production, or treat other conditions—and corrective surgical procedures. Sperm-related disorders may be treated with intrauterine insemination (IUI) using the husband's sperm or donor sperm. For damage to the fallopian tubes, the two medically recognized options are microsurgery and in vitro fertilization (IVF). The success rates are low. In 1994, less than 50 per cent of American women using infertility services of any kind delivered a live baby.[12]

In IVF, the woman is given drugs to stimulate her ovaries into producing two or more ova. These are surgically extracted and mixed with sperm in a chemical medium. Fertilized embryos are placed in her uterus, in the hope that one or more implant and develop. The procedure involves repeated injections of drugs, and various surgical procedures, mostly performed on the woman. The technology gave rise to a number of related procedures, including one for male infertility. Today IVF and other Assisted Reproductive Technologies (ARTs) are promoted for all forms of infertility.

Treatment Risks

Infertility treatment also has its risks. Surgical procedures for diagnosis or therapy for suspected infertility can cause internal damage or introduce infection—with health consequences which might, ironically, include infertility. The drugs can be harmful, especially if prescribed carelessly. Among their known adverse effects are: multiple pregnancy which puts both pregnancy and the mother at risk, and ovarian hyper-stimulation syndrome, a potentially life-threatening condition. Suspected adverse effects are: extra uterine pregnancy, congenital ab-

[12] Collins, J. and Collins A. (1994),"Reproductive Technology—The Price of Progress" *New England Journal of Medicine,* Volume 331, Number 4, July.

normalities, and hormonally dependent cancers.[13] Such risks are minimized if infertility diagnosis and treatment follow a well-defined protocol, and if treatment facilities are well equipped, and ensure access to treatment for complications. And, of course, the couple must know the risks and then provide consent. Couples also need to be counselled about adoption as an option that they might wish to consider.

"The only treatment at the village level is traditional remedies," says Dr Iyengar. "At the district level, infertility is treated mostly by men who do 'homoeopathy': they ask some questions and prescribe remedies without examining the couple. People spend a lot of money on faith healers." Or on pilgrimages. Or they take vows, make sacrifices. Many just wait and hope. In fact, many couples cannot think about spending on health services of any kind.

Government Services Indifferent

Only the poorest and most desperate visit government hospitals for treatment: a visit can mean losing a day's wages, and the services available there depend on the interests of the doctors. "It can take up to a year for a couple to get a complete diagnostic work-up in most public hospitals," says Dr Kamala Ganesh, who worked in one for more than thirty years.

While, in theory, some infertility treatment is available in government hospitals, "there are problems at every stage," says Dr Ganesh. Effective infertility services require access to and coordination between gynaecologists, male infertility specialists, surgeons and lab technicians—all with some time and interest in the subject. This is rarely the case. "For example, the department will schedule just three endometrial biopsies in a week. When the woman turns up, the doctor is busy elsewhere, the postgraduate student or the ayah is absent, or there is an

[13]Stephenson, P. (1993), " Ovulation Induction During Treatment of Infertility: An Assessment of the Risks", in Wagner M.G. and P. Stephenson, (Eds), *Tough Choices: IVF and Reproductive Technologies*, Philadelphia, Temple University.

electricity failure. The next appointment can be four-five months away. Or supplies for an essential test have run out, and a tender has to be called for." Those who can afford it will get the tests done at private clinics. Those who can't may just give up altogether. And doctors in public hospitals can't provide the necessary monitoring, even if they want to.

The government hospitals, starved for funds, minimize investigations, often making do without necessary ones. The flip side is that they also generally do not advocate unnecessary investigations, as in the private sector.

Infertility Research in India

Since the 1980s, contraceptive research has been accompanied by research into infertility. One centre for such work is the Institute for Research in Reproduction (IRR) in Mumbai (now the National Institute for Research in Reproductive Health). Funded by the Indian Council for Medical Research (ICMR), the IRR is also one of the WHO's clinical collaboration centres for multi-centric clinical trials in reproductive health.

In August 1982, barely three years after the birth of the world's first documented 'test-tube' baby, the IRR began work on an IVF programme. This venture represents the most direct government subsidy of private IVF services. A write-up in the *ICMR Bulletin* presents an interesting justification for spending public money on a prohibitively expensive, and experimental, procedure:

> In India, tubal sterilization is a widely used method for control of fertility. However, due to high infant and child mortality, several women who have undergone tubal sterilization do seek tubal recanalization. Recanalization involves major surgical intervention (microsurgery), the subsequent pregnancy rate being 12 to 70 per cent, depending on the type of sterilization and the method of reversal. IVF/ET requires comparatively less surgical intervention than tubal recanalization. If a couple is convinced that pregnancy could be achieved with certainty by the IVF/ET technique, in the event of their losing the existing children, they might read-

ily accept tubal sterilization as a method of family planning. *Thus in vitro fertilization could be of great relevance to our national family welfare programme.*[14] (emphasis mine)

The programme was set up in August 1984, in collaboration with a Mumbai municipal hospital, and the first documented "test-tube" baby in India was born on August 6, 1986. Harsha was born to the wife of a municipal sweeper. Her birth was heralded by large sections of the Indian media as a triumph for Indian medicine, though some commented on the high costs and poor success rates of this technique. Eventually, the enthusiasm petered out and so did the programme. Present staffers say the venture was secretive, and of poor quality. Dr Indira Hinduja, one of the doctors on the IVF team (now in private practice for some years), blames the KEM hospital for not being able to translate the research into a regular service.

"I was in the IRR when Harsha was born," says Dr Karkal. "Both the parents were less than five feet tall. In normal circumstances, their baby would be just one more of the 36 per cent of Indian babies born with low birth weight, doomed to poor health if they manage to survive the first five years of life. Because Indira Hinduja was interested, the baby was born weighing more than 2,500 grams. Why can't every baby receive this care?"

The NIRR continues to run an infertility clinic, though it doesn't offer IVF at present. Couples come there from the city and all over the country, travelling by bus and train, staying with relatives and friends, coping with financial limitations, the demands of household, family and jobs in their search for a child.

Snehal and Ravindra are in their early 40s. They say they earn about Rs 5,500 a month between them; she as an insurance agent, he as a rickshaw driver. Married a year earlier,

---

[14] Peter, J. (1984), *Indian Council of Medical Research Bulletin,* Vol. 14. 14, No. 10. October. (The author also mentions the potential of IVF for sexing embryos "to control sex-linked disease" and for investigating new forms of contraception.)

they've come to the IRR after spending approximately, 10,000 in a "five-star" hospital. But they were not happy: "The doctor did not give us proper attention because we were 'free' patients." They came to the IRR because it worked for a relative. They say the doctor here gives them an "80 per cent guarantee". They have to pay for their drugs, which are expensive, but they feel they are treated better here.

Besides the government's questionable investment of public money in the IRR's IVF programme, the public sector has indirectly collaborated in the diffusion of expensive and irrational health treatments in India. Health analyst Ravi Duggal has argued that public resources (such as medical education, soft loans and tax concessions) are used to develop the private sector, which appropriates the profits.[15] The public sector's connivance continues today, going by the suggestions of an article in the *ICMR Bulletin* on the "need and feasibility of providing assisted technologies for infertility management in resource-poor settings".[16] The paper, written by a senior ICMR scientist, together with two private infertility specialists, proposes a "public-private collaboration" to provide assisted reproductive technologies such as in vitro-fertilization to those who can't afford them.

This collaboration would include waiving duties for expensive IVF equipment and drugs, public-private pooling of some supplies, government support for some facilities, introducing specialized teaching programmes in assisted reproductive technologies in government hospitals, and insurance cover for infertility treatment. The article estimates a "need" for 400,000 cycles of IVF in India, costing Rs 50–75,000 per cycle (separate from obstetric costs for any consequent pregnancy,

---

[15]Duggal, R. (1988), "Privatisation and New Medical Technology", *Foundation for Research in Community Health Newsletter* , September–December.
[16]Puri, Chander, Indira Hinduja and Kusum Jhaveri. (2000), "Need and Feasibility of Providing Assisted Technologies for Infertility Management in Resource-Poor Settings." *Indian Council of Medical Research Bulletin*, Volume 30, No. 6–7. June–July.

which is termed high risk), with a 30 per cent "take home baby" rate.

This collaboration is proposed when the public sector is consciously curbing access to basic health services. Municipal hospitals charge for everything from case papers to diagnostic tests to life-saving treatments like heart surgery. If implemented, such a proposal would not provide care to the poor who anyway do not get access to other care. All it would do is enable private infertility specialists to find opportunities to benefit from the public sector's support.

Surprisingly, and with no data, most policy makers and media commentators, believing their own experience is valid for everyone else, make claims about the efficiency and efficacy of the private sector. It is, however, the private sector that is largely indulging in unethical practices with reproductive technologies. This has led to the marked 'masculinization' of sex ratios in the country with the result that there are only 927 girls for every 1,000 boys. It is also because of large-scale, often inappropriate, use of the private sector that medical expenditure is emerging as a leading cause of indebtedness in the country.

The Private Health Care Industry

Health care is a huge and unregulated industry in India estimated at Rs 126,270 crores in 1998. It is growing at the expense of essential public services and through various government subsidies. It is estimated that 80 per cent of all expenditure on health care in the country is on private facilities, spent by individuals without health insurance. These range from the corner x-ray clinic to the drug-company-funded corporate hospital. They are used because they are more accessible than government services. A household survey of health care costs in an Indian district found 77 per cent of those who fell ill, went to a private doctor and only 13 per cent to a government doctor. Up to 6 per cent ignored the problem, presumably because they couldn't pay for treatment. [17]

One might argue that the public sector is full of various money-making rackets, from selling hospital drugs in the open market to charging for free services. However, in the absence of external regulation by the government, self-regulation by professional bodies or accountability to the public in any other form, decisions in the private sector seem to be guided almost exclusively by profit. Further, decisions on health care are made not by the person who pays but by the doctor. As a result, doctors may be tempted to prescribe unnecessary—and expensive—investigations, unnecessary and often irrational treatment procedures. And above all, here there is even less accountability than in the government sector.

Role of Corporate Hospitals

The 1980s saw the rise of corporate hospitals with resources to invest in sophisticated medical technologies. Simultaneously, there has been a country-wide diffusion of stand-alone units providing technologies of various levels of sophistication, mostly financed by loans from banks or financial institutions. Imports became easier after the liberalization of the economy.[18] Doctors earlier needed special contacts to obtain the necessary drugs, machinery and disposable material. "Now we can get anything we want," said a specialist.

"Many medical choices are provider-specific, and the provider often has a vested interest," says Dr Puneet Bedi, an infertility specialist in Delhi. This analysis of high-tech health care is particularly true of assisted reproductive technologies. "The doctor, the pharmacist and the diagnostic unit all represent investments—in education, inventory, real estate—which

---

[17]Duggal, R. and Amin, S. (1989), *Cost of Health Care: A Household Survey in an Indian District*, The Foundation for Research in Community Health, Mumbai.

[18] Sukanya, S. (1996), "Investing in Medical Equipment: Study of Private Hospitals in Madras City", *The Radical Journal of Health,* 1996 January–March.

must show profits," notes Dr Bedi. Specialists offering IVF and related procedures have spent a minimum of Rs 20,00,000 on equipment alone.

"Any bank will give between forty and fifty lakh rupees [Rs 40,00,000–50,00,000] to set up IVF facilities, at 20 per cent a month," continues Dr Bedi. "For that, the infertility specialist needs to treat 20-30 couples with IVF each month. IVF is appropriate in barely two per cent of couples coming for treatment. It's the 20th of the month, five lakh rupees have to be raised before the 30th. What's to prevent the doctor from telling the next patient she needs IVF?"

What is more, the costs of infertility therapy are levied in instalments. If the first treatment fails, try once more, or try another variation. And then something else. After all, you've already spent so much money, taken so many drugs. . . . Once they've started, patients are reluctant to stop. It would be a waste of all that money, time, trauma.

The costs of assisted reproductive technologies would seem to put them beyond the reach of all but the very rich in India. In Mumbai, the costs can be as high as Rs 100,000 per treatment cycle—with a not more than 15 per cent chance that a couple entering the programme will leave with a baby. But IVF is not restricted to the wealthy.

"The women I spoke to spent between a few hundred rupees and a few hundred thousands for treatment," says Dr Prakasamma. "One couple sold three acres of land..." Recently, a public sector company, Bharat Petroleum, started reimbursing employees for infertility treatment, including three cycles of IVF. Infertility Friends, a support group based in Mumbai, is petitioning medical insurance companies to follow suit.

A decade ago, IVF was limited to metropolitan cities like Mumbai and Delhi. Today, the Indian Society for Assisted Reproduction, a voluntary body, lists 186 members, from all parts of the country. "If two years ago, there were 50 centres offering some form of assisted reproductive technology, today there are 107," says infertility specialist Dr Sadhna Desai. "Many of them advertise the latest in technology, like intracytoplasmic sperm injection, embryo freezing, and pre-implantational genetic diagnosis."

"Has anyone stopped to think why there are so many IVF centres here despite the fact that India has one of the lowest prevalences (of infertility) in the world?" asked Dr Karkal at a public meeting.

The crowd starts gathering early in the morning at the clinic of one of the best-known infertility specialists in the country. The harried receptionist responds brusquely to various timid inquiries. "You'll have to wait," she tells a couple, with ill-disguised irritation. On the phone she tells someone, "No, we have no idea when the doctor is coming in." For those who believe that IVF is a rich person's luxury, the nylon saris and plastic sandals label most of the women here middle-class. Some of the tense faces could be from any of Mumbai's slums.

A couple sits anxiously in the waiting room of one of Mumbai's expensive hospitals—which double as "research centres" to avail of various tax concessions. The man earns about Rs 11,000 a month as a college lecturer in a small town outside the city. They've seen six doctors so far, spent over Rs 70,000 on two laparoscopies, various other tests, and three intrauterine inseminations. "This doctor is very decent, she kept our costs to a minimum." Here, they have spent Rs 50,000 on one IVF cycle. When that didn't work they went back home ("for some peace"). Now they're back for their second try at IVF, for which they're organizing a second set of loans, adding to debts from previous treatments. "The success rate is 30–40 per cent, the doctor tells us. I am confident things will work out, I only wish we had come here first," he says, as she breaks down at the thought of failing once again.

The doctor says their's is a hopeless case. If that is so, why is she doing the procedure? At first she has no answer. Then she says, "If I don't do it, they'll go somewhere else."

Couple after couple in IVF centres quoted the "40 per cent success rate"; it's the mantra of hope. It refers only to the percentage of 'biochemical pregnancies' out of those ovarian stimulation cycles that resulted in oocyte (egg) retrieval, fertilization and embryo transfer. Stimulation cycles don't necessarily result in oocyte retrieval; retrievals don't necessarily result in fertilized embryos; fertilized embryos don't necessarily implant when transferred to the uterus; and, finally, an implanted embryo does not necessarily develop into a healthy baby. The bottom line, the "take-home baby rate" is not more than 15 per cent in the best of clinics. Yet some doctors tell their patients that the success rate gets better with each attempt, so that by the third try, it becomes 70 per cent. This mathematical manipulation, called the "cumulative pregnancy rate", can only serve to mislead the desperate couple, into trying again and again.

Like most Indian doctors, Dr N maintains no medical records; patients bring the records with them for each appointment. He has no idea how many of the couples who visit him end up with a baby. He guesses that 50 per cent of his patients come back for a second visit and undergo a complete work-up. In turn, many of his patients have come to him after unsuccessful treatment elsewhere.

Many of the couples in plush IVF clinics like Dr F's office get a "subsidized" treatment: "I use fewer drugs for them," she says, even though it might reduce their chances of success. Or she asks them to donate embryos to rich couples who pay for their treatment. There has been no discussion in the profession about such unofficial cutting of corners and trade-offs.

This is one area where Say's Law, that supply creates its own demand, operates freely, and unfettered by any regulations. Meanwhile, public relations firms hired by infertility doctors (in violation of the Code of Medical Ethics) flood reporters with write-ups and photographs of beaming couples flanking a serene doctor holding the latest IVF/GIFT/ZIFT baby/twins/triplets.... Human interest stories in the press—woven around the mother's bliss and fulfilment and the doctor's commitment to her dreams—drum up more business for such doctors.

A 25-year-old woman from Bhiwandi, a town near Mumbai, was underweight and six-and-a-half-months pregnant when she delivered quadruplets at the state-government-run Cama hospital. The babies died within 12 hours of birth. Were ovulation-inducing drugs responsible? "I'm one hundred and fifty per cent sure," says a specialist. Multiple pregnancies are a common complication of infertility treatment; such drugs must be used with restraint, and monitored. "Triplets have a less than 10 per cent chance of surviving the pregnancy," says Dr Bedi. Yet doctors will often try to maintain multiple pregnancies, and when they succeed, send off press releases about their "achievements". When they fail, all the couple is left with are a lot of bills.

With no uniform protocol, no auditing, no one to answer to, doctors can do just about anything they want, and it is almost impossible to evaluate the quality and effect of infertility treatments. Still, doctors are more than willing to comment on their colleagues. They tell stories of patients who have been administered a hodgepodge of tests and treatments, often omitting basic tests like a semen analysis. Many women undergo dilation and curettage—a procedure which can introduce infection, and is of limited, and doubtful, value. "Patients are often put on potentially dangerous drugs without preliminary investigation, and without monitoring," says Dr Daisy Dharmaraj. Other doctors report being called in to treat critically ill women with ovarian cysts caused by another doctor's drug overdoses.

Every infertility specialist knows about the chemical pregnancy scam: give high doses of certain hormones to obtain test results which can be interpreted as a "chemical pregnancy". Later on, the woman will be told she had a spontaneous abortion. Infertility doctors claiming to be trained in cryopreservation are reportedly known to reuse contaminated equipment. There are reports of donor sperm being used in artificial insemination and IVF—without the couple's knowledge. "IVF babies' parentage should be verified with DNA testing," according to Dr Shaukat Sadikot, a Mumbai-based endocrinologist.

There is the story of the careless doctor who missed diseased tissue and removed a healthy ovary. Yet another about a doctor who injected a clot-dissolving drug to dissolve fibrous tissue—a creative, if useless, therapy. Some gynaecologists are known to test a woman's fallopian tubes by injecting them with air, which can be fatal. "Some doctors will do a laparoscopy on a woman before doing a semen test on her husband, because of the pressure from her husband and in-laws," says Dr Bedi.

If stand-alone infertility clinics promote expensive and unnecessary treatments, in-fighting in hospital-based set-ups has its own hazards: women in one hospital were forced to undergo a month of hormone therapy only to find out that the embryologist was not available to extract the ova when needed; she had left the country on a holiday without telling the gynaecologist.

Women are submitted to treatments which are totally unnecessary. Dr Pervin Meherji, who runs the IRR's clinic, mentions cases of women who underwent expensive IVF with private doctors, and then succeeded in getting pregnant with more conservative treatment at the IRR. Others undergo intrauterine insemination repeatedly only to find out later that their tubes are damaged, and the treatment could never have worked. One couple was prescribed IUI 11 times even though doctors say if it hasn't worked for six tries, it should be abandoned.

Why don't we read about couples outraged by such malpractices? "There is no anger because they never stop hoping," says Dr Bedi. "The craziness for a child is fuelled by the medical profession," says Dr Srinath, of Sudatta, an association of adoptive parents in Bangalore. Sudatta regularly sends doctors information about the association for their patients. "But no one has even bothered to acknowledge our letter, leave alone reply, or make enquiries."

If adoption is seen as the last option for couples wanting children, the medical profession has managed to find a way to profit here as well. In January 2003, Jawahar and Janaki Bijlani were arrested for selling an infant to a couple from New Delhi. Investigations have led to evidence that a number of doctors run "maternity homes" for pregnant women. The women are given medical care until they deliver their babies who they then hand over to the doctor for a price.

The ARTs are not always used only for infertility. Dr N is one of the many doctors who "help" couples wanting a son: Y-bearing sperm are separated and inseminated to increase the chances of a boy. Another doctor actually advises this for his patients undergoing IUI: of course, he makes money in the process.

SJ and his wife had a daughter after 12 years of trying. She has had enough of infertility doctors, but he says, "I'm from a conservative family, and I'd like a male heir." Their doctor has offered them IVF with a difference: a technique called pre-implantational genetic diagnosis (PGD) will screen the fertilized embryos identifying male embryos for implanting into the woman. "I see it as an opportunity for the parents," says the specialist. "It is paternalistic of doctors to refuse such requests."

PGD is the latest in sex selection techniques marketed nationwide but banned following an extensive campaign by women's and health activists. However, despite the Prenatal Diagnostic Techniques (Regulation and Misuse) Act, 1994, sex selection clinics continued to flourish openly, even in small towns. It was only following public interest litigation in 2000 that the Supreme Court ordered state governments to implement the law. The writ petition was filed by health activist Sabu George, the Mumbai-based NGO Centre for Enquiry into Health and Allied Themes (Cehat) and the Pune-based NGO Mahila Sarvangeen Utkarsh Mandal (Masum).

The petitioners also asked for the law to be amended to include newer sex selection techniques such as PGD. Infertility specialist Aniruddha Malpani, who has openly advertised sex selection on his website, intervened in the court case and argued that a ban on PGD violated parents' right to choose the sex of their child. However, the amended Preconception and

Prenatal Diagnostic Techniques (Prohibition of Sex Selection) Act, bans all sex selection including PGD. Dr Malpani now faces legal action for omitting to remove the advertisement for sex selection from his website.

A public meeting organized by the ICMR revealed that infertility specialists have done little thinking on the ethical issues relating to infertility treatment. Some senior infertility doctors declared that poor women could benefit from paid surrogacy. Others felt affronted by the many complaints of unethical practice. True, a standardized infertility work-up should be promoted, clinics accredited with a national registry, properly equipped, and with confidential records. Yes, couples must get better information about their condition, the chances for successful treatment, and about other options such as adoption. But doctors don't need policing, thank you. They'll get their act together, on their own, in their own time.

In September 2002, the ICMR released draft guidelines to regulate infertility treatment. The guidelines specify infrastructure requirements and a code of practice for infertility clinics, and stipulate additional training for gynaecologists who specialize in infertility treatment through ARTs. The ICMR also proposed the creation of a government agency to license infertility clinics. This agency would be mandated to ensure that clinics conform to standards. It would also fix the upper limit of charges for gamete donation and surrogacy—in other words giving legal sanction to a trade in human ova. Currently a number of infertility specialists advertise for egg "donors", paying up to Rs 20,000 per procedure.

"You can't make people spend if they don't want to," says one specialist. "The drugs may have risks, but they can improve the couple's quality of life," declares another. "If they want the treatment, who are we to decide?" A third is shocked at the suggestion that infertility treatment is a waste of time. "Helping a woman have a baby is a doctor's greatest accomplishment."

"In a commodity where consumer resistance is at its lowest, the rapid increase in the uncontrolled private sector which operates on the profit motive may divert scarce resources from food to doctors and medicines." notes health analyst Ravi Duggal.[19] In fact the infertility industry shockingly illustrates the lopsidedness of the priorities set by private interests in health care.

[19]Duggal R and Amin S (1989), *Op cit.*

Grass Widows of Bihar

DHIRENDRA K JHA

Amidst the golden rice fields of Mainhi village in the Madhubani district of Bihar, better known among the cognosceti outside the state for the delicate and colourful line paintings by its women, a heavily pregnant Khajni almost faints with pain as she works in the fields. Soon after, a baby boy is born under the open sky. Khajni is still holding a sickle in her hands as it is harvest time and she cannot afford to lose a day's wages—two kilograms of paddy. Other women help her with her delivery and to arrange herself. Slowly, Khajni gets up, takes the baby in her arms, and limps back to her desolate shack. Her husband Panch Lal is thousands of kilometers away in Punjab. He's been there for the last several months. The rare remittances he sends from there are not enough to feed her three-year-old daughter, her old parents-in-law and herself.

In Kiratpur village in adjoining Darbhanga district, Dai Sunnair, a Dalit landless labourer, has not slept for the last three months. She spends the days toiling in the nearby fields and the nights tending to her 10-year-old son who is suffering from tuberculosis of the bones. But work is scarce and the wages are not sufficient to meet her needs. The loan Dai Sunnair took for the treatment of her ailing son is unpaid. Her husband Basant Mukhia, who migrated as a labourer to Assam eight years back, is scared to face moneylenders back home. The unpaid debt has sealed the possibility of his return even as the interest piles up.

For Nirmala, who lives in Darbhanga district, the future is uncertain. Her husband, a migrant labourer, tested positive for the Human Immunodeficiency Virus (HIV) and died of tuberculosis three months ago. Nirmala, who is pregnant, does not know if she too is infected or what the future holds in store for her.

Rural Bihar is dotted with numerous Khajnis, Dai Sunnairs and Nirmalas, especially in the northern districts of Darbhanga, Madhubani, Saharsa, Supaul, Madhepura and Purnea.These women are frequently referred to as grass widows. With their husbands away for long spells in distant lands where they work as labourers, these women struggle for survival without the moral or financial support of a spouse. They work as agricultural labourers to make ends meet, run households and single-handedly look after their aged in-laws and little children. These are women not seen or heard of; they are absent from all discourses. Few policy makers, academics or journalists pay attention to their plight.

Migrant Labour

Conventional definitions of migration describe the intensity of labour migration from these districts of the country as very low. The two major sources of data on migration in India—the Census of India and the National Sample Survey (NSS)—cover only permanent or semi-permanent migration, omitting seasonal migration as it falls in neither category.The result is a restricted coverage of migration by the two data sources. They have, in fact, reported declining trends of outmigration from north Bihar over recent years, despite evidence to the contrary. Several experts have started pointing out this dichotomy.[1]

A recent study by Bharatiya Khet Mazdoor Union (BKMU) or the Indian Farm Labourers Union found a 22 per cent increase in seasonal migration of labour between 1989 and 1999, chiefly from the rural areas of the flood-prone districts of north Bihar. The BKMU study, which covered 50 villages from five

[1] Srivastava, Ravi (1999), "Migration and Labour Market in India", *Indian Journal of Labour Economics*, Vol 41, No 4. ; Kundu, Amitabh and Shalini, Gupta (1996), "Migration , Urbanisation and Regional Inequality", *Economic and Political Weekly*, Vol.XXXI, No.52, December.

districts of Saharsa, Supaul, Darbhanga, Madhubani and Madhepura, also found that, on average, about 60 per cent of the landless labour from these districts migrated during lean agricultural seasons in 1999.

Migration of male agricultural labourers from north Bihar villages to the more industrially or agriculturally developed parts of the country has risen sharply in the past decade. At present, the seasonal labour exodus is so intense that village after village is left without male labourers for certain parts of the year. Gunnar Myrdal, in his book *Asian Drama,* might have discovered that "the poorer the people, the stronger the barrier to migration", but in Bihar the number of households sending migratory workers increases as one goes down the socio-economic ladder. The grass widows of Bihar are the wives of the lowest rung.

For the landless poor in Bihar, migration is a way out of the exploitation emanating from agrarian structural anomalies. The agrarian landscape is characterized by the large-scale prevalence of landlessness, extremely low wages, too many hands competing for too few jobs in the fields, near absence of agro-industries in the region, and the continuing practice of bonded or unpaid labour forced by upper caste landlords. There has also been little by way of State intervention in the agricultural sector in the form of infrastructure development or land reforms.

Grass Widows—Left Alone

With the men away for six to nine months of the year, and often for years on end, the onus of running the household is on the grass widows. On the one hand, the traditional patriarchal society in India expects a woman to be under "male protection", on the other, grass widows are expected to run families without this "male protection". The anomaly causes a crisis in the traditional production structures, in which a woman's role as a breadwinner for the family has remained secondary to her role as a wife and mother. Additionally, it leaves these women vulnerable to traditional as well as newer forms of exploitation, both within the family and outside.

For the grass widows, the so-called benefits of migration—the remittances—are yet to outweigh the losses. The remittance has not mitigated the poverty of these families, nor has it made up in any way for the problems faced by the grass widows during the absence of the men. A substantial part of the remittance is pocketed by moneylenders and other middlemen. It also goes to pay bribes to petty officials in both Bihar and the migrants' destination states of Punjab, Haryana etc.

The absence of State intervention has also meant that there are no institutions for credit for even agricultural activities as in other parts of the country.Thus moneylenders occupy a key place in the agrarian economy of the region. With the rise in migration over the last decade there has also been a perceptible increase in the number and influence of the moneylenders who not only lend money to labourers eager to migrate in search of jobs, but also to take care of the day-to-day monetary needs of the families left behind. The rates that these "patrons" charge from the hapless labourers are so exorbitant that most of the earning of the migrants goes straight into the pockets of these moneylenders. The rates of interest in these villages vary from five rupees to ten rupees per month for every hundred rupees borrowed. In annual terms, the rate of interest turns out to be anything between 60 per cent and 120 per cent!

The method evolved by these "masters" to corner the "benefits" of migration is foolproof. In the majority of cases, migrant labourers are directed to send the remittance not to their families but directly to the moneylenders. Consequently, while the moneylenders get the earnings, the earners' families remain in utter penury.The grass widows—largely illiterate and thus unable to receive money orders—are at the moneylenders' mercy and vulnerable to exploitation by them, both physical and fiscal.

Migrant's Travails

As seasonal migration has increased, a chain of extorters and cheats who thrive on the migrant labourers' lack of awareness and insecurity has emerged. In their native Bihar, they have to cope with exorbitant interest rates on loans taken from moneylenders, while in the states they migrate to, they have to pay middlemen and contractors who arrange jobs for them and pocket a good part of their earnings. Added to this are extortions by corrupt policemen all along the route. In the trains in which they travel, the migrants have to keep hiding their goods from the searching eyes of ticket checkers who force them to pay unnecessary surcharges, all illegal. And yet unemployment is so high and wages are so low in the villages of Bihar that men have no option but to migrate for work.

In Bihar the statutory minimum wage for an "unskilled" labourer is Rs 46 a day. In reality, the agricultural labourers in these villages do not get even half of this amount. In Dahia-Kharwair village, for example, the average daily wage for an agricultural labourer is five *sier*[2] of rice. Here a kilogram of medium-quality rice does not cost more than ten rupees. Thus, the average wage is never more than Rs 22.50 per day. Even this is a highly liberal conversion of kind into cash because the rice given in wages is of such poor quality that it normally costs less than Rs 10 per kilogram.

"Although the absence of my husband is not easy to cope with, I cannot afford to ask him to stay back because that will mean unemployment and starvation. The one bigha of land we share for cropping is not enough to feed us all," says Imarti Devi of Dahia-Kharwair village in Madhubani district. Imarti has to look after her two-year-old son and 85-year-old widowed mother-in-law. Her husband Bhikhu Ram migrates to Punjab for almost six months every year, especially when there is a lean agricultural season back home. "Most of his earnings go straight to the moneylender from whom we borrow every

---

[2]One *sier* equals 450 grams.

time my husband goes to Punjab. And still I do not have the courage to stop him (Bhikhu) because whatever is left is more than what he can earn here in months," she adds.

Ailments and Shackles

Grass widows who are left behind to run the households in the absence of their husbands are mainly Dalit (belonging to castes like Musahar, Chamar, Pasi, Keot, Dhanuk, Dusadh, Mallah, etc.) landless labourers, toiling on lands and in the households of the landed sections for meagre wages. Devoid of any familial and social security, they have to work hard, and for long hours, to merely survive from day to day. With such meagre earnings, they have virtually no money to spend on treatment for illnesses. They continue to work even when they are seriously ill as they are the main breadwinners for their families.

"I don't have money even for food. How will I buy medicines for myself?" asks Banarsi Devi of Dighiapar village in Kusheshar Asthan block of Darbhanga district. Suffering from Kala Azar[3] (Leishmaniasis) for the last one year, Banarsi Devi has not taken any medicine. Not because she is ignorant and does not know what is good for her, but simply because she cannot afford to buy medicines. Caught between disease and deprivation, she slogs in the fields to feed herself and her one-year-old child. She is landless, belongs to the Musahar community and has no one to look after her and her baby. Seasonal migration of men is most common in the Musahar community—a community so poor that it derives its name from the *moos* or rat, which forms the staple diet of its members.

Banarsi's husband Kari Sadai, who also suffers from Kala Azar, left her when she was with their baby. "My husband is a

[3]Transmitted by the sandfly, Kala Azar or Leishmaniasis epidemics are frequent and widespread in Bihar. The disease is characterised by chronic and recurrent high fever, extreme weakness, wasting, anaemia, and swelling of the liver and spleen. Untreated, it carries a huge mortality.

rickshaw puller in Allahabad. He is also ill. He is not able to send us any money because whatever he earns is spent on his food and medicines. Earlier, he used to send me money," says Banarsi.

The Primary Health Centre (PHC) at Kusheshar Asthan, about four kilometres from Dighiapar, does not have sodium antimony gluconate, the medicine for Kala Azar, even though this disease has turned into an epidemic in this block and in some nearby areas. The incidence of Kala Azar is high in parts of Darbhanga, Madhubani, Supaul, Saharsa and Madhepura. The villages in East Kusheshar Asthan (Dighiapar falls in this block), West Kusheshar Asthan and Kiratpur blocks of Darbhanga district are the worst affected. Nestled between Kamla and Kosi rivers, the region is soggy with water that seeps through cracks in unattended embankments. Waterlogged all year the land remains damp providing a perfect breeding ground for the sandflies (*Phlebotomus*) that transmit the disease.

In Dighiapar, a village of about 200 Musahar and Mallah households, 85 people have died due to Kala Azar between mid 1999 and March 2002, according to official records. This is likely to be an underestimate since many deaths are never recorded. "The consignments of sodium antimony gluconate which came last year (2001) were found to be spurious and were therefore sealed. There has been no replacement so far," says Darbhanga's Civil Surgeon, Dr Mani Bhushan Srivastava.

Given the absence of medical care—either private or public—quacks have turned the situation to their advantage. "Here quacks take on contracts for treating Kala Azar. Depending on the condition of the patients, the contract amount varies from ten to fiteen thousand rupees. Those who can manage the amount go for the treatment, the others remain without medicine," says Laxmi Naik, a political activist at Kusheshar Asthan. Banarsi cannot afford the quacks and the government won't provide her with the medicine. She has long forgotten that she needs care and treatment. What is uppermost in her mind is how to keep herself and her baby alive.

Most grass widows face similar problems. A study by Action Aid in 2000 on health issues of Dalit and Muslim women in rural areas of north Bihar found that "in spite of ill health 61 per cent women continue to work."[4]

In the case of women whose earnings are an absolute necessity for their families, not attending their daily wage earning duties (however onerous these may be), because of ill health is unthinkable. This worsens the ailment and raises the cost of medicines and treatment for them. Gradually it affects their capacity to earn. The vicious cycle ultimately cripples a large number of grass widows. The Action Aid study says the women who perform triple roles—reproductive, wage-earning and domestic—as indeed most poor women in rural areas do, suffer from health problems over a prolonged period of time.

Even the grass widows' perception of their well-being and health is based on the extent to which their ailments affect their ability to work. "The health status of these women is so crucial for the family that they do not consider themselves ill until they become totally incapacitated," says Rana Mukherjee, an NGO activist working for the Darbhanga chapter of Discipleship Centre, which is engaged in educational and health related programmes for the empowerment of women.

And yet the health of grass widows is often not on the priority agenda of either the State or indeed their own families. As a result, the majority of them suffer from undernutrition, anaemia, goitre, night blindness and communicable diseases like malaria, Kala Azar and tuberculosis, the quintessential diseases of hunger and poverty.

Given their low wages, and long hours of back-breaking work, the majority of grass widows are unable to afford two square meals a day and suffer from varying degrees of undernutrition and hunger. According to a study conducted in 2001 by a Patna-based NGO, Centre for Health and Resource Man-

[4] Action Aid (2000), *Women's Health: A Benighted Truth*, New Delhi.

agement (CHARM), this is compounded by a lack of proteins.[5] Given the overall lack of food, it is not surprising that over 90 per cent of the respondents, women belonging to the Musahar community, have no access to protein in their food and 67 per cent of them do not eat green vegetables or eat them rarely (less than two times a week). Almost 90 per cent of Dalit women in the reproductive age-group (a significant number of them being grass widows) in rural areas of north Bihar suffer from moderate or severe anemia. They are also severely undernourished.

There is also a near total absence of government health facilities in these villages. "The health centre in the village is meaningless. The doctor posted here rarely shows up and medicines are never available. The gap is filled by ojhas or village shamans and quacks," says Raghu Sadai, a resident of Hatni village in Madhubani district in Bihar. The desolate health centre in the village confirms Raghu's assertion.

Originally, the ojhas were traditional healers who combined the use of herbs and roots with medico-religious practices. In remote rural areas with little access to health care facilities, ojhas exercise tremendous influence over local communities—as often they are the only medical help available for the sick. The local poor find their services affordable too—they do not charge consultation fees and accept "offerings" which may be in kind, such as rice or other foodgrains. Even if some poor people cannot afford to give anything in kind, ojhas defer payment till they are able to so.

The 2001 study by CHARM on the health status and preferences of people belonging to the Musahar community in north Bihar villages found, "About 94 per cent of the respondents depend on quacks and ojhas."

This is despite the fact that on paper India has an elaborate three-tier primary health care delivery system for rural areas, with sub-centres, Primary Health Centres (PHCs) and Community Health Centres (CHCs). Sub-centres, catering to

[5] CHARM (2001), "Musahars: Health Status and Preferences", Patna.

populations of up to 5000, are the most peripheral contact point between the health care system and the community. These centres are supposed to be attended by one male multi-purpose worker and one female worker or Auxiliary Nurse-Midwife (ANM). PHCs are to be headed by a medical officer (MO) and act as a referral system for six sub-centres. They are to have up to six beds for patients. CHCs are to act as referral centres for four PHCs with four medical specialists in attendance—a surgeon, a physician, a gynaecologist and a paediatrician—supported by over 20 paramedical and other staff. CHCs are supposed to have up to 30 beds, in addition to facilities like operation theatres, X-ray machines, labour rooms and pathological laboratories.All government programmes and schemes are to be implemented through this health care delivery system. The three-tier public health system is, however, hardly visible in rural areas of north Bihar. Either they simply don't exist or are ramshackle facilities without staff and medicines.

The quacks and ojhas are of course accountable to no one. They can prescribe anything and get away with it. They even try their hands at surgery, often with disastrous consequences. And yet because of the non-availability of health care services such as medical personnel, medicines and treatment in the government health centres, most poor villagers have no other option but to depend on them.

In the case of grass widows, this dependence is often fatal. Living in utter penury and in the absence of effective State health services at their doorsteps, they turn to quacks and ojhas even for serious ailments. Most often they have to take loans from moneylenders for treatment. In order to avoid this, they often remain silent and, in the majority of cases, ailments remain undetected and unattended till it is too late.Untreated illnesses affect the women's capacity to work and earn, pushing them further down the economic ladder.

Often faulty or complete absence of treatment unleashes further suffering and pain as women become victims of their husbands' wrath and apathy. Take the case of Ramdai of Hatni village in Madhubani district. She is destitute now. But she was happily living with her husband, a migrant labourer, till about two years back, when she had an eruption on her right leg. It was operated upon by an ojha, Mohan Thakur, but predictably the infection spread to the whole leg. Soon she was unable to walk as, according to her, the "leg dried up". Her husband Ghuran Sadai, who was in the Punjab at that time, returned after a few months and instead of getting Ramdai treated, abandoned her.Today, Ramdai has lost the use of her leg and drags herself. Stoically, she holds her fate responsible for her plight, rather than blame the ojha or her husband.

Ramdai does not even know that her problem was a simple infection that could have been cured by proper medical treatment. She sincerely believes that supernatural forces are against her and that she is a victim of *agnivaan* (a divine curse), as her ojha had said. She finds nothing wrong in the attitude of the husband who deserted her and firmly believes that she had become "useless" for him.

Misplaced Health Priorities

The migration of male labour in search of jobs and the consequent responsibility of the grass widows to run households leads to a dichotomy in which, on the one hand, these women act as the sole—or at least the main—breadwinners for their families and, on the other, continue to have no say, or at best, only a marginal say in decision-making, including decisions relating to their health and reproduction.

As with most women in India, bearing children is not necessarily a choice for the grass widows, but a "responsibility" towards their husbands and their families. Their only asset—their physical strength—becomes diminished usually after several childbirths and miscarriages, worsened by malnutrition and continuous stress.

While the government is prompt in sending family planning workers to the doorsteps of villagers, usually to persuade or coerce them to opt for sterilization to limit their family size in accordance with family planning norms, it has singularly failed in providing primary health care, including maternal health programmes to the women in rural Bihar. In Rasiabharna village in Darbhanga district, for example, none of the 15 grass widows this writer talked to had ever received any pre- or post-natal assistance from the health centre in the village. Nor were they aware that any such facility existed. Only two were immunized against tetanus during their last pregnancy and that too by quacks. The absence of tetanus vaccination is especially significant in view of the fact that a majority of the deliveries here are carried out at home, mostly by family members or untrained dais or traditional birth attendants, locally known as *chamains*.

The Action Aid study on the health issues of Dalit and Muslim women in rural areas of north Bihar found that the majority of them depend on dais for delivery and that only 17 per cent of the pregnant women received some ante-natal care. According to the study: "This means that over four-fifths of the pregnant women are exposed to pre- and post-natal risk and their children to neo-natal and infant mortality,"

A major health problem central to the grass widows' life is the unusually high infant and child mortality rate in this part of the country, a fact borne out clearly by a recent survey conducted in the villages of Kiratpur block of Darbhanga by a local NGO, Mithila Gram Vikas Parishad (MGVP). Although the MGVP is in the final stages of processing the data, it shared its findings on three villages of the block.

According to their survey, the under-five mortality rate in village Kiratpur, is as high as 290 per thousand live births. In two other villages, Rasiari-Pauni and Jhagarua, it is 241 per thousand live births. "Among Dalits in these villages, the child mortality rate is more than 300 per thousand live births," says MGVP coordinator Narainji Choudhary.[6] The all India figure is

[6] Mithila Gram Vikas Parishad (2003),"Child Mortality: A Case Study of Kiratpur", Darbhanga, Bihar (forthcoming).

110 per thousand, indicating the level of sheer deprivation among these people. Even the average under-five mortality rate in the rural areas of Bihar is much less than in this part of the state.

The National Family Health Survey-II (NFHS-II) released in November 2000, which puts the under-five mortality rate in rural Bihar at 114 per thousand, says, "Despite the overall decline in infant and child mortality, one in every 14 children born in Bihar during the five years before NFHS-II died within the first year of life, and one in every 10 children died before reaching age five. Clearly, child-survival programmes in Bihar need to be intensified to achieve further reductions in infant and child mortality."[7]

Kiratpur, Rasiari-Pauni and Jhagarua are among the most backward villages of Bihar. About 90 per cent of the population of these villages is made up of landless labourers or marginal farmers, who have employment for not more than three to four months a year.

The MGVP survey shows that diarrhoea, upper respiratory tract infections, diphtheria, measles and pneumonia account for most of the child deaths in these villages. And yet the routine immunization of children against diphtheria, measles, tuberculosis, whooping cough and tetanus—the cornerstone of child health care—has not only remained abysmally low but in certain cases the coverage has even declined in the last few years. One reason for this could perhaps be the health budget cuts under the structural adjustment programme.

According to the immunization schedule, all primary vaccinations should be completed by the time a child is 12 months old. Data from the NFHS-II, however, indicates that in Bihar only 7 per cent of all children are fully vaccinated by the time they are 12 months of age. In the case of rural areas the coverage is a mere 6 per cent. "In the age-group of 12–23 months, the routine immunization has come down to 11 per cent (in

[7] International Institute of Population Sciences (1999), *National Family Health Survey II*, Mumbai.

1998–99) from 30 per cent in 1994–95," the NFHS observes. The Government's apathy is not restricted to the immunization of children alone; it is visible in case of other health problems too. Diarrhoea, for example, accounts for one-fourth of the total deaths of under five children. The central government has even launched an Oral Rehydration Therapy Programme as "one of its priority activities for child survival". The programme seeks to make Oral Rehydration Salt (ORS) packets widely available, and to create awareness among mothers about how to use them.

According to NFHS-II, "The knowledge of ORS packets among mothers has not improved much in Bihar since NFHS-I (1994–95), when 37 per cent of mothers with births during the three years preceding the survey had reported knowledge of ORS packets." The situation is much worse in the case of grass widows. In fact, none of the grass widows in the reproductive age group in 12 villages in Darbhanga and Madhubani districts that I visited had received any such packet, nor had any health personnel ever visited their huts in this regard.

It is not as though government services are completely absent from rural areas of Bihar. The government, in fact, makes its presence felt in a big way for family planning and for pulse polio vaccination—which only puzzles the villagers. "Everyone asks me to protect my child from polio, but I say polio will pose a threat only if my child survives diarrhoea," complains Bachia Devi of Kiratpur village. Bachia, an illiterate grass widow, has lost four babies to diarrhoea and jaundice. The fourth baby died six days after receiving pulse polio drops. Bachia now refuses to get her fifth child—one-year-old Banaiya—vaccinated. An unknown fear grips her whenever polio vaccinators visit her hut. For her, polio is not a life threatening disease but diarrhoea is.

"Polio vaccinators have visited my home several times but no one has ever come to help me save my babies from diarrhoea," Bachia complains.

"To work on polio on such a large scale is possible because this disease demands only a technical solution. This is not so in the case of other diseases. For example, diarrhoeal diseases will require not only a technical solution but also intervention at the level of sanitation, housing, safe drinking water, nutrition and finally affordability for such measures which would involve steps towards development of the overall economic status," says Dr Shakil-ur-Rahman, a physician and a consultant with the UNICEF in Patna. The gap persists. What is important for Bachia is cumbersome for the government. For her, the first priority is to save her baby's life, and then worry about polio.

Ailments Migrate Too

An equally serious health problem of the grass widows is their vulnerability to various infectious diseases like TB, Sexually Transmitted Diseases (STDs) and HIV that their husbands often bring from distant places.

"The migration of male labour in search of employment to Delhi and other big cities has worsened the already fragile health of the wives who stay back. The men bring home not only money but also several infections like TB and HIV that they contract in other places. In the last few years there has been a sharp increase in the number of migrant labourers who have tested HIV positive in Darbhanga district," says a local activist Krishna Kumar Kashyap, whose NGO Mithila Vikas teaches Dalit women (most of them belonging to the Musahar caste) traditional Mithila painting as a means of livelihood.

Between 1997 and 2001, a leading private pathological lab in Darbhanga—Sharma Diagnostic Centre—tested about 500 HIV positive cases and almost all of them were migrant labourers. Two other private laboratories in the town with testing facilities for HIV could not give the exact figure in the absence of proper records and the district hospital refused to give out any figures, possibly because they didn't have them, although they do claim to be doing the tests. But the findings of Sharma Diagnostic Centre are enough indication of the growing HIV problem among migrant labourers in the state.

According to Dr Jagdeo Sharma, who runs the Sharma Diagnostic Centre, "Over the years the number of HIV positive cases detected at our lab has been increasing. In 1997 the number was only 17, in 1998 there were 42 new cases, in 1999 we detected 76 more HIV positive cases, in 2000 our lab identified 144 new cases and in 2001 a total of 200 new persons were reported HIV positive. All these cases were below the age of 40 years, the majority being in the age group of 20 to 30 years."

What is also to be borne in mind is that only those who are reasonably well off would have approached the Centre. Although no data, official or private, are available on the extent of the spread of HIV among the grass widows, the fact that the majority of HIV positive cases among men are in the reproductive age group increases the vulnerability of their wives.

The vulnerability of grass widows increases further as most of them are illiterate with hardly any knowledge of the virus or the infection. The NFHS-II found that only 8 per cent of rural women in Bihar have heard of AIDS and among the households belonging to lower strata (from which most of the migrant labour come), this figure is as low as 3 per cent.

Even among the grass widows who have heard of HIV and AIDS, the percentage of those aware of how to avoid getting infected is pathetically low. According to the NFHS-II, in Bihar 50 per cent of the women who have heard of HIV do not know how to protect themselves from being infected. Women belonging to Scheduled Castes, Scheduled Tribes and Other Backward Classes (social categories sending most of the migrant labour) are less likely to know any means to avoid the infection. The survey further reveals that the level of education and the standard of living have a strong bearing on the women's capacity to avoid infection. The percentage of women in rural Bihar who do not know any means to avoid the infection is substantially higher among those belonging to lower educational and economic strata, the NFHS-II found. The government, on its part, does not seem to have grasped the gravity of the situation. "We are planning to take up programmes to increase the awareness regarding HIV and AIDS," comments Dr Srivastava.

According to the CHARM study, "Most of the women respondents belonging to households with intense male labour migration are suffering from Sexually Transmitted Diseases (STDs). The presence of STDs increases their susceptibility to HIV." The CHARM study also found a very high incidence of tuberculosis among grass-widows. The real estimate could be much higher, partly due to the absence of diagnostic and treatment facilities, partly because these women just cannot afford treatment as it exists and partly because of the social stigma attached to the disease. "In the backdrop of extreme poverty and widespread prevalence of tuberculosis, infection with HIV can lead to high morbidity and mortality in the community," the study adds.

What seems to have worsened the situation is the near total absence of any follow-up, counselling, care and support activities on the part of the government. Of the 500 HIV positive cases detected by Sharma Diagnostics between 1997 and 2001 in Darbhanga, none was known to the official health machinery. Obviously none of them has received any counselling from the government setup. Whether or not these people went back to the private doctors who referred them to Sharma Diagnostics is also not known. Put simply, they have just fallen off the map. There could thus have been no effort to provide testing facilities—especially needed for the wives and the offspring of these patients—to confirm the extent and spread of infection. Treatment is of course not on the cards for anyone.

Jolt to the Old Order

The migration of labour has given a major jolt to the remnants of agrarian bondage, though not without a price. The downtrodden, who for generations lived at the mercy of landowning upper castes, have suddenly found new sources of employment and the old order, which was so meticulously preserved till recently, has started to crumble. This has created tension in several villages in north Bihar. The hidden anger of the upper castes keeps exploding in caste wars from time to time and from village to village. Since many of the attacks by armies of the upper castes on Dalit families take place when male labourers have migrated, that cross too is borne by the grass widows.

With migration, labour has become scarce in these villages, forcing the upper caste landlords to manage their fields with women and children. Sometimes they themselves have to work in the fields. The upper caste landlords resent the fact that their grip over the lower castes has loosened, more so because the "*begar*" or unpaid labour system, can no longer be effectively enforced by them. Earlier, the landlords tried to forcibly prevent labour migration, but this failed.

The change is not limited to the agrarian structure alone; it has affected family structures as well. Often migration to distant places and exposure to a new socio-cultural environment generates new expectations from their wives among the men. As the grass widows—who do not get the opportunity to experience the world outside their village—find it difficult to respond to the changing needs of their husbands, they face new insecurities. There are several instances of migrant labourers settling down with new wives at their new places of work. The result is a rise in the number of deserted women in rural north Bihar. With little choice left, these women are made to slog for the whole day for meagre wages. However, their needs are so simple, and their expectations from life so little, that they often do not realize that they are being exploited by their employers.

What is most disturbing in the entire socio-economic structure—which forms the basis for migration of male labour and exploitation of grass widows—is the complete absence of the State, its laws and its machinery. Whether it is in the form of employment generation through various government programmes or providing them foodgrain under the Public Distribution System (PDS) or providing security cover to grass widows and their families, or extending them a formal credit facility which is desperately needed by this section and which has the potential of reducing their dependence on moneylenders, the State is conspicuous by its absence, its acts of omission rather than those of commission. Even the Minimum Wages Act, which was legislated as early as 1948 and revised several times thereafter, exists only on paper. Any demand for the prescribed minimum wages arouses violent reaction on the part of the employers, and the State continues to keep its eyes closed, or only partially open.

Take the example of how the State functions in the rural areas of Bihar. The Swarnjayanti Gram Swarojgar Yojna (SGSY)—the major self-employment programme aimed at pushing the rural poor above the poverty line—has proved itself no better than its predecessor, the Integrated Rural Development Programme (IRDP) under which a large number of individual beneficiaries belonging to the Below Poverty Line (BPL) families were given subsidized loans apart from skill development training under TRYSEM (Training of Rural Youth for Self-employment). The IRDP was, however, discontinued on April 1, 1999. This was partly due to the economic measures initiated under the SAP and partly because it was realized that the programme had turned into a money-minting racket for officials who were slicing off substantial portions of loans meant for the rural poor. The "beneficiaries", who were made to thumbprint documents saying they had received amounts much larger than what they had actually got, now had to repay full amounts. Obviously, the majority of these "beneficiaries" in the rural areas of Bihar could not clear their dues and became "defaulters". The SGSY, which focuses on a group approach for self-employment, excludes the households of these IRDP victims while deciding on beneficiaries simply because bank loans cannot be extended to "defaulters". Not only are the beneficiaries-turned-defaulters left to the mercy of moneylenders, their ranks are, in fact, swelling as the SGSY has started working overtime.

This is only one aspect of the rot in a state like Bihar where most rural development programmes meant for the poor end up benefiting officials and middlemen.

For the grass widows of Bihar, it is evident that the migration of their husbands in search of work and a better life has not improved matters in any way. They are left to fend for themselves and their families, continue to be exploited by the upper castes and receive no attention from the government or from policy planners.

Women as Vectors
Health and the Rights of Sex Workers in India

GEETANJALI GANGOLI

"What we need is better working conditions, clean roads, good doctors who don't treat us like we are untouchables. Actually, we are untouchables only when we go as patients to their clinics, otherwise, they don't seem to mind coming to our rooms in the evenings!" says Prema, a 24-year-old sex worker in Kamathipura, Mumbai's well-known red light area.

Prema is one among the estimated 2,000,000 sex workers in the country today. There are no reliable statistics, but a study conducted the by Central Social Welfare Board (CSWB) in 1996[1] in six cities places the number of sex workers there between 70,000 and 100,000. The Delhi-based NGO, Bhartiya Patita Udhar Samiti, estimates that there are as many as 1,100 red light areas in India where nearly 2,300,000 sex workers, and their children, reside. The CSWB estimates that 35 per cent of sex workers enter the profession before the age of 18, as minors, and nearly 30 per cent are under 20 years. The annual turnover from the sex trade in the city of Calcutta alone is estimated at a whopping Rs 7,200 crores.

Most sex workers live and work in appalling conditions which have a deleterious effect on their health. A walk down two of the country's most famous red light districts—Kamathipura in Mumbai and Bowbazaar in Kolkata—reveals narrow pot-holed dark streets with garbage piled along the sidewalks. In the monsoon, rain water collects on the streets as the drainage system is less than adequate—clearly drainage in red light areas is not a priority for the municipality. The

[1]Central Social Welfare Board (1996), *Commercial Sex Work in Metropolitan Cities in India,* New Delhi.

"houses", piled upon each other, are mostly made up of several tiny, poorly lit cubicles with little or no light and sanitation, with women cooking in the same room that they sleep and work in.

Within the last decade, sex workers have suddenly found themselves to be the focus of health care attention from the government, medical practitioners and NGOs because of the world-wide AIDS scare. However, the emphasis has more or less been on treating them as "vectors" for the spread of HIV and other sexually transmitted infections, while ignoring their other, perhaps more legitimate, health needs.

The most glaring instance of this attitude is a bill proposed by the Maharashtra state government in 1994 that calls for the registration of all sex workers under a board constituted by the government. The bill proposes that the board conduct compulsory periodic medical testing for sexually transmitted diseases (STDs) and brand all suffering from them with indelible ink. "If this bill is ever passed, it will legalize widespread human rights violations against sex workers, who are anyway subjected to surveillance from the police under existing laws," says Sujata Gothoskar of the Forum Against Oppression of Women in Mumbai.

Real Health Needs

A large cross-section of sex workers interviewed in Mumbai, Delhi and Kolkata agreed that their most pressing health needs include reliable health care systems for themselves and their children, dependable contraception, protection from sexual violence within the profession, and from STDs and AIDS.

There is a marked absence of adequate health care facilities in red light areas. As Gita, a sex worker attached to the Mumbai Municipal Corporation's HIV/ AIDS Prevention Cell points out, "Private doctors are no good, they charge us a lot of money, and the treatment is not always good. Municipal hospitals are cheaper, but sometimes the doctors treat us badly if they realize that we are commercial sex workers. And I have seen them being rude and uncaring with AIDS patients." Gita, however prefers government hospitals in spite of the doctors being rude, perhaps because it saves her money. Like many sex workers living on a limited income, spending money on health care seems a luxury. Other sex workers in Kolkata believe that doctors in public hospitals offer a higher standard of care. Padma, a brothel keeper in Sonagachi, Kolkata, says that she takes the women in her brothel to the government run health care centres. "Those in the area who have money go to private doctors, because they feel that they might give them better care. But I don't think so. Even though I don't lack money, I prefer government clinics, because the doctors are more thorough."

Not all states run Primary Health Centres (PHCs) in urban areas; where they exist, as in Kolkata as Urban Health Centres (UHCs), they are poorly funded and falling apart. UHCs in Sonagachi are ill-equipped and lack essential drugs. Sex workers point out that the staff does not come to work regularly. Often, sex workers are forced to pay "donations" or have sex with the doctors or social workers to get access to some services. And, the timings are usually not convenient for them, as these centres are not open in the afternoon.[2]

A Condom is not a Panacea

Protection from STDs and HIV remains a significant health issue for sex workers. The overwhelming focus on condom use to prevent AIDS and STDs does not take into account the realities of women in the profession. It is not always possible for powerless sex workers to insist that the client wears a condom. According to Anju Pawar, Community Development Officer at the Mumbai Municipal Corporation Cell that works in the red light areas in Mumbai: "We tell women to use condoms with all their clients. But it is not always possible. How

[2]Government of India, National Commission for Women (1996), *Societal Violence on Women and Children in Commercial Sex Work—A Report*, New Delhi.

can they? If the woman is very young, and the man is aggressive, she can't refuse him. Also, if the woman is hungry and needs money desperately, she doesn't dare insist that the man use a condom." The Mumbai Municipal Corporation's HIV/AIDS Prevention Cell, therefore, feels that male clients should be targeted. They conduct puppet shows in theatres and public places in the area to promote the use of condoms.

Another major problem that women face is the unreliability of condoms as only the cheaper varieties are supplied in red light areas. Shanti, from Sonagachi, who is certain that she doesn't want children, says, "It's all too easy for doctors to say we should insist on clients using condoms. I do insist that the man uses a condom, since I am terrified of falling ill. But, many condoms supplied to us in the dispensaries are thin, and often break. So, to make sure that I don't get pregnant, I take (the pill) Mala D."

Another issue is that sex workers are conditioned to believe that condom use is essential only in their professional life. Sex workers interviewed in Mumbai, Delhi and Kolkata say most of them use prophylactics only with their clients, not with their husbands or babus. The babu can sometimes be a pimp, but he is more often a long- standing client who the sex worker may accept as her husband or long-term partner. While the relationship with one babu lasts, the woman rarely accepts another man as her babu. He may have other sources of income and sometimes is married to another woman, but is an important source of emotional support for the sex worker.

One woman who admitted she had been infected with syphilis by her babu pointed out, "I had to undergo long and expensive treatment, during which time, my children had to do without books for their school". When she confronted her partner, he denied having passed on the infection, accusing her of infecting him instead. "I know that it is not my fault. I make sure that I don't sleep with a client unless he uses a condom. But how can I force my babu?" Skewed power relationships between the babu and the women make it difficult for them to assert themselves—or even to want to—on the issue of using condoms.

The relationships between babus and women in red light areas are often as oppressive as many traditional marriages. According to Sarboni of Sanlaap, an NGO for sex workers in Kolkata, "Some women do go through some kind of ceremony with their babus, and say that they are married. The babus often live off their earnings, and subject them to violence. Women seem to need these relationships desperately." Sujata Gothoskhar adds, "Commercial sex workers are as keen as 'other' women to settle down into a quasi- marriage, which sometimes replicates all the oppressive conditions of a 'real' marriage, without the social sanction. It merely reiterates the pervasiveness of marriage, especially to a category of women placed outside the margins of conventional marriage and family life."

The exclusive focus on condom use has other drawbacks. Preeti Patkar of the NGO Prerana that works for the prevention of second-generation commercial sex work says, "I agree that using condoms is the only way of preventing AIDS and a host of other STDs. But has anyone ever considered what using condoms all the time for sex workers can do to them? Some sex workers service three to four men every day. The repeated use of condoms can often cause allergies and rashes at the very least." In addition, women in commercial sex work often want children, and at such points, condom use is not possible.

In spite of these problems, sex workers take steps to prevent getting infected. As the National Commission for Women recognizes, sex workers have played a significant role in combating AIDS.[3] Sanlaap has formed self-regulatory boards that encourage sex workers not to work without the use of condoms. The HIV/AIDS Prevention Cell at the Mumbai Municipal Corporation has similar aims.

But AIDS is not the only health issue for sex workers. Organizations such as the HIV/ AIDS Cell in Mumbai have real-

---

[3]*Ibid.*

ized that it is impossible to focus exclusively on AIDS prevention. Manisha, a sex worker working with the Cell, points out: "Sex workers have a host of reproductive tract infections. Seventy five per cent of women practising the sex trade have some form of STDs. White discharge and a burning sensation with urination are common health problems, as is tuberculosis." Dr Kannai Banerjee, attached to the Kolkata Medical College, says that in his experience, Reproductive Tract Infections (RTIs) like genital ulcers and discharge are common among sex workers. There is a high incidence of skin infections, such as scabies, and illnesses like Hepatitis B.

One point of view is that there is a link between AIDS and other sexually transmitted diseases. Dr Smarajit Jana, who works with an AIDS prevention project in Kolkata, says, "People without venereal diseases have only a 0.1 per cent chance of acquiring AIDS. Most venereal diseases are curable, but people, including sex workers often don't approach doctors in the initial stages, as they think it is not a serious illness."

No Control Over Birth Control

Reliable contraception is another important unmet health need of sex workers. Contraceptive use is erratic and uncertain. Alpana, a 45-year-old sex worker from Kamathipura says that while today many women insist that their clients use condoms, ten years ago, things were different. "I got into the profession when I was 17-years-old. I got pregnant three months later. I had three children by the time I was 22, and then decided that enough was enough. So I went in for sterilization."

Preeti Patkar says that from her experience of working in Kamathipura, many women do not use contraception regularly. "They get pregnant and then have a Medical Termination of Pregnancy (MTP) in the second or third month, or even later. What happens often is that they become infertile as a result of some STD that they contract. Once they figure out that they can't conceive, they stop using any contraceptive method." Contraceptive pills are often used by women in the trade, many times in combination with condoms. MTPs are used as a last resort. But there is some fear of the side effects of using pills and one sex worker I spoke to said: "I used Mala D for a few months initially but then I was told that I had to use a condom as well. I was putting on weight and losing my hair; I was worried about losing my clients so I stopped the pill."

Some women use Intra Uterine Devices (IUDs). A representative of the Population Council points out that IUDs can cause, and aggravate, infections of the reproductive tract, and are unsuitable for sex workers. Condoms, due to poor quality, and reluctance of the client to use them, are not always reliable. She claims that long acting hormonal contraceptives, such as NET-EN, Depo-Provera, Norplant and Anti Fertility Vaccines, are perhaps more suited to the needs of sex workers. When quizzed about the side effects of such methods, she says, "It is far more dangerous for commercial sex workers to get pregnant repeatedly, given the high incidence of STDs. Pregnancies are followed by MTPs, which are probably worse for their health than these contraceptives."

Jayashree Velankar, a member of the Mumbai-based Forum for Women's Health, is horrified at this proposal. A pamphlet brought out by Forum for Women's Health, titled "Pros and Cons of Contraception Available in India", points out that these methods have many possible side effects. These include, heart problems, depression, menstrual irregularities, effects on future fertility, including irreversible sterility, premature menopause and effects on the immune system. They need sophisticated screening and monitoring, which is not available in India. Nor is removal easy or possible. Control over the method is thus vested with the medical practitioner, not the woman.

Dr C Sathyamala, a health activist with the Medico Friends' Circle, elaborates, "Contraceptives are not therapeutic drugs. Side effects for these can't be condoned as they can be for say, cancer-fighting drugs. Of course, sex workers, like most other women in the reproductive age group, need contraceptives. But that need can't be exploited to push dangerous measures like Depo-Provera and NET-EN on them." The idea that long-acting contraceptives are ideal for sex-workers is thus deeply controversial. It represents too a "fix-it and forget-it approach" to their needs simply because they are considered marginal to mainstream society.

Non-sexual Ailments

Women in the industry are vulnerable to a host of other non-sexual ailments. Dr Jana points out that constant exposure to social stigmatizing leaves women with low self-esteem. Drug abuse and alcohol dependence are thus quite common. Women who may want to leave the profession are unable to do so because they believe their families will not accept them. Prema, who joined the sex trade after being abandoned by her husband and parents-in-law, says, "I dream of going back to my family, not my husband, but I do miss my son. But, since they've thrown me out, they are not going to take me back if I tell them that I've been in Kamathipura these four years."

In addition, violence from clients, especially at the point of entry into the profession, and later from babus, is a part of their lives. While practising the profession, some women are raped and beaten by their clients, including regular customers. Customers often impose their sexual fantasies on women in commercial sex work. They are forced to perform sexual acts that they are reluctant to, often out of fear of losing a customer.[4]

The rape of a commercial sex worker is never seen as possible in a court of law. As one woman pointed out: "If women like us go to a police station to complain of rape, the police ask us if we are married or single. They ask us why we stay with a *gharwali* (woman brothel owner) if we want to complain about rape." In some areas in Mumbai, there have been cases of local lumpen elements beating and attacking women.[5] Fear of arrests and of the police adds to a sense of vulnerability. The police beat and harass them regularly, aided as they

[4]Gangoli, Geetanjali (1999), *Report of Conceptual Clarity Workshop.* Oganized by Prerana. March 30—April 2, Khandala.
[5]*Ibid.*

are by the provisions of the law on commercial sex work. Others in the area often do not help a woman in distress, even if she is being assaulted publicly. The situation leaves women in commercial sex work feeling very vulnerable, especially since they lack community support.

Trafficking the Girl Child

Minors find it even more difficult to cope with the demands of sex work. Most women entering the profession as adults, or of their own accord, seem to accept the situation in which they find themselves with some degree of helplessness but nevertheless conscious that they have made the decision. According to Shraddha, a 35-year-old worker from Kohlapur, "I got into the profession after I had three children. My husband left me. Though I was educated, I couldn't get a job. So, to look after my children, I came here. Today, my son is a doctor."

However, those who come in as children face more agony that continues even as they grow older. As Vimla from Kamathipura points out, "I was brought to the city 15 years ago when I was 12. My parents were told by someone in our village that I would get a job in someone's house. So they sent me here. I still send money home. But I still have nightmares about the beatings that I suffered from the brothel keeper till I accepted my first client."

A study by Sanlaap on child commercial sex work in Kolkata testifies to the extensive use of violence to coerce minor children into commercial sex work.[6] The violence includes sexual assault by agents or customers, and physical violence. Interviews show that minors are sold by parents or family members, or more rarely, kidnapped and brought to red light areas. Child sex workers have a low awareness of the causes and consequences of certain illnesses, especially STDs and RTIs. The Sanlaap report elaborates, "Even where awareness exists,

[6]Sanlaap (1998), *Child Commercial Sex Work in Calcutta: A Situational Analysis*, Kolkata.

there is little that they can do to prevent or treat them. Whether it is the use of a condom, or taking some other precautionary measures, sex workers, especially child sex workers, are particularly helpless *vis a vis* their clients. When a disease actually occurs, follow up is not always regular."

Meenu De works as a warden in a home for minor girls who have been rescued from commercial sex work. The home is run by Sanlaap in Ambola, a suburb of Kolkata. She says many girls in the home suffer from respiratory illnesses, headaches and depression. "The girls are desperately in need of affection and care. Their life is so difficult, and at a young age, they are subjected to sexual abuse, which is nothing short of rape. They end up feeling ashamed and insecure and fall prey to a host of psychosomatic illnesses." Many girls are separated from their families, adding to a sense of isolation. For minors in the profession, the risks attached to rape are high, as their reproductive tracts are not ready for sexual activity. Interviews conducted with minor girls in the profession reveal a sense of dejection. Says Priti, a 16-year-old, who was kidnapped from her village in rural West Bengal by her uncle, worked in Kamathipura, and was sent to a shelter in Kolkata after police raids in 1996, "I was forced to do very bad things with clients. The police took me away from there, but I can't go back to my parents. They will not accept me."

Priti testified to the ill-treatment that she had suffered at the hands of the brothel keeper. "I was starved and beaten by the *malkin* if I refused to work. Sometimes the men used to beat me because they enjoyed it. There were 25-30 girls in the brothel. Only the older girls were allowed to go out of the building, we weren't. The malkin didn't give me any money. I was only allowed to keep the baksheesh with me." Priti does not have much faith in the police, in spite of being "rescued" by them. "The police took away my money. I had saved Rs 1,200 and they gave me only five hundred. Nobody listened to me when I tried to complain."

In addition, there is the risk of pregnancy and early childbearing. As Sarboni pointed out, the brothel owners encourage young girls not to abort during their first pregnancy, as they know that their options will be further reduced once they have a child. "Most sex workers get little care during their pregnancy, even though some other women in the *badi* (brothel) try to look after the girl if it is her first pregnancy. What is worse is that many are forced to keep on working through their pregnancies and even when they are lactating. They have no choice, they need the money."

While there is a widespread misconception that sex workers force their daughters to enter the sex trade, a study conducted in Kolkata in 1992 reveals that less than 5 per cent of the sex workers surveyed were born in the city.[7] As Indrani Sinha from Sanlaap points out, "It is a stereotyped impression, completely false, of the commercial sex worker that she wants daughters only to push them into sex work. The fact is that most new entrants into sex work are trafficked from outside the red light area. But I will not deny that there are gross human rights violations that these children suffer from." These violations may include an early exposure to sexual activity, especially if the woman operates independently, and from a small room. In addition, as Kinsuk Roy, a social worker from Kolkata, points out, the daughters of sex workers are often vulnerable to sexual harassment and assault from clients. Besides, as we have seen, some women are pushed into alcoholism and drug abuse, which have an adverse effect on the children.

In addition, there are the problems that children of sex workers in red light areas share with other children belonging to poor families. That is, living in small, overcrowded, badly ventilated rooms, and lack of fresh and nutritious food. Malnutrition and poor ventilation lead to a host of health problems that their mothers cannot cope with.[8]

---

[7]Durbar Mahila Samanwaya Committee (1996), *The Fallen Learn to Rise: The Social Impact of STD-HIV Intervention Programme*. Kolkata

[8]Government of India, Central Social Welfare Board (1990), *Commercial Sex Workers and Their Children: Report of a National Workshop*, New Delhi.

Archaic Laws

Laws relating to sex work in India, for example, the Immoral Trafficking in Women and Girls (Prevention) Act, 1986 (PITA), focus on trafficking as the entry point. The logic is that entry into commercial sex work is seen as trafficking, synonymous with coercion, force, kidnapping, and/or sale of young women and children into the field. The focus is on "prevention" of commercial sex work. While commercial sex work *per se* is not illegal under the act, working as a sex worker is rendered difficult. Under PITA, soliciting, brothel keeping, and living off the earnings of a commercial sex worker and child sex workers are illegal. But PITA is largely used by the police to harass women on the streets. As the police inspector, Crime, Nagpada Police Station in Mumbai, states, "The police needs a search warrant to search a brothel. No such legality is needed to book a single woman out there 'soliciting'." The term soliciting is also undefined. The police admit that sitting at a window, standing on a balcony, smoking in a public place and gesturing are interpreted as soliciting. The Act gives the police the right to arrest women under these charges. In addition, the police also enjoy extra-legal powers that help them collect bribes from the women, beat and often rape them.

State policies on health for sex workers are grossly inadequate. The focus has been on the prevention of AIDS and STDs. A study by the National Commission for Women points out that sex workers are being tested for HIV without their consent in some hospitals. Lawyers Anand Grover and Priti Patel, who work on the area of legality and ethics, explain that consent is needed for HIV testing, as it involves removal of an individual's body fluids. Compulsory and forced testing is clearly illegal and violates World Health Organization (WHO) guidelines. At a 1993 regional workshop organized by WHO, and attended by Indian representatives, a recommendation was passed that: "Governments should adopt national policies on HIV testing, including confidentiality. There is no medical, or public health rationale for screening or routine testing of specific risk groups or patient groups." [9]

Although earlier there had been controversies about NGOs conducting so-called AIDS vaccine trials illegally in the country, the Government of India approved an AIDS vaccine trial to commence by the end of 2003 to be conducted by the National AIDS Control Organization (NACO). According to officials of NACO "Over 2,500 people representing commercial sex workers and clients of STD clinics have been recruited in Pune (for the trial)."[10] Significantly, in 1994, the US took a decision to indefinitely postpone its scheduled trials of two HIV vaccines on the grounds that there was not enough evidence regarding their effectiveness to justify the trials.

The net result of targeting women in red light areas, as the NCW report elaborates, is that it "increases public and police violence upon them; decreases their ability to assert themselves; allows customers to demand and force unsafe sex upon them; and increases the rate of HIV infection among women ... customers and the family of the customers." In addition, a near exclusive focus on sex workers ignores the fact that any part of the population is at risk, hence it "creates a false sense of security (among) ...other groups." Indeed as many feminists in India have pointed out, targeting sex workers for AIDS makes very little sense as the greatest danger to women's health is from arranged marriages—to partners they have no relationship of equality with. They have pointed out that few women in the country can exercise agency about who they marry, when they marry, and within marriage, insist on safe sex.

What is most significant is that a mindless focus on sex work as a high-risk activity means that other activities and categories, even in the lives of sex workers, are ignored in intervention programmes. As we have seen, women in commercial sex work face various problems even when they want to protect themselves from infection. However, state efforts to im-

[9]National Commission for Women, (1996) *op-cit.*

[10]*The Times of India*, "India Okays AIDS Vaccine Trial", November 10,1998.

prove the conditions of sex workers often ignore these nuances and complexities.

A report brought out in May 1998 by a committee commissioned by the Department of Women and Child Development, Ministry of Human Resource Development, makes several useful recommendations to improve the health of sex workers.[11] These include issuing health cards to sex workers and their children to ensure free medical treatment, drugs and medication; setting up health care centres in or near red light areas, and preventing and banning unethical, illegal and uninformed medical testing for HIV/AIDS/ STDs. However, the report refers to sex workers as "women and child victims", thus displaying a rather patronising attitude.

Children of a Lesser God

An area of concern for policy makers and activists is improving the conditions within which children of commercial sex workers live. Many children of commercial sex workers have problems accessing schools and obtaining health care. They tend not to receive immunization for example, and as activists working in the area point out, it is rare that the local government hospitals run an ongoing campaign on the issue. Often children are immunized once or twice, but the course is not completed.

In addition, sex workers have found it difficult to get their children admitted in schools, because school authorities insist on having the father's name on the admission form. NGOs like the Bhartiya Patita Udhar Samiti in Delhi try to help the children in red light areas by starting classes locally to provide non-formal education. However, Sujata Gothoskar feels that

[11]Government of India, Ministry of Human Resource Development (1998), *Report of the Committee on Commercial Sex Work, Child Commercial Sex Workers and Children of Commercial Sex Workers and Plan Action to Combat Trafficking and Commercial Sexual Exploitation of Women and Children*, New Delhi.

this leads to ghettoization. "The children of commercial sex workers, like anyone else, have the right to education in main-stream schools. It is ridiculous that non-formal education is good enough only for the poorest, and most marginalized in our society."

The situation was redressed—legally—by a Supreme Court judgment in 1992, which states that in the case of children of sex workers, the name of the father or male guardian will not be insisted upon for the purposes of admission in a school. The Department of Women and Child Welfare, Human Resource Development Ministry, has sent relevant instructions to the Education Ministry to be implemented in each state.[12] This, however, is still to be done.

Significantly, policy makers feel that sex workers are incapable of looking after their children. Khairati Ram Bhola, who runs a school in Delhi's GB Road, speaks of how he is forced to follow the government schedule that if a sex worker has more than two children, and has not had herself sterilized, her children will not be admitted into schools. A Supreme Court judgment in 1997 recommended that children of sex workers, especially their daughters, should not be allowed to live in red light areas, and should be segregated from their mothers.[13] The judgment supports the logic of the Juvenile Justice Act, 1986. Under this Act, the State is empowered to evolve a system for the protection, development and rehabilitation of those defined as "neglected juveniles". While defining a neglected juvenile, the Act makes a distinction between all other destitute and vulnerable children, and children of sex workers. The latter, by virtue of their parentage, are deemed "neglected juveniles". The report by the Department of Women and Child Welfare examines ways in which children can be removed from red light areas, using "persuasion and motivation", rather than coercion.

---

[12]Interview with T M Vijay Bhaskar, Director, Department of Women and Child Development, Ministry of Human Resource Development, Government of India, September 3, 1998.

[13]Gaurav Jain Vs Union of India. *AIR 1997 SC 3021.*

As reported earlier, most sex workers do not allow their daughters to enter the trade. The solution, then, might perhaps lie in not forcibly separating children from their mothers, but in creating an infrastructure where children in red light areas are safe. The efforts of some NGOs in this direction have been significant. CINI-ASHA, a Kolkata-based organization, has set up crèches where sex workers can leave their children in the evenings while they practise their trade. At another level, interviews with sex workers reveal that they focus almost exclusively on looking after their children. Lachmi, a sex worker in Khidirpur, a red light area near the Kolkata port, bristles at the suggestion that sex workers make bad mothers. "Like all mothers, we have dreams for our children. Why do people think that just because we are sex workers, we exploit our children? Most of us are in this line for the sake of our children."

NGOs Chip in

This dismal picture is only partly redeemed by the efforts of some good Samaritans working on a variety of issues in the red light areas. The need for health services in red light areas has prompted Khairati Ram Bhola's organization to put pressure on the government to extend the services of government run mobile vans to operate at times convenient to the residents of the area, but without success. CINI-ASHA, Kolkata, combines work on sexual health issues, providing services like crèches for children of sex workers, non-formal education and improving the general health of children in the red light area by providing nutritive food and food supplements.

NGOs like the Mumbai Municipal Corporation Cell and Sexual Health Intervention Programme in Kolkata run clinics in red light areas that try to address the varied health needs of sex workers. Dr Amar Kumar Singh, who volunteers for the clinic run by the Sexual Health Intervention Programme, agrees that the health needs of sex workers are not met by State-run programmes. This is true even in West Bengal, where the public health system is said to be better than in other states. As he puts it, "To a large extent, the NGOs are taking over the responsibilities of the State. The proportion of India's GDP allocated for health is as low as 1 per cent and is shrinking further. But health is the most essential sector of society." Well meaning as these NGOs are, this means that the State can ignore its responsibility to provide basic amenities to the poor and marginalized in society, which includes sex workers.

Also, large-scale social change is necessary. It is not just the police who harass sex workers or the health care system that does not reach out to them. A study conducted by the Social Welfare Board, reveals that sex workers believe that members of the judiciary are insensitive to their plight. "They do not consider us human beings. . . they add to our harassment and humiliation. . . they fail to understand the human aspects of the problem. They perceive it as a law and order problem."[14]

This feeling is not unjustified. A recent judgment reveals the prurient and voyeuristic attitude of some judges. According to Justice Ratnavel Pandian, children within commercial sex work are seen as "unfortunate" and as "girls in full bloom" being blighted. Speaking of the Immoral Trafficking in Women and Girls (Prevention) Act, 1986, Justice Pandian states that the Act aims to "rescue the fallen women and girls. . . and also to provide an opportunity to these fallen victims so that they could become decent members of society." The judgment focuses on "violations of all canons of morality, decency and dignity of humankind."[15] Nowhere in the judgment is there any reference to the physical and mental violence that children experience within commercial sex work. This is, in a sense, double victimization in that victims are condemned for being victims.

---

[14]Central Social Welfare Board (1996), *Commercial Sex Work in Metropolitan Cities in India*, New Delhi, 1996.

[15]In the Supreme Court of India. Criminal Original Jurisdiction. Writ Petition (Criminal) No 421 of 1989.

Decriminalization or Legalization?

The major area of concern is how the current situation can be redeemed. Existing law hardly offers a solution. Social workers in the field often focus on prevention of trafficking of women and children into commercial sex work. International conventions on trafficking, such as the 1998 SAARC Convention,[16] are based on preventing and restricting the passage of women between countries in South Asia.

The Convention fails to make a distinction between trafficking of women and children. There can be no question of consent or agency as far as trafficking of children into hazardous industries, including bangle making, commercial sex work or camel jockeying, is concerned. But, as far as women are concerned, the issue needs to be seen slightly differently. Many women seek a livelihood, for supporting themselves and their families, through sex work. Difficult and exploitative as their lives and experiences undeniably are, they may not be able or willing to leave their profession. Different guidelines and strategies are needed to withdraw children from hazardous work conditions and to improve the working conditions of women within commercial sex work, as in other professions, say experts. The focus on commercial sex work through the prism of trafficking means that it is not seen as work, or an occupation that might be difficult, even hazardous, but nevertheless an occupation. Where the focus is on trafficking, as it is in India, issues of rights of sex workers are hardly ever seen as significant.

Some social workers in this sector have expressed an opinion that legalization of commercial sex work is one way to improve the health and socio economic conditions of sex workers. Khairati Ram Bhola feels that the status of sex workers cannot improve unless the profession is legalized. As he puts

[16]SAARC (1998), *Convention on Preventing and Combating Trafficking in Women and Children for Commercial sex work*, Available at http://www.hsph.harvard.edu/Organizations/healthnet/SAsia/repro2/SAARC.htm.

it, "Under existing conditions, commercial sex workers lose up to 75 per cent of their income to the police and pimps. They do not have enough money, and end up being indebted to moneylenders. Nor do they have a health card." He goes on to say that licensed brothels can lead to regular health tests. Bhola's demand is based on the assumption that while most women do not enter the profession out of choice, once in, they have the right to basic amenities.

I H Gilada, of the Mumbai-based Asahaya Tirskrut Nari Sangh argues similarly. He holds that commercial sex work is a necessary evil that preserves the family and prevents rape of women. These attitudes are prompted not out of concern for the health of sex workers, but to prevent them from "infecting" a healthy population. Khairati Ram Bhola says, "If commercial sex workers are unhealthy, they will infect our children, the young boys who go to them for gratification." This ties in with his view that commercial sex workers have the right to good health and living conditions as they fulfil a social need. "All men feel hungry—for sex. Commercial sex workers prevent women from good families from getting raped. If commercial sex workers were not there, women would not be able to walk on the road. Unmarried young men would attack any woman on the road. In fact in my opinion, commercial sex workers are social workers, next only to mothers and should be treated with respect." The argument seems a trifle suspect. It is not only unmarried and young men who frequent brothels. Men of all ages and social classes are seen in red light areas. It also seems to imply that patriarchy—in all its worst exploitative aspects—is somehow natural.

In response to Bhola's views, Nandita Gandhi from the Forum Against Oppression of Women, Mumbai, retorts, "We are very happy that Bhola considers commercial sex workers to be individuals in their own right. But to equate them with social workers is to demean both. Commercial sex workers should be given respect because they are doing work. The point, however, is that the work they do is of a perverted kind. This is not because of their immorality, but because of economic factors."

Gandhi points to double standards that accept and condone only the sexual needs of men, not of women.

Some women in the profession feel that legalization can only increase stigmatization. In a workshop with sex workers, the issue of licensing was discussed in some detail. Some women saw a connection between the move—from the State—to license sex work, and the HIV/ AIDS scare in the nation. They pointed out that licensing would lead to increased control by the State, and that they would be subjected to increased surveillance and restriction of mobility. It would also lead to a division between "legal" and "illegal" commercial sex workers.[17] The experience of the Netherlands, for example, has not been equivocally positive. Indeed it only affects the tip of the iceberg, with a large number of commercial sex workers outside the purview of the State and of health authorities. It has also been argued that in countries where economic policies such as the Structural Adjustment Programmes have led to a decline in the living conditions of large numbers of people, the largest proportion of entrants to the sex profession are housewives and students seeking to supplement their income. That there has been an increase in prostitution consequent to these policies has been documented in a number of countries. Activists further argue that in the Indian context, given the high degree of vulnerability of women within the profession, the reality of large-scale coercion, trafficking of minor girls into commercial sex work and the inhuman conditions of life within brothels, licensing will merely legitimize these violations.[18]

Another objection that women in the profession had to licensing was that it would be tantamount to being "stamped" as commercial sex workers. Being given a "legal" status would permanently fix their status. Besides, their experience with the law enforcing machinery and the rampant corruption there

---

[17]Gangoli (1999), Report, *op-cit.*

[18]Activists of Prerana cited in Rajeshwari Sunder Rajan (1996), "The Commercial Sex Work Question(s): (Female) Agency, Sexuality and Work",. *Research in Progress Paper, History and Society. Third Series,* New Delhi, Nehru Memorial Museum and Library.

made them feel that licensing would lead to a fresh set of problems with the police and the judiciary. It may not stop violence by the police—which is illegal anyway—but may actually aggravate it.

Organized sex workers feel that rather than the State regulating their lives through licenses, it is important that sex workers themselves make efforts to improve their lives, at least in some fields. Sanlaap has formed self-regulatory boards that do not allow the entry of minor girls into the profession, while providing services. The Kolkata Sex Workers Union, which grew out of the Durbar Mahila Samanwaya Committee (DMSC), in Sonagachi now includes both male and female sex workers in the city of Kolkata. DMSC also expresses the view that: "We do not want any legalization—we want our right to regulate our own lives. . .".[19]

One point of view among sex workers is that though licensing would not improve their working conditions there is a need to make some demands from the State. The most important demand is that children should be stopped from entering the profession. As it is, corrupt officials collude in allowing children to be recruited for sex work. Second, they also demand that their children be provided with basic educational and vocational skills by the State.

Other than the State, the *gharwali* should take some responsibility to provide the women in her brothel with safe living and working conditions. The brothel should be treated as a workplace and women in the brothel given certain rights, including the right to safety and crèches for children.

A manifesto, floated by the Union in 1997 argues that contrary to the opinion expressed by social workers, police and State officials, commercial sex workers are not a homogenous category. The manifesto argues that commercial sex work should be treated as work, and commercial sex workers not seen as "victims" who need to be rescued. Thus, they believe

---

[19]Durbar Mahila Samanwaya Committee (1997), *Sex Workers Right to Self Determination*, Kolkata.

that "rehabilitation" seen as the only feasible solution, is not desirable for two reasons. One, given the existing socio-economic situation, the large number of men and women in the profession cannot be easily integrated into other professions. Second, that sex workers, like workers in other professions, have the right to demand improvement in their working conditions while staying within the profession.

It argues that criminal provisions against commercial sex work should, therefore, be removed, while there should be stricter implementation of laws for the prevention of child sex work. In other words, the group believes that there needs to be a shift from the attitude manifested in existing law, that is, blaming and penalising the victim, to improving the conditions within which women live their lives. As the manifesto puts it, "Women take up commercial sex work for the same reason as they may take up any other livelihood option available to them. Our stories are not fundamentally different from the labourer from Bihar who pulls a rickshaw in Kolkata. . .when do most women have a choice within or outside the family? Do we become casual domestic workers willingly? Do we have a choice about whom we want to marry and when?"

The range of options available to anyone wanting to take a stand on the issue is confusing. What is perhaps necessary is that the people who matter listen to women in the profession, and not treat them either as criminals, or as victims, but allow them the right to choose from—and enlarge—these options. Some activists argue that the first step might well be to remove criminal provisions against sex workers. Decriminalization may not transform the lives of commercial sex workers. But what it can do is to create a context within which sex workers can unionise and fight for better working and living conditions, and regulate the injustices within their profession.

(The names of all the sex workers have been changed.)

Even If We Shout There is No One to Hear

Reproductive Health Issues among the Marginalized Population of Nagaland

RUPA CHINAI

Busy hands prepare a woman for a Caesarian section in the Zunheboto district hospital situated in the remote hills of Nagaland. Her delivery is two weeks overdue. Her face is covered by a mask which is sprinkled with ether. She writhes in agony till she loses consciousness. This primitive, highly risky, "open air anaesthesia" is routine in the hospital. The hospital has not owned a single cylinder of oxygen for the past 12 years. If the woman's pulse rate weakens or she has a cardiac arrest, there is no apparatus to monitor her, or make breathing easier.

The mother and baby are lucky to survive the ordeal. But many Naga women are not so fortunate and succumb to the grossly inadequate health infrastructure and care in the state. Maternal and infant mortality rates continue to be high, despite the state government's claims to the contrary.

The Numbers Game

If Nagaland's official records are to be believed, health indicators in this remote hilly state surpass even those of the affluent Scandinavian countries. The health department in the state capital of Kohima claims that maternal mortality is below one per 1,00,000, while infant mortality is 7 per 1,000 live births. The female literacy rate is said to be 55.7 per cent and immunization coverage is 60 per cent. Says a senior health official: "Our women are strong, they have stamina. They hardly ever go to a doctor with complications. They deliver their children safely at home."

The state's complacency is at variance with the Second National Family Health Survey for 1998–99, that reveals that less than 20 per cent of women in Nagaland receive any ante-natal care, and only 14 per cent of children receive their complete course of vaccinations. Hospital-based data do not reflect the reality of illness and death in the villages, say independent researchers. Patients have no faith in the services there and come only when they are really critical.

In rural areas there is no system of record keeping unless a patient reports to the government hospital—and that seldom happens. Access to health services remains difficult because of the long distances patients have to travel, compounded by the absence of roads and transportation. Death or birth certificates are not issued.

In this scenario, the only ones with access to some figures are the churches and women's organizations. The Konyak Baptist Church, with 45,000 members belonging to the Konyak tribe, the largest among Nagaland's 15 indigenous groups, reveals that 384 women died in Mon district in 1998, mostly, it is said, in childbirth. Members of the Konyak Women's Association in Aboi block point to the large number of infant and child deaths in the last two years since 1997.

Compounding the problem of high maternal and infant deaths is the high rate of miscarriages in the state, most of which are of course unreported. A survey by independent health researcher Monisha Behal reveals an alarmingly high incidence of miscarriages amongst rural women during the course of their reproductive years. Women do not readily talk about the problem, and because it takes place in the privacy of their homes, it is seldom recorded in official data, she says. In Shoipu village of Zunheboto district, with a largely Sema population, a survey of 47 households revealed 76 miscarriages, with some women recalling they had suffered as many as ten. Similarly in Kivikhu village with 52 households, there were 71 miscarriages, and in Khukiye Lukhai village with 24 households, the figure was 41. This information is based on women recalling their lifetime reproductive experiences, and does not conform to any time frame. Thus although these figures do not give an idea about reproductive wastage rate or the still birth rate, they nevertheless do give some indication of the extent of reproductive problems.

Similar findings emanate from Phek district. In Leshemi village, a survey of 100 households revealed a total of 83 miscarriages amongst 46 women. Nearly two-thirds of women's complaints here are, however, related to backache, weakness and abdominal pain caused by heavy workloads and low nutritional status.

Doubly Burdened

The risk of miscarriages and death among pregnant women in the three remote districts of Mon, Phek and Zunheboto reflect both the overall lack of socio-economic development and the neglect of the health sector in Nagaland. The Nagas have been fighting a relentless struggle for independence from India for the past 50 years. Many Nagas firmly believe that historically and culturally they are different from Indians. Apart from their image as rebels, most Indians know nothing about the Nagas, how they live or what they think. Many think of them as "primitive tribals".

Most of the country's development programmes have made little inroads into these inaccessible hills. Although the central government in New Delhi has poured in millions of rupees for the state's development, there is little evidence of its legitimate use. Naga society, on its part, has been unable to demand accountability from its political leaders and bureaucrats because of their preoccupation with finding a solution to the "Naga political problem".

The centre's new health policy thrust on "reproductive health", which aims to safeguard the health of women and children and encourage birth control, has little meaning in the context of the Nagas' lives. Nor do other key aspects of the policy such as reducing maternal and infant deaths. These small communities, amongst the most marginalized on the Indian map, provide a rare insight into what is going wrong with India's public health policy and programmes.

Four weeks of travel in Mon, Phek and Zunheboto districts revealed how women in these communities perceive their health needs. One afternoon, three middle-aged women walked from Tamlu village, 65 kilometres away to Mon town for a visit. Mon, inhabited by the Konyaks, is one of the least developed and most isolated districts of Nagaland. When asked what their main health problem was, they said, "We always feel so weak and tired." Virtually every interview with Naga women elsewhere in the interior districts of the state produced the same reply. Behind this general complaint lies a story of excessive workloads, inadequate food, frequent illnesses and disease, repeated child bearing, lack of access to preventive and curative health services, and stress due to the political and economic turmoil that grips this troubled area.

For the Konyak women, the day starts long before dawn. Deforestation and depletion of ground water has caused havoc in their daily lives, forcing them to walk miles in search of fuel and water. Collection of firewood takes at least three hours, and fetching water requires one hour. Apart from all the household chores, the women work throughout the day in the fields on the steep hillsides, slashing and burning old crop residues and growing new ones, in the *jhum* or "shifting" system of cultivation typical of the area. At dusk, when they return home, the women collect wild jungle leaves, which garnish their supper of rice, chillies and some meat, if the husband has been successful in the day's hunt. In the midst of this back-breaking routine, they bear an average of five to ten children.

In Longwa, a picturesque Konyak village, women gathered in the palm leaf thatched house of the powerful *angh* (hereditary chief), confirm this story. This village marks the international boundary line. The angh's kitchen is in India and his living room is in Myanmar. With the local Primary Health Centre (PHC) securely locked, the Longwa villagers have to trek a whole day to reach the nearest medical facility in Mon town. But they might as well not bother, for the district referral hospital is devoid of competent doctors, essential drugs and equipment.

In Chizami village in the state's Phek district, a toilet in a PHC has been converted into a makeshift delivery room for high-risk pregnancies.[1] The 12-bedded centre services a population of 2,500, with no microscope, no laboratory technician, essential drugs or vaccines. With no connecting roads, it takes the doctor at least three hours to walk to the farthest village to conduct a home delivery.

Precarious Lives

Nagaland's health infrastructure is so poor that sometimes a simple fall from a tree can lead to the death of a child. In Mon district, a six-year-old boy died four days after falling from a tree and breaking his leg. There is no X-ray machine in the district and a doctor from the Mon Civil Hospital who examined the boy failed to detect internal injuries. With no faith in the government doctor, the parents rushed the boy to Sonari in neighbouring Assam state, a six hour drive on a potholed road. There, a quack tightly bound the leg in plaster and sent him back home. Toxemia developed, and everyone watched helplessly as the child breathed his last.

When basic survival cannot be guaranteed, the resistance to having fewer children, despite the toll on their health, has a logic rooted in local compulsions. Says Phekao, a newly married woman: "I want at least five children. We are farmers. We have to help one another in cooking, agriculture, and firewood and water collection. If there are not enough people in the family how are we going to finish all these things? To get this help I need more children. If we do not work, we cannot eat.

Following the publication of this story, the Nagaland health authorities did visit the Chizami health centre and arrange for the establishment of a proper delivery room.

If I don't have brothers and sisters, who will come to help me when I need it?"

Ngupkhao, a mother of seven children, says women in Longwa do not want family planning methods, even if they are available. The birth of children should not be prevented "because they are God's gift", she says, adding that some of the children will not survive. The aversion to birth control in Longwa, one of the more primitive and isolated amongst Naga villages, however, sharply contrasted with the great desire for information amongst young women elsewhere, where new realities are impinging.

"Even If We Shout There is No One to Hear"

Says Nungkem, a pastoralist from Tamlu, "Villagers do realize that they cannot look after so many children. This is a competitive world. We want to give our children good education, but it is expensive. Parents cannot support all their children, and many are becoming vagabonds. These children are frustrated and are fighting, stealing and becoming drug addicts. As such social problems increase, the importance of family planning is now realized."

How deeply younger women feel the need for health information was strikingly demonstrated at Longchang, another village in Mon district. Young women hung back after a meeting organized by the village council while the men left. "We have many questions that we cannot ask in front of the men, that is why we have stayed back," said one.

Surprisingly, in all such discussions, the very first question invariably was about modern methods of contraception. Most of them did not know about temporary methods of birth control—or their possible side effects. The women in Longchang had never seen a condom and said they would not dare to suggest its use to their husbands. This is extremely surprising since the popular perception is that women among the Scheduled Tribes are more "autonomous" than their caste-Hindu counterparts. They were also eager to discuss whether a woman should marry before she is 20 years old, and whether becoming a mother within a year of marriage is advantageous.

The NFHS reveals that AIDS awareness among Naga women has increased from 41 per cent of married women six years ago to 72 per cent in 1999. But almost a quarter of the Naga women who have heard about AIDS do not know how to avoid this disease. Despite their interest in planning families, only 24 per cent of married women in Nagaland used some modern method of contraception—far below the national average of 43, according to the latest National Family Health Survey. And, almost 30 per cent of married women in Nagaland have an unmet need for contraception.Unlike the women of Longchang, their men had no interest in discussing birth control. Their interest centred on technologies to grow vegetables. This, they felt would help generate income to educate their children and improve health standards.

According to the second National Family Health Survey, almost half of married Naga women suffer from reproductive health problems that could be symptomatic of a more serious reproductive tract infection. If left untreated, which is often the case, reproductive tract infections can cause pregnancy-related complications, infertility and chronic pain. They are also risk factors for pelvic inflammatory and sexually transmitted diseases.

Recalling her experience of working in Nagaland, studying women's reproductive health issues, health researcher Monisha Behal says, "Women often spoke about the problem of frequent childbirth and the hardship of those who experience complicated pregnancies. Some women are carried all the way to the district headquarters for treatment or deliveries. There is simply no knowledge of controlling one's own reproductive health".

Lacking access to health education and services, Naga women are left to invent their own devices of protection. Behal reports the case of Shoipu village, in Zunheboto district, where Sema women know they are taking a grave risk in using an oral contraceptive, Mala D, to abort an unwanted foetus. They stumbled upon this method of abortion when one of them accidentally consumed the pill without knowing she was pregnant, and suffered an abortion. This of course was an happenstance, but many among them believe that the pill can be used as an abortifacient.

Sterilization is the only widely known method of family planning. It is available only in district hospitals. But women fear this because they believe it causes weakness and will impair their ability to work. The men refuse vasectomies for the same reason.

Behal's interviews with 703 women in Zunheboto district show that only 73 women (10.4 per cent) used contraceptives, while 630 made no attempt to control childbirth, and neither did their husbands. Thirty per cent said they would not like to use contraceptives, another 30 per cent said that "children are a gift of God", while the rest said they did not know what to do. The average number of children per woman is between four and seven, while the maximum rises to ten.

Notwithstanding this, the absence of suitable contraceptive services support is forcing many women to abort each time they conceive, says Hokheli Sema, a senior nurse at the Dimapur Civil Hospital. But since the past five years, the health department has ordered a stoppage of abortions, unless linked to sterilization, she says. Consequently this is promoting quackery, and the hospital receives many serious cases where poor and illiterate peasant women have tried to abort through self-medication with leaves and roots, or massage or insertion of a stick into the cervix by a quack.

In Mon town, patients say government doctors perform abortions in the civil hospital for a fee. "It is just a small expression of their *khushi* (satisfaction)," says a government doctor. If secrecy is required, these doctors are equally willing to perform the operation in a curtained cubbyhole offered by the local pharmacies, alleges K Tonlih, an office bearer of the Konyak Women's Association. "Women do want birth control. Many come for sterilization, but hospitals have no equipment or medicines, and send them back. Last year a woman died in an auto-rickshaw, as she was returning from the clinic of a quack after an abortion. The government is not interested in the plight of women. Even if we shout, there is no one to hear," says Tonlih.

Changing Food Patterns

A shift away from traditional diets to modern foods is adding to the poor nutritional status of the Nagas. Traditionally Naga women knew how to recognize nutritious edible herbs and leaves and collected up to a hundred wild vegetables and fruits from the forest. Their social life revolved around gathering food and medicinal plants from the forest. But amongst many Nagas today, such traditions are fast eroding with a younger generation that prefers mass-produced food popular in urban areas. While some villagers in interior districts continue to produce naturally grown millet, corn, kidney beans and unique strains of wild rice, these vital sources of nutrition and energy are lost to urban housewives who are turning to commercial products bearing dubious labels such as "the complete health food".

According to Naga elders, the commercial exploitation of the forests has resulted in a limited variety of green leaves and vegetables in the cooking pot, and there is an excessive reliance on red meat to accompany the staple, rice. Besides, many communities in the interior are still in the process of emerging from the hunter-gatherer stage and have yet to master the art of cultivation. Levels of anaemia are high in women, touching almost 40 per cent, according to official figures. In children, anaemia is even higher, ranging between 40 and 49 per cent, according to the second National Family Health Survey. A two-year study conducted by Behal, however, found that anaemia affects over 96 per cent of the women interviewed in seven districts of the state. Linked to anaemia are a range of complaints like weakness and irregular menstruation.

In some cases, lack of health education adds to irrational food habits. In Chizami village of Phek district, for example, Chakhesang women do not encourage their children to eat the juicy peaches and plums growing in profusion around the village, because they believe these fruits cause diarrhoea. They do not associate their children's diarrhoea with the flies that sit on the fruit, and the need to wash the fruit before eating, says Seno Tsuhah, a health worker.

Mothers lack knowledge of how to wean their babies. While breast feeding is widely practised, weaning either starts too early or too late. If a mother is ill or does not produce enough milk, weaning could start as early as two months, or within a week if the mother dies, says Ngippo, President of the Konyak Women's Association in Aboi, Mon district. Sema tribal women in Chekiya village near Dimapur, say their babies are weaned with rice and milk powder. By the time the infants are around seven months, they are also given morsels of meat that the mother has first chewed to a pulp. In the anganwadis that sporadically function, poor nutrition is further promoted through the distribution of biscuits and weevil-infested milk powder.

Some Nagas still retain traditions that foster the health of women and children. For instance, men of the Chakhesang tribe aid their wives during childbirth. Most men in the picture-postcard village of Chizami in Phek district believe it is shameful to depend on a neighbour's help when such a momentous event is taking place in their family. There are several rituals connected with the birth of the baby in which the father plays a nurturing role. Some groups strictly enforce the custom where a woman, after giving birth to a baby, must rest at home for at least five days before returning to the field. But amongst other groups, poverty compels the woman to immediately get back to work, carrying the baby with her, resulting in severe health consequences for both.

Diseases of Poverty

While reproductive problems contribute to illness and death amongst women, Naga society is also burdened by the high incidence of communicable and infectious diseases. Records from a private clinic in Kohima, run by Joyce Angami, show that malaria and typhoid are now taking precedence over diseases like urinary tract infections and worm infestations, which dominated four years ago.

Meanwhile, Behal's survey shows that in 200 households surveyed in Chizami village, Phek district, women recalled the names of 88 children who had died from treatable problems like tetanus, followed by diarrhoea, fever and measles. These incidents did not take place during a specific time frame, and the survey was an attempt to know what the main diseases killing children were. In July–August of 1999, large-scale deaths took place in isolated villages of Mon district from malaria, typhoid and jaundice, reports Nyamto Wangsha, principal of the Konjong School in Mon.

The collapse of health infrastructure throughout Nagaland, never very strong, is starkly evident. Says K. Mero, Chairman Chizami Village Council , "The Centre is giving a lot of money for the Nagas. On paper we see that so much is sanctioned, but it never reaches us. The state government always says it has no money. When we do a thorough check with the concerned authorities, we find it is misappropriated. The public is fed up." This depressing story continues in Zunheboto, where 80 per cent of the population lives in poverty. Pulmonary tuberculosis (TB) is rampant here, while diarrhoea, skin infections and anaemia are common.

The medicine chest of the Satakha PHC in Zunheboto district contains only 200 tablets of paracetamol, which arrive every four months. "Patients are admitted here only when there are medicines. At present we have neither," (patients nor medicines) says Khiheto Sema, the "computer analyst" who passes his time playing chess in this deserted facility. His post was created in anticipation of a computer that is yet to arrive!

The Zunheboto Civil Hospital has been gifted an incubator by UNICEF, but the machine lies unused in the absence of an oxygen cylinder and electricity, which is "regularly irregular", according to the hospital superintendent. The operation theatre needs a mobile, shadow-less lamp. The generator for the operation theatre has come after the superintendent virtually coerced a gift from a private donor. The labour room has one rusted bed and there is no baby-weighing machine. The hospital has no facility for issuing birth certificates.

Tali Longkumer, Nagaland's minister for social welfare however insists, "You have gone to the most extreme areas of Nagaland and you cannot generalize for the whole state". But even urban areas like Kohima and Dimapur belie his claim. In the Naga Hospital, the state's main referral hospital in Kohima, the superintendent, Dr Kepelhusie, says the budget is controlled by the Directorate of Health Services, and he does not know how much money is sanctioned for the hospital, let alone see any of it. He is concerned by the huge number of TB patients coming from interior districts, for whom no medicines are available. The hospital medical store has only 26 drugs available, most of them of little value in emergencies.

Even as the government's PHC system is collapsing, there is a huge growth of NGOs in the state. Dr Kepelhusie says he faces an uphill battle in trying to hold on to his best doctors. "All our doctors are being drawn into NGOs and specialized programmes such as AIDS control. Nowhere else in the country is a government doctor deputed to an NGO, where they receive higher pay and have better service conditions. Who will be left to work in the hospital? We cannot function unless there is a good team."

In view of the resources flowing into the NGO sector, it is not surprising that hundreds of NGOs have sprung up, many dealing with AIDS. Nor, given the lack of overall development, is it surprising that Nagaland lacks the thriving private sector in health care evident all over the country. What is also clear is that doctors in private practice—as much as NGOs—also stick to towns with a substantial population and buying power, avoiding the more remote and poorer rural areas.

Drugs and AIDS

Poverty, lack of development, the crushing impact of insurgency conditions, also contribute to a flourishing drug culture. Situated next to "The Golden Triangle" in Myanmar—the world's largest source of illicitly grown pure grade heroin—opium is used as a means of barter on both sides of the border. Drug addiction is having a crippling impact on youth in states like Nagaland and neighbouring Manipur, while contributing to an alarming incidence of AIDS.

Here in Mon district is proof of the cross-border opium trade. Hordes of Myanmarese Konyak youth walk for days to get to Mon through the Longwa border post, to stay and study. But many bring with them opium which is the only currency they have to purchase goods in India. It is also their succour back home in Myanmar.

A refugee from Yenjung village in the eastern Konyak area of Myanmar, a two day walk from Mon said, "There are 100 houses in my village. Everyone grows opium. Everyone is an addict. There is no doctor or medical facilities. That is why many people are dying. We have no medicine but opium".

Reverend T.W. Yamyap Konyak of the Konyak Baptist Churches Association has a church mission operating since 1972 in 37 villages in the Khamti area across the border from Mon. Describing this as the "most backward area", he says there is no food, schools, medical care or road communications. Basic tablets like dispirin are not available. Many people are dying, primarily from diseases like tuberculosis and leprosy. "If you stop opium cultivation the economy of the entire area will be affected. When a cow is sold, payment is made with opium. Without the opium economy, even the pastor would not get a salary", Rev. Yamyap said.

The Myanmarese youth escape the economic repression only to serve as agents of AIDS in India's north-east. State government records show that the first AIDS case in Manipur was a citizen of Myanmar. Manipur heads the list of Indian states where intra-venous drug abuse and AIDS amongst the youth is of serious consequence. The road from Imphal, Manipur's capital, to Moreh, the border town through which trade with Myanmar is conducted, is the famous "Number Four" route.

This refers to pure white heroin, which is trafficked through this corridor into other parts of India, and thereafter to international markets. Police and customs officials in the state say that in the absence of basic infrastructure to check such smuggling, they have no control over this and other entry points on this open stretch of border where patrolling must take place on foot tracks and through thick jungle. Others, however, say that the politicians, the police and the insurgents are all involved in the lucrative trade.

In Mon town, social organizations involved in drug rehabilitation estimate that almost 50 per cent of the youth are opium addicts or practise some form of drug abuse. Through the calendar year 1996, a total of 28 youngsters died in Mon from drug abuse according to the Konyak Mothers' Association. A high drop-out rate marks the functioning of both government and private schools here, because opium addiction is rampant in virtually every home. Locals are forced to sell their belongings so that addicts can sustain their habit, and families can survive, says Nyamto Wangsha, headmaster of Konjong High School in Mon. In the absence of medical and HIV-testing facilities here, the incidence of AIDS can only be guessed at. The estimates of the National AIDS Control Organization however indicate that IV drug abuse and AIDS is having a catastrophic impact on small, ethnic populations.

War Wounds

The enormous physical hardships faced by Nagas are further compounded by the 50 years of political and social strife they have lived with. Ordinary Nagas have been caught in the crossfire between the Indian army that tries to put an end to "insurgency" in the area and the now-divided Naga militant groups. Though peace talks between key underground insurgent groups and the Indian government have been initiated, the decades of "insurgency" – Naga's themselves view this as a "freedom struggle"—have had devastating effect on their lives.

In Longwa village of Mon district, the Naga underground stealthily emerges after nightfall. The villagers, including the women, are systematically selected from each home to carry their rations and luggage to hideouts across the border, or to feed them. Schoolchildren are forcibly recruited by the dominant militant factions in villages like Tizit. Each family, despite grinding poverty, is forced to pay the militants a tax of Rs 500 a year. And when the armies of India or Myanmar discover this the locals face their wrath as well.

Chakhesang women of Chizami village, Phek district, say their lives are full of tension. These women say they are bothered by the loss of work culture, love, respect and dignity in their social dealings. Insecurity is writ large, with an increase in crime. Their homes cannot be left unlocked as in the recent past, and women cannot move around freely for fear of extortion or rape. Poor families are apprehensive about the lack of food security. According to P Ngully, a psychiatrist, many Nagas are in the grip of "post-traumatic stress disorder". It started in the 1950s at the height of the Naga movement for an independent country. During this time villages were burnt, many people were killed or wounded, and women were molested. Seeing a uniformed person still evokes fear and terror, he says. Dr Ngully cites the example of December 1994, when the civilian population in Mokokchung town was caught in a severe clash between the Naga underground factions and the Maratha Light Infantry division of the Indian army. A study conducted 11 months after the incident showed that the population was suffering from stress disorders. People would complain of pain or discomfort that seemed real enough to them, but could not be diagnosed despite extensive investigations.

According to Dr Ngully, "These persons are filled with anxiety, worry, and unhappiness. There is no joy or verve in their life. They look at the future with a sense of doom. For the Nagas, their village was like a nation by itself. When it was reduced to ashes and they were herded into concentration camps, their sense of belonging and security was shaken." The signs of stress are manifest in several ways, says Dr Ngully.

In parents, it could be anxiety over the safety of their children or excessive pressure on them to succeed. In others, there is a tendency to keep to themselves and then explode in violence when the situation becomes intolerable. Many join underground factions, which are sharply divided according to tribal affiliations. Yet another trend is to turn to religion, evident in the large number of Naga youth turning to theology studies. Finally, of course, is the oblivion of drugs.

The women have suffered severely, but they do not talk about it easily, says Dr. Ngully. "Their insecurity coincides with the lack of any expectation of what life has to offer them. They usually come with some intangible physical complaint, but deeper probing soon reveals that it is a subjective disorder that invariably leads to their anxiety over children or husbands who have gone astray due to alcoholism and drugs," he says.

Stagnant Economy

Developmental stagnation, and the absence of any creative means of finding economic independence, are key factors inhibiting Naga progress. According to a senior non-Naga bureaucrat in Kohima, the state has 90,000 government servants, but the main problem is that jobs are cornered by the educationally advanced tribes. Information on development schemes does not filter down to the less developed groups. In rural Nagaland, the majority of the population is dependent on agriculture, which is the only source of employment in the state.

While neglect and poverty fuel insurgency, development money is utilized to pay the salaries of a white elephant bureaucracy, or filtered away in corruption. The Naga militant groups also extract their pound of flesh, and it is an open secret that "underground tax" is routinely extracted from the salaries of even top officials, and collected by the various factions directly from government cashiers.

The absence of basic infrastructure—communication and transport—is another major hurdle in improvement of the state's economy, which further prevents the Nagas from taking responsibility for their health, education and developmental needs. Take the instance of a woman entrepreneur in Mon town who set up a cooking gas agency. Despite the enormous effort required in trucking cylinders over potholed mountain roads for seven hours, she succeeded in filling her warehouse with stocks. Even then sales remain low, because the women who need this facility the most, do not have purchasing power, access to roads and means of cheap transportation.

The Konyak Women's Association has tried to solve the problem of the community's lack of access to emergency transport. The nearest, reliable source of medical care for Mon district requires a seven hour drive to Jorhat Medical College in Assam. The women raised money for an ambulance to transport patients. But at Rs 2,500 half the rate charged by private car owners, there are still no takers. Private enterprise cannot fill this need, which clearly calls for subsidized government intervention.

The Konyaks are amongst the most backward and isolated of Nagaland's indigenous peoples. Their long isolation has however served to keep alive knowledge of traditional medicinal plants, skills in crafts and weaves—skills and knowledge that are now dying out amongst other advanced groups. But the absence of any link with people and markets elsewhere in India, prevents the Konyaks from directly reaching urban customers who place a high value on their beautifully woven cane baskets, hand crafted jewellery, weaves and wood carving. It is in families of such gifted craftspeople that women are dying of TB for lack of medicines, and where children are pulled out of school because there is no money for education.

Meanwhile, the high cost of raw material and transportation to and from the north-east, ensures that the product remains unviable for markets elsewhere in the country. Women in virtually every rural household in this region know how to weave. But the cost of yarn from the cotton producing areas of the country is phenomenally high by the time it reaches them. This is both because of transportation charges and the chain of middlemen involved. Local government agencies for handloom or handicraft development, who were meant to counter the stranglehold of middlemen, are themselves riddled with corruption and inefficiency.

Similarly, while the juiciest and sweetest of fruits abound in the north-east, along with unique strains of wild rice and other naturally grown agricultural products, there is no viable means of reaching these to consumers. If an individual Naga wants to truck his products from the urban centre of Dimapur to Mumbai, he has to hire an entire truck, costing Rs 30,000. While he could join hands with other entrepreneurs, he lacks access to credit, organizational skills and the business contacts required for such an operation. Private trucking companies in Mumbai meanwhile, readily accept a single carton for delivery to Dimapur, at the rate of six rupees per kilo, but do not offer the same facility out of the region. All kinds of goods including pharmaceuticals and textiles are trucked to north-eastern markets from the rest of the country. They also reach the border posts of Myanmar and Bangladesh where there are ready buyers. But the people of the north-east receive no benefit from this booming exchange.

With geography, ideas of race and "mainstream" indifference stacked against them, Nagaland remains a mirror to how India, in its march towards "development" and "health for all", treats the most marginalized segments of its population. And it appears unlikely that the voices of the beleaguered women will be heard anytime soon.

The Silent Transition
Indian Women and Menopause

Lyla Bavadam

In most Indian languages, the word for menopause translates, quite literally, as cessation of menstruation. None of them expresses the complex range of biological, psychological and social changes this phase in life signifies for an Indian woman. While possibly in the West, the word is associated with loss of beauty and youth, and the pain of this loss, it appears that in contrast in India, these negative connotations are not so widespread. Words like "freedom" and "liberation" were commonly used by a large cross-section of women in different parts of the country to describe their experience of menopause. For Mira, a slum dweller in Ahmedabad, the freedom came when she did not have to sit outside her hut while her mother-in-law said her prayers. "I never got used to the embarrassment of knowing that everyone realized I had my periods because I was outside"

For Laxmibai, who lives in a village in Maharashtra, the sense of freedom came with her husband allowing her to travel alone by bus to visit her sister in the next village. "When I asked him why he no longer minded me going alone, he said, 'You are old now, who will look at you?'"

Reactions to menopause were influenced not only by social class, but by the presence of a mother-in-law or, especially, the husband, giving credence to the possibility that negative social and emotional aspects of menopause are often male created. For instance, in Gujarat a 40 year-old woman speaking of her menopause in front of her mother-in-law said she had done all that she was born to do, by bearing children, and to that extent, her life was over. Her mother-in-law nodded approvingly, adding that this was the fate of all women. Later, when spoken to privately, the mother-in-law talked at length of "the relief from monthly periods and all the accompanying rules". Her daughter-in-law expressed the same sentiments privately, adding that she felt much safer because men had ceased to look at her with desire. A number of rural women also expressed this perceived change in their sexual image by men.

Linking Sexual Attraction and Fertility

This would seem to highlight the link that most men in the country make between sexual attraction and fecundity. It is a link internalized by most women in the form of the deeply held social belief that a woman is a woman only if she bears a child. So dominated are women's lives by this social demand that it sometimes emerges as a strange psychological phenomenon of possession, more common in rural India.

Social activist Manisha Gupte, working with women in Maharashtra's Purandar district, noticed the phenomenon of women claiming to be "possessed" by spirits. She found that they were in two distinct age groups—women in their late teens and women between the ages of 40 and 45. The former age group was either unmarried, or if married, had no children. The older group of women was peri-menopausal. There were no cases of women being possessed in the intervening years. When the older women were asked if this had happened to them before, some of them said it had, but only when they were very young. Asked why it had not happened in the intervening years, they said, "We had no time for it".

Gupte, however, is cautious, explaining: "It is very difficult to say whether this is a reaction to menopause or not. It all depends on their emotional health." She adds, "These women do not have a voice in the community and they find that when they are 'possessed' they get attention and people listen to them. There are also other factors that have to be considered with this behaviour. You have to see their marital happiness, whether they have children who are still at home, whether there is a daughter-in-law at home and so on."

Menopause in the Indian Context

Biologically, menopause (derived from the Latin *meno* for month and *pausia* meaning halt) marks the end of a woman's natural fertility. As a woman approaches menopause, the number of ovarian follicles declines, producing less oestrogen, causing irregular periods. Eventually, the amount of oestrogen produced is too low to maintain the monthly cycle. Because of the complex nature of this process it is often difficult to distinguish whether the symptoms arise from physiological or social causes. That is, between the symptoms which are consequent to ageing and the resulting loss of ovarian functions, and those arising out of social and environmental conditions.

Some women report vasomotor and/or psychological changes at this stage of life. The vasomotor symptoms could be hot flushes, vaginal irritation, vaginal dryness or a burning sensation while urinating. These are all clearly related to menopause and most complaints vanish as the body accustoms itself to the new stage. Psychological symptoms could range from vague feelings of worthlessness to depression to insomnia. Together, the physical and psychological symptoms are referred to as the menopausal syndrome.

In the case of Indian women, as indeed perhaps women all over the world, it is important to understand that the sociocultural events in their lives are more influential than the milestones of chronological age. Grey hair, loss of teeth and menopause are seen as marking the passage of time, but they have no real relevance in themselves. Transitions related to the development cycle of the family are much more important in defining the major periods of a woman's life, for instance, marriage, the birth of children, the marriage of children etc.[1]

One factor that determines the general perception of menopause is the extent to which women report it and in this re-

[1]Vatuk, Sylvia (1995), "The Indian Woman in Later Life: Some Social and Cultural Considerations", in Monica Das Gupta, Lincoln C. Chen, and T.N. Krishnan (Eds.), *Women's Health in India: Risk and Vulnerability*,New Delhi, Oxford University Press.

spect it is true that Indian women by and large do not make "an issue" of menopause. Dr B S Anklesaria, an Ahmedabad-based gynaecologist, who is among the very few doctors to have conducted clinical studies on older women in the country, says he has "so far found only 30 per cent of Indian women subjectively complaining of vasomotor instability." His study was still ongoing at the time of writing.

In another study, the researcher reports fewer acute symptoms among Rajput women and concludes that this is probably because menopause is perceived as a positive event in Rajput culture since this stage of life marks more social freedom for women.[2] And, in his study Anklesaria says, "In Asia, by and large, fewer vasomotor and psychological symptoms are reported due to social, cultural and economic factors. However, the better educated and more affluent among these women report these same symptoms more frequently."[3]

Lower Age at Menopause

Research on menopause has been extensive in the West, but in India it is still an emerging subject, gaining research recognition only at a few institutes. Dr Rashmi Shah is Assistant Director of the Institute for Research in Reproduction (IRR) in Mumbai, which is one of the centres of the Indian Council for Medical Research (ICMR). Shah has carried out a study of menopausal women in India and established that the mean age for menopause is at 44.3 years. The IRR study was conducted with a sample survey of 500 women who were urban and belonged to the lower economic bracket.

Studies in India conducted by Wyon *et al*, Randhawa *et al* and Kaw *et al* indicate that Indian women reach menopause at a lower age as compared to those in the West. Most Indian

[2]Flint, M. (1995), "The Menopause: Reward or Punishment?", *Psychomatics*, 15.

[3]Anklesaria, B.S.(1996), " Climacteric Symptoms and Urogenital Problems" in Usha R.Krishna and Duru Shah (Eds), *Menopause*, Chennai, Orient Longman.

studies show the median age at menopause at 48 years, while those from the West reveal the age to be about 51.[4] Anklesaria is himself conducting studies and "in an ongoing analysis of 250 subjects, the median age was found to be 44.35 years with a range of 36–55 years." The low nutritional levels among Indian women and the high prevalence of anaemia could be factors contributing to this. "Undernourished women appear to have menopause four years earlier compared with those who are not (undernourished)", says a recent study.[5] This is also supported by another study on the subject by Mahadevan *et al.*[6]

Perceptions of Rural Women on Menopause

Dr Rani Bang is a gynaecologist, a public health activist and co-founder of the NGO, Society for Education, Action & Research in Community Health (SEARCH) in Maharashtra. Bang has conducted an informal study of 100 post-menopausal women aged 40 to 70 years living in Gadchiroli district of Maharashtra. The women were illiterate farm workers of all castes. She believes that rural women are "definitely affected by psychosomatic factors but they have so many other problems to deal with, like high infant mortality rates, the health of their in-laws, alcoholism among spouses and economic problems, that menopause is small in comparison and so they don't notice it." In fact, one woman said, "It came and went so fast that I did not even have time to notice any differences." Bang also noted that when she persuaded women to talk more about themselves and less about their families, they did mention problems like prolonged periods, vaginal itching, decrease in appetite, depression and a sense of isolation, all part of the meno-

[4]WHO Scientific Group (1981), *Research on the Menopause*, Technical Report Series 670.

[5]Shah, Rashmi S (1998), "Menopause and HRT: Growing Public Health challenges". *ICMR Bulletin* Vol 28 No. 1 January.

[6]Mahadevan, K, M. Murthy, P, Reddy and S. Bhaskaran (1992), "Early Menopause and its Determinates", *Journal of Biosocial Science* 14.

pausal syndrome. A frequent complaint was stomach pain. Bang explains this, saying, "They are unfamiliar with physiology. So they think that if they've stopped bleeding the blood must be hardening inside the body forming a ball and that this causes them pain."

The women also said that they hesitated to complain because, as Bang explains, "In a village everything depends on your working and earning capacity. Once you are a burden no one tolerates you." According to Bang's study, 78 per cent of the women did not discuss their menopause problems with anyone and 90 per cent did not visit a doctor. At a late stage when their husbands did find out their menopausal status, 75 per cent of them "did not react in any manner."

The women said they did not feel the need to inform their husbands since "it is not a husband's business." Likewise, men disassociated themselves from their wives' menopausal condition, saying that was "a matter for women to discuss" and expressed bewilderment that such a question was even asked of them.

Bang feels "children can be a great support to a menopausal woman" and has started a special session in the sex education sessions she holds for rural youth. After one session, a woman told Bang, her son came home from the workshop, embraced his mother, and begged forgiveness for not understanding the problems she must have undergone. Speaking of another case where she counselled the family of a woman who was going through menopause and was suffering from depression, Bang says, "The husband and sons had no idea of the reason for her depression and there was a lot of tension in the family. I told the elder boy of his mother's problem and he had tears in his eyes. In an attempt to cheer up their mother, the boys decorated the house cheerfully, played cheerful music and took their mother to the cinema—for a comedy. The change in her outlook was drastic."

Most interesting of all was the reaction to Bang's questions on sexuality. Fifty five per cent of the persons who were asked if there was any change in their sexual desire said it had decreased. Some of these said, "I'm too weak for sex" and "I'm now a mother-in-law; it is not seemly at my age." Bang says the explanations are pointers to the old belief that sex is meant for procreation. An idea so ingrained in women that one woman even claimed, "My desire died when I got my menopause", while another said menopause had affected her feeling of femininity. "I feel like a man" was the way she put it. Another woman said her post-menopausal state made her feel like a "dry tree that can no longer produce gum."

But there are exceptions like Chabbubai of Saswad village in Maharashtra. She is in her late fifties and a grandmother of eight. On sexual relations with her husband, she laughs, "I thought desire was only meant for producing children. Now I can't have any more, but still my husband and I sleep together. You think we are two bad old people still doing this in our old age, but what can we do—he desires me and I desire him."

Reactions to the onset of menopause among rural women were largely those of relief. They ranged from the tragic story of the farm labourer who said that on the first two days of her period she had to stand the entire day so that she would not stain the only sari she owned, to the story of Yashodhabai in Gadchiroli. Yashodhabai is something of an exception in her radical attitude. The cessation of her period was like the beginning of a new life for her. "I had this strong urge to do something useful," she says. She approached Rani Bang for some informal training as a dai and plunged into village social work. Her husband however, was unhappy with her newfound enthusiasm and Yashodhabai says she realized that unless she did something he would keep "following" her (the unsaid thought was that her husband expected their sexual relations to continue). "He needed to be kept busy and needed to be looked after. I had no time for that. I had done it all my life and now I was too involved in this new job of mine. So I found him a young woman and got the two of them married." The easy relationship was accepted by the entire village and Yashodhabai, her husband and his new wife, and their offspring literally lived happily ever after.

Livelihood and a woman's capacity to contribute to the home are the primary issues for poor rural women as they age. Menopause *per se* is not as much an issue as loss of health in old age. By and large, they see menopausal complaints in this context. As Manjulabai in Dibna village of Maharashtra says, "If you can't work in the house and field then even your own daughter won't look after you." And Vacchalabai, also from Dibna, adds, "I'd have to be dying not to get up from bed in the morning." In extremely poor families in India, old women are workhorses to the last and are not even spared the strenuous task of collecting wood.

Similar findings on the perceptions of semi-urban women were reported by Professor P. V. Ramamurti and Dr D. Jamuna of the Centre for Research on Ageing at the Sri Venkateshwara University in Tirupati, Andhra Pradesh. Their study was conducted among semi-urban, literate women of the middle socio-economic bracket of Cuddapah, Nellore and Chittoor districts of Andhra Pradesh. Ramamurti and Jamuna have reported that women found the early stages of menopause to be more psychologically stressful than was presumed by the researchers. A separate study by Jamuna in which she compared three groups—pre-menopausal, menopausal and post-menopausal—indicated that women in the pre-menopausal group reported satisfaction with their lives in terms of health, emotional state, self esteem, home life, social status and responsibility and even sex life. Women in the post-menopausal and menopausal stages were dissatisfied with these areas of their life with the exception of a sex life in which post-menopausal women said there was an "improvement" as compared with their pre-menopausal stage. The meaning of "improved", says Jamuna, could either refer to resuming of sexual relations which had stopped while the woman was undergoing menopause, or could refer to a cessation of all sexual activities.

Poonam Kathuria of the Gujarat NGO, Society for Women's Action and Training Initiative, says that when she held discussions on menopause with local women, "the response was limited." Kathuria says, "Perhaps this indicates the lack of understanding of menopause as well as the low significance attached to it. Unlike menstruation which is celebrated, a woman enters her menopause privately and silently." At the same time, it is also true that even in rural areas functions to celebrate menarche are not as visible on the social calendar as they used to be. As lower castes are increasingly "Sanskritized" this ritual is not as important as it used to be earlier.

Adding a slightly different perspective are the findings of the Rural Women's Social Education Centre in Chengalpattu, Tamil Nadu. A report on older women and their stresses shows "the hardships of poverty, the menace of alcoholism amongst men which sparked daily quarrels, the separation from children and the need to be dependent on them caused frustrations in the women.... Pressures of daily existence impel many women to speak of ending their lives."[7]

In short then, menopause among women in rural areas, especially the poor, is dealt with matter of factly, as a way of life, something that every woman experiences, indeed sometimes something liberatory. While all this may indeed be admirable, it also means that when there is a problem related to this phase of their lives, women are not likely to pay any attention to it. So just as patriarchy demands that it be the norm that they eat last in their homes, it also demands that female illnesses and diseases are not to be given any attention.

Perceptions of Menopause Among Urban Women

Almost in direct contrast to the rural woman are women living in urban areas where factors like social status, economic level, education and access to information come into play. While rural women spoke unhesitatingly even on intimate matters, women in urban areas were reticent about their menopausal experiences. With the exception of two women, all those spoken to said they would prefer not to be identified.

[7]Meena Gopal, A. Caries and U. Kalpagam (1997),"Latent Burdens: Women's Health in Middle and Later Life', Unpublished Report, Rural Women's Social Education Centre, Chengalpattu

The preservation of youth (expressed primarily in terms of glowing skin and lustrous dark hair) is a big concern for a large section of urban women of all economic classes. The concern was most noticeable among those of a higher economic and social level. Despite conversations where cliches such as "looks are superficial" and "beauty is skin deep" were mouthed, it emerged that Hormone Replacement Therapy (HRT) was a major attraction, mainly to retain youth. HRT is a clinical alternative offered by doctors to women whose bodies no longer produce the same levels of oestrogen as they used to—either because of natural or surgical menopause. In a nutshell, HRT replaces the body's decreasing oestrogen and can provide relief for many symptoms for the women who experience them. When asked what they hoped the treatment would do for them, the women parroted the list of health benefits which they had learnt from their doctors, but it was clear that they were also banking on benefits to their skin, hair and muscle tone.

Attitudes to ageing among this class of women arose from a complicated mixture of factors. One was, of course, the dread of losing youth, beauty and hence their sexuality, although they claimed these were superficialities. More significant, perhaps, was some knowledge of HRT derived from family and friends as well as conversations with their gynaecologists. Some had read about the wonders of HRT in the agony aunt columns of newspapers and magazines.

This attitude seems to be due to two factors. One is the exposure to western literature on menopause (generally via women's magazines) and the other is related to the workplace. On the whole, magazine articles in India on menopause concentrate on how to overcome this stage. This is especially true of women's magazines in English which have an elite readership. Cosmetic, surgical, clinical and therapeutic alternatives are offered to women, along with exhortations to "take an interest in your looks", " use makeup that hides wrinkles", and "wear the correct colours for the older woman". All these are aimed at keeping women continually attractive for men and thus keeping their husbands in thrall. This is not surprising given that the post-liberalization years have seen a massive boom in the business of beauty along with the fetishization of the lifestyles of the beautiful. To a certain extent these influence the dread with which some middle class urban women view menopause.

More important perhaps for the working urban woman—lucky enough to be in the organized sector of employment—is that as she approaches menopause, she also nears the retirement age for most jobs. While the government has raised the retirement age for its employees to 60, a number of private organizations retire their employees in their fifties. Loss of a salary, loss of a daily routine as well as the feeling that a career has come to an end, all play on the minds of such women. While financial security is important regardless of whether the woman is urban or rural, the urban middle class woman does depend on it more because it often gives her a sense of identity.

The lower and lower middle class urban women carry the heaviest workloads and this, in turn, leaves them little space for themselves. Gajra Hire is a 50-year-old woman who lives in a slum in Worli, Mumbai. Every evening she tutors young mothers in basic hygiene. When asked what she did for her own health care she shrugged and said, "I lost my first son to tuberculosis. All I know is that I have to feed my family every day and I pray that my husband stops drinking."

Sarita Jadhav is 48 years old and works as a telephone operator for a State-run company. Her workplace is two hours away by train from her home and she has to brave the crush of peak hour crowds for her journey to and fro. She wakes up at 4 a.m. to fill water, cook and pack lunch for herself, her husband and sons. By 7 a.m. she has served breakfast to her family and prepared lunch for her mother-in-law. She catches the 7.30 a.m. train to the city. After a day's work she shops for vegetables on the way to the station, and, if she gets a seat on the train, peels and cuts them during the journey. She sleeps at midnight. Sarita knows about menopause because she discusses "all sorts of problems" every day with her friends in the ladies compartment in the train. "My periods are very irregular and I'm tired all the time. Who has time to go to the doctor? Work, eat and sleep... never enough of sleep. Some days I don't have the time to oil my hair," she says. Sarita exemplifies the typical Indian woman who is brought up believing that she has to look after others and not think of herself. Though the kind of workload she is subjected to is quite unimaginable for those better off, it also appears to give her enormous reserves of strength to deal with any emotional upheaval she might experience during menopause.

No Public Health Recourse

India's overburdened and under-funded public health care system has no special programmes for older women. Even the International Conference on Population and Development (ICPD)-inspired Reproductive and Child Health Care approach only looks after a woman during her reproductive years. The main government bodies responsible for the public health care system not only have no current health programme that caters to the specific reproductive health needs of ageing women, but have no intention of starting any either. An important document in this field, the Introductory Report to the National Family Health Survey, does not even mention menopause as an issue. Dr Ashok Kumar, Deputy Commissioner at the Department of Family Welfare in Delhi, says, "After a woman has passed the childbearing stage she becomes the responsibility of the primary health care programme. I agree that in reality she has very specific health care needs and the primary health care system is really very primary (basic) in what it offers."

Representing the public health care system is an official who is at the top of the rung in the Directorate of Health, Delhi. Declining to be identified, he says, the health needs of older women are "actually not a priority for India's public health system, which is still grappling with deadly diseases and infant mortality." Where women are concerned, the priority is on controlling fertility. But the fact is that India has a rapidly greying population. According to the *Statistical Outline of India*[8], the average Indian woman's lifespan in the 1940s was 31 years. The 2002–2003 edition of the same publication calculates that current life spans are much higher, with women living up to an average of 65 years. This means that women will live approximately one third of their lives in a post-menopause stage. Currently, men and women in India in the 60-plus age group number about 60 million; that is nearly six per cent of the population. Projections for the year 2025 show that this is expected to increase to approximately 165 million. Judging by current gender proportions about half of this population will be women. The problem arises because of the lack of special health care for this ageing population and especially the lack of understanding of the special health needs of older women.

Government officials are not wrong when they say that for the majority of Indian women menopause is not an issue. It would, however, be closer to reality to say that Indian women do not, as a rule, medicalise their menopausal problems. Some of them experience the menopausal syndrome but choose to rely on support from their families and communities instead of public health care facilities. But the rapid erosion of the social structures that have provided relief to menopausal women now means that the government might have to step in with alternative programmes like counselling and maybe basic clinical management for some cases with severe symptoms.

The Economics of Hormone Replacement Therapy

Such programmes be would undoubtedly better than allowing free reign to the unregulated private sector which is much more likely to be swayed by large pharmaceutical concerns waiting to reap the benefits of prescribing expensive HRT. In-

[8]Tata Services, Department of Statistics and Economic Services, (1999), *Statistical Outline of India 1998–99*, Mumbai.

dia's growing population and expanding middle class[9] make it a target for manufacturers of all kinds of consumer goods, including HRT. Thus newspapers, which advocate wilful consumerism, also carry lavish articles on the lifestyles of the rich and powerful. Amidst these are lifestyle articles glorifying food, fashions, and the virtues of HRT.

But what are the likely costs? In an article discussing the controversies in HRT, doctors N D Motashaw and S Dave quote a USA study, which states that by the year 2005 there will be 25.3 million women between the ages of 50–64 in the USA who would be potentially eligible for HRT. The estimated cost of treating these women, considering only drug cost and monitoring, is US$ 5 billion .[10]

In a paper entitled, "The Menopause and HRT: Growing Public Health Challenges", Dr Rashmi Shah has said, "76 per cent of the world's post-menopausal women will be in developing countries." [11]A growing area of concern among activists is the promotion of HRT by corporate medical giants. Examples of corporate influenced research on HRT are well documented in the West and Indian activists now express the fear that western corporations are showing an interest in the growing youth consciousness of Indian women. HRT advertising has so far been restricted to medical journals. But there are indications that HRT manufacturers are interested in the Indian market. The multinational drug giant, Novartis, a major manufacturer of HRT, sponsors the meetings and seminars of the Indian Menopause Society, an organization run entirely by the medical profession. So far however, the sheer expense of HRT has gone a long way in containing its prescription and usage in India and it seems likely that this will remain so for

[9]Currently the Indian middle class numbers 200 million, according to the *Statistical Outline of India.*

[10]Tosteson, A., M.C. Weinstein and I. Schift (1994) "Cost Effectiveness Analysis of Hormone Replacement Therapy", in Lobo, R.A. (Ed) *Treatment of the Postmenopausal Woman: Basic and Clinical Aspects,* Raven Press, New York.

[11]Shah, Rashmi (1998), *op cit.*

the near future. But the industry is making a determined bid to saturate the existing market.

The HRT Debate

There are two categories of HRT that doctors routinely recommend for women. One is short-term use for relief of symptoms caused by lowered oestrogen. The other is that long-term use is believed to be preventive in nature.

Short-term HRT has a higher acceptance and compliance from women. Such use of HRT has been found to be effective in cases of burning while urinating, dry vaginal passage, hot flushes, incontinence, insomnia, dizziness; collectively known as vasomotor symptoms that appear and disappear in the early stages of menopause. A study of 500 women undertaken by the IRR to elicit views of those on HRT showed that only 40.1 per cent agreed to take short-term therapy for up to one year. As regards long-term therapy for more than five years, 67.8 per cent refused the HRT. Among the common reasons stated for refusal was the nuisance of vaginal bleeding and a feeling that menopause was a natural occurrence and therefore needed no treatment. Lack of awareness was also a reason for low usage.

This is not something that would please doctors. And indeed it doesn't. Dr Usha Sriram, an endocrinologist practising in Chennai, says, "The number one problem with HRT is patient resistance to it. So our main thrust should be to increase patient acceptance and compliance." Sriram believes that "the menopausal scene is at a crossroads in India and if we do not get the message across now it may be too late."

The same study undertaken by the IRR showed that of the 156 women who agreed to use it on a long term basis 55.1 per cent were willing to take it provided the per month cost was between Rs 50–100. At present the costs are in the range of Rs 200–300 hundred per month.

Western research has focused on the links between menopause, HRT use, and Alzheimer's disease, osteoporosis, heart disease, breast cancer and uterine cancer. However since there are no baseline studies in India that establish the mean age or even the prevalence of these diseases there is no research in the Indian context. Thus treatment involving long-term use of HRT has generated more controversy than cures.

An 83-year-old gynaecologist who chose HRT for herself over the past 30 years after having a hysterectomy and developing a crack in her femur, says, "The earlier response of doctors was to dismiss symptoms like hot flushes as psychological. There was no acceptance even of the possibility of it being a physiological reaction. They used to say the woman was hysterical and give her sedatives. It's a very sensible change now to give hormones instead of sedatives. I believe every woman should be on HRT." But Rani Bang objects to the widespread tendency to promote HRT without there being substantial studies to prove its long-term effects. Bang says, "People are more exposed to deadly pathogens today from pesticides in food, to chemicals in water, to air and noise pollution. These take their toll on the body, especially the liver which is the main organ for 'digesting' medication. Doctors presently treat HRT as some sort of miracle medicine. It is frightening."

Many pro-HRT physicians believe that it has a big role to play in preventive medicine. Anklesaria is all for "universal HRT" saying, "it can prevent complications in mature women." Speaking to doctors at a function of the Indian Menopause Society in Delhi, Anklesaria said, "You are guilty of malpractice if you haven't put your patients on HRT." It is thus not surprising that there is an ongoing medicalization of the normal in urban middle class India. In this, as in so many other instances, doctors, perhaps unwittingly, end up acting as salespersons for the pharmaceutical industry. But is this surprising given that the industry is the chief source of continuing education for doctors in our country?

Perhaps the final question to pro-HRT physicians is: how many of them take HRT themselves or recommend it to near relatives? The question was asked by Dr R. Kaul at a Delhi meeting of gynaecologists and the answer was startling: none of the female doctors present at that time took HRT even though many qualified for it in terms of age. Their reason? They say those who are gainfully employed do not need HRT.

Most activists believe a healthy diet and active lifestyle are much more instrumental in ensuring a trouble-free menopausal transition than any HRT. Rani Bang believes that the government health care programmes should not even consider HRT treatment. She says "the money spent on HRT would be better spent ensuring an adequate and healthy diet for women throughout their lives."

Alternative Therapies for Menopause Management

Latha R, 49, is a college professor in Mumbai. Single and living alone, she says she went through a patch of great depression some months ago. "It was the worst phase of my life. I felt I had no control over my life. I wouldn't want to get up in the mornings. My work was at its lowest and I lost eight kilos." Her general practitioner advised her to visit a gynaecologist who told her she was approaching menopause. Latha was advised to go on HRT but "shied off because I didn't want to mess around with hormones." Instead she visited a naturopath who first made dietary changes that, Latha says, helped her overcome her depression. She was also put on Bach Flower remedies: a system where distilled essences of various flowers are administered to users. The results were dramatic. After a fortnight of this treatment Latha says, "Life looked bright again." She is now being instructed in yoga. She says the combination therapy has worked wonders for her. "I don't have any explanation for this. Perhaps it was the fact that I had a routine for my treatment and this gave me sense of stability. Perhaps it was the fact that I was taking things in hand."

Menopausal complaints are not foreign to traditional fields of medicine. Dr S K Sharma, advisor Ayurveda, Ministry of Health, says, "The post-graduate teaching universities of Gujarat Ayurvedic University, Benaras Hindu University and the National Institute of Ayurveda in Jaipur have brought out Ph.D.

theses on the management of menopausal symptoms. The most useful medicines are (the plant derivatives) *ashwagandha* (*Withania somnifera*), *ashoka*, and *chandan*. Their advantage is that they are non-hormonal. They are suitable for menopausal symptoms like hot flushes, irregular periods, excessive bleeding, and change in temperament and sexual behaviour. The medication is usually given to women between the ages of 40–50 years for a period of two months and there is usually no need to repeat it."

For women who experience the symptoms and are uncomfortable with HRT, there is a large menu of alternative therapies including vitamins, minerals and herbs that provide relief from initial symptoms like hot flushes, mood swings, anxiety, vaginal dryness, lack of sexual interest and insomnia. As oestrogen levels fall, medical research has shown that phytoestrogens are an excellent source of replacement. Phytoestrogens are a diverse group of plant substances that have some of the effects of oestrogen. Soya, seaweed, algae, some nuts and dark green leafy vegetables produce phytoestrogen. Preliminary studies indicate that a high intake of phytoestrogens also reduce hot flushes and vaginal dryness. The studies are supported by observations that women from the "far east" who have a rich diet of phytoestrogens throughout their lives report few menopausal symptoms.

Counselling is another alternative to clinical intervention in the treatment of menopausal symptoms. In fact, physicians and social workers who work with women, believe counselling is more effective, since women are more affected by the social changes brought on by menopause than by the actual hormonal change. Unfortunately counselling has been completely under-utilized as part of treatment. In rural India counselling is informal. As Bang says, "For most women menopausal discomforts are too trivial to demand the attention of a doctor. For many, a listening ear, sympathy and reassurance about what is happening to her are all that is necessary."

In Kolkata, Dr D. Leelaram runs a private "Well Woman Clinic" at the Woodlands Old Age Home. She profiles a typical case. "The patient is usually about 43 years old. She is either childless or her children are away. Her parents are not alive. Her husband is completely involved in his work and has no interest in her. She frequently has stress incontinence. She feels isolated and she's lost interest in herself. My patients are essentially rich, demoralised women." Leelaram says her treatment is oriented towards providing relief as well as prevention of diseases. But she also counsels women on cosmetic care and dressing, believing these to be as important.

Predisposing Factors for the Menopausal Syndrome

Increasing research on menopause has meant more information. For instance, are some women more susceptible to menopausal syndrome than others? Yes, say researchers and doctors. Based on research and observation, doctors present a broad profile of women who might suffer the menopausal syndrome. As mentioned earlier, undernourished women often have premature menopause.

In an article, Doctors F Parikh and S Nadkarni, quote a study that showed dose related effects of smoking on the age at menopause.[12] According to an article in the Indian Council of Medical Research (ICMR) Bulletin, "Smokers have menopause on an average one to two years earlier than non-smokers". [13] And regular drinkers are more likely to be prone to osteoporosis or brittle bone disease since heavy intake of alcohol inhibits the accumulation of calcium, increasing the chances of this bone degenerative disorder. Dr R K Bhathena says, in an article on osteoporosis, "With alcohol abuse and excessive cigarette smoking, there is a reduction in bone density through lowering of plasma oestrogen concentrations."[14]

---

[12]Parikh F. Nadkarni, S. (1996), "Premature Menopause" in Usha R Krishnan, Duru Shah (Eds), *op cit.*

[13]Shah, Rashmi (1998), *op cit.*

[14]Bhathena, RK (1996), "Osteoporosis—Prevention and Management"in Usha R Krishnan, Duru Shah (Eds), *op cit.*

In the same article, Bhathena writes "bone density increases through the growth years reaching a peak in the late twenties. Some time after the age of 35, healthy men and women lose bone mass at a far greater rate, about 3–5 per cent per year, showing a ten-fold increase. The accelerated period of bone loss generally lasts for 6–10 years after which the loss continues at a much slower rate." It must be made clear that though osteoporosis is not restricted to women, menopausal women certainly do stand a greater chance of this "silent epidemic" because of the loss of oestrogen support as well as the fact that women have a lower peak bone mass than men and therefore tend to develop osteoporosis earlier than men. Bhathena says, "The incidence of osteoporotic fracture is 2–3 times greater in women than in men" because of this lowered peak bone mass.

Genetically, women who are tall, fair skinned and slim are more prone to osteoporosis. "Racial" typecasting has shown Parsis to have the highest incidence of osteoporosis in the world followed by Jews. Dr Bhavin Jankharia, a Mumbai-based radiologist, regularly scans patients referred to him on his DEXA (Dual Energy X-ray Absorptiometry) machine, one of the few in the country. He says the data available in India on the incidence of osteoporosis are limited, but believes that "50 per cent of the population over the age of 50 could be affected (by osteoporosis)." Shah and Jankharia are planning a sample survey aimed at setting the norms for Indian women and osteoporosis. This will be done using the DEXA machine to get precise measuring of bone density of the hip and spine regions of Indian women, thereby establishing a baseline study.

Culture and ethnicity in combination with dietary influences can also be factors that predetermine osteoporotic cases but Jankharia cautions that this is still in the realm of unscientific observation. Doctors have informally noted that Keralites have a high bone mass, a fact attributed to the high intake of calcium and seafood, along with marked exposure to sunlight. Dr Anklesaria bears out this observation, saying women from the Far East countries with their high seafood intake report few menopausal symptoms. He also observes that "all along the coast osteoporosis is low." Veiled or burkha-clad Muslims, whose dietaries are also inadequate, have a tendency to osteomalacia (one of the causes of osteoporosis) due to Vitamin D deficiency related to lack of exposure to sunlight. And people from the northern state of Punjab have a high bone mass which could be due to their heavy milk intake.

Obviously more significant in India than smoking and alcohol however is undernutrition. Jankharia also notes that people from the lower socio-economic strata have a low bone mass because of poor nutrition. While all these conditions are not gender specific it logically follows that Indian women will be more affected because of poverty and poor diets and the fact that they tend to put a low priority on their own nutrition and health care.

Adopting a low-fat diet rich in calcium, frequent intake of green leafy vegetables, exercising regularly and avoiding smoking help in reducing menopausal symptoms. In turn these measures will reduce risks for osteoporosis and cardiovascular diseases—both high-risk diseases for menopausal women, especially in the higher socio-economic groups.

In conclusion, there is a need to understand and accept that the menopausal experience is not just a biological phenomenon but one that is strongly influenced by socio-cultural factors. A wholesome approach to menopause would be to see it, not as a medical issue, but a social one—a natural transition that may be temporarily problematic for some women. There is certainly a lot to be learnt—especially by the medical profession—from Chabbubai of Saswad village in Maharashtra.

The Gulf Wife Syndrome

K P M Basheer

"I never wanted to marry. I wanted to study and become a doctor ... I don't want to be a mother. I hate it," Shabna, 15 years old and five months pregnant, at a gynaecologist's clinic.

"This (pointing to her swollen abdomen) is my school certificate.... Two months before my final examination, I was married off." Zuhra, 16, and six months pregnant, recovering from depression at a psychiatrist's clinic.

"One day, when I returned home from school, my father told me matter-of-factly, 'Daughter, I've fixed your marriage'. It was so sudden." Naseema, 17 years old.

Teenage marriage and adolescent childbirth among Muslims in the verdant Malappuram district of Kerala, exposing them to both physical ailments and psychiatric disorders, is not new. But paradoxically, the phenomenon is on the rise over the last decade or so because of the influx of money and prosperity from young Keralan men with jobs in the Arabian Gulf. A "Gulf man" is considered a prize catch for parents eager to get their daughters married off as soon as possible. The prospective Gulf grooms, usually in their early 20s, also seek young brides. These marriages set standards for other families in the district to emulate, with the result that young girls are plucked out of school and pushed into wedlock long before they are ready, either physically or emotionally.

Teenage marriage and adolescent pregnancy are the biggest blots on the reproductive health scenario of Malappuram district, says Professor K Abubacker, principal investigator of a UN Population Fund (UNFPA) study. The study, carried out in 1998 by the district reproductive health project, found 53 per cent of the ever-married women it contacted had entered wedlock between the ages of 15 and 17. Indeed, the baseline study that surveyed 2,400 random households, identified seven married girls in the age group of 10 to 14. Says psychiatrist Manoj Kumar Therayil, many of whose patients are teenage wives, "Early marriage and early pregnancy hamper the natural development of a girl. It's a pity that at the time when a girl should be playing with her schoolmates, she is changing her baby's nappies."

According to a recent Rapid Household Survey commissioned by the World Bank-funded Reproductive and Child Health Project that studied 1000 households, 35 per cent of all women married in the three years before the survey date were below 18, the legal age of marriage. It also showed that 61 per cent of all the married women had consummated their marriages before 18.[1] The survey was carried out by the Bangalore-based Institute for Social and Economic Change. Professor T V Sekher, who headed the survey, pointed out that over 90 per cent of the teenage marriages that took place in the district were in Muslim families.[2]

Dr Shabna

There is a cruel joke in Malappuram: "A Muslim girl attains her *sastipoorthi* (ceremony held to celebrate 60th birthday) by age 20—she marries at age 14, has her first baby at 15, the second at 16, the third at 17 and so on..." The joke implies that by age 20, a Muslim girl is drained of her youth, health and beauty and she looks like a 60-year-old. Though exaggerated, it highlights the reality of many ordinary Muslim girls in the district.

Fifteen-year-old Shabna of Pullangod village is a case in point. Her swollen belly rests incongruously on her tall, lean frame as she waits for her turn for a check-up at a gynaecologist's office. A cream scarf is tied casually round her head, as is now mandatory for Muslim women in Malabar. She speaks in

---

[1]Population Research Centre, Institute for Social and Economic Change (2001), *Reproductive and Child Health Project Rapid Household Survey, 1998-99*, Bangalore.

[2]Sekher, T.V.(2000), *Migration and Social Change*, Rawat Publications, Jaipur.

fits and starts—about her marriage, about her deep longing for her school and friends, of how her marriage put an end to her secret dream of becoming a doctor. "I never wanted to marry. I wanted to study and become a doctor," she says bitterly. Doctors had always fascinated her, especially stately women doctors moving about hospital wards with stethoscopes hanging from their necks. When alone as a child, she often used to call herself "Dr. Shabna".

But last summer her cherished childhood dream was shattered. A fortnight after she passed her ninth class exam with honours, her parents married her off to a 24-year-old Keralite working in one of the Arabian Gulf countries. She had protested with all the teenage fury she could command, but protests by a girl in a Muslim family in the male-dominated social milieu of Malappuram lead nowhere. "The wedding took place so suddenly that I did not even get the time and privacy to commit suicide," she says chillingly.

Barely two months after her marriage, her husband left for the Gulf. Shabna was left in a new household with his parents, brothers and sisters-in-law and their children, all of whom live together in a small house. She feels terribly lonely in the crowded house where her role is that of an exalted housemaid. Instead of duties in a hospital ward, from daybreak until late in the evening she has an endless round of household chores.

"In the evenings, sometimes I have this sudden feeling that I am still a schoolgirl and that I have not finished my homework. I get up and go to fetch my books, then reality strikes and I realize that I am no longer a student; that in another five months I will be a mother." A moment later, the girl says calmly: " I hate the idea of being a mother."

Excluded from the Kerala Miracle

The Kerala model of development— that of attaining high human development indicators without a corresponding rise in per capita income—is often held up as an example to the world.

Kerala is the first state in India to become totally literate, its overall population growth rate is below the replacement level (two children per couple), and it has achieved several national health and demographic targets years ahead of national deadlines. But Malappuram hovers on the fringes of this miracle.

Bordering the Arabian Sea, Malappuram with 3550 square kilometres of hills, rivers, coconut plantations and rice fields, is the third largest of the 14 administrative districts of Kerala. In terms of population it is home to some four million people, making it the largest. The main occupation is agriculture and the district has only a handful of industrial units.[3] It also has the highest rate of unemployment in the state. A low-paid job in an Arabian Gulf country is often the only hope for young men.

Judging by all indicators of development, Malappuram is the least developed district in the state, says Mohammed Rasheed, the district information officer and an active social worker. "This is manifested in a relatively high rate of population growth, comparatively low public health status, families of a larger size than is now the norm in Kerala, comparatively low levels of education and very low agricultural and industrial growth."

"In terms of physical quality of life, Malappuram is one of the most backward districts in Kerala" says Prof. Abubacker, who hails from the district and teaches economics at the local government college. It has the highest fertility and mortality rates in Kerala. Its annual rate of population growth during 1981–91 was 2.9 while the state average was a mere 1.3.[4] Healthcare facilities are inadequate compared to other districts. The central government's Ministry of Health has identified Malappuram as one of the 90 problem districts in the country.

Two-thirds of the district's population is Muslim. In fact, at 2.6 million, Malappuram represents one of the highest con-

[3]Government of Kerala, Department of Public Relations, (1996), *District Handbook of Kerala Malappuram*,Thiruvananthapuram.

[4]UNFPA(1999) *Reproductive and Child Health Scenario—Baseline Survey 1998, Malappuram District*, New Delhi.

centrations of Muslims in India. The rest of the district's population comprises Hindus and Christians. The social milieu is more male-dominated in the Muslim community compared to non-Muslim communities and women have very little say in social affairs.

Says Fouzia Jabbar, a school teacher and one of the few Muslim feminist activists of Malappuram: "The patriarchal family set-up and the community's general lack of education and economic advancement deny Muslim women access to personal freedom and women's rights. What is not even spoken about is reproductive rights: when and whom to marry and how many times to conceive."

Although these are not particular to the Muslim community, they are nevertheless more entrenched among them for a variety of reasons. Practices like polygamy, dowry, men's right to divorce at will, early marriage, adolescent childbirth, frequent childbirths and reluctance to adopt family planning methods are quite prevalent among the community. "All these practices militate against women's rights and freedoms," Jabbar argues.

Historical Background

Historically the marriage of men before age 21 and women before age 18 was quite common throughout India and continues at places despite the Indian government's ban on it through the Child Marriage Restraint Act of 1928. Even today in India over a half of women get married each year before they are 18. In the north Indian states of Rajasthan, Uttar Pradesh, Bihar and Madhya Pradesh, evocatively called the BIMARU (sick) states, this percentage is over 60. Seven and eight year old brides are not uncommon in these areas. In Kerala too, until a few decades back, child marriage was widespread in all communities, especially among Muslims in northern Keralan districts and among the Namboodiri Brahmins at the top rung of the Hindu caste system.

V T Bhattathirippad, who waged a relentless war for the liberation of Namboodiri women and E M S Namboodiripad, who headed the first communist government in Kerala in 1956, recall in their autobiographies several incidents of 70-or 80-year-old Namboodiri men taking teenagers as their fourth or fifth wives.[5] Professor M N Karasseri of Calicut University, a Muslim intellectual, says he recollects instances of girls below 10 years being married off in his community. Manu Musaliyar, a leading Muslim cleric and key functionary of the All Kerala Muslim Religious Education Board, says that four decades ago, he had, as a 30-year-old, married his wife when she was only 10. Until the mid-20th century, teenage marriage was common among the educationally advanced Catholics too. But in the past few decades the situation has changed drastically in Kerala. The average age at marriage of women is now 23.5 years, the highest in the country.

Although it is often said that this is a consequence of female literacy and the resultant women's empowerment, it is also frequently a fact that women are forced to marry later than they would wish to because of sharp increases in the amount of dowry. Women are then forced to work to earn their own and their sisters' dowries. Among certain Christian communities in south-central Kerala, the mean age at marriage of women is now 25. A substantial section of professional Christian women, mainly nurses who work abroad as well as in other parts of India, marry after 30. Annamma Cherian of Thiruvalla, a nurse in the army, married when she was 32. Her younger sister, a nurse in a Kuwait hospital, married at 34. Annamma says that her mother had married at 16. "My generation of Christian women realized that a career was as important as a stable married life," she says. "Marriage can wait, but if you do not acquire an education and start a career in time, the career will not wait for you."

---

[5]Bhattatiripad, V.T. (1972), *Kannerum Kinavu* ("Tears and Dreams"), Kottayam D.C. Books Namboodiripad, E.M.S. (1970), *Atmakatha* ("Autobiography"), Kottayam, D.C.Books.

The Christian community in Kerala is now one of the most socially, economically and educationally advanced communities in the whole country. The first woman judge of the Kerala High Court, the first surgeon-general and many other firsts among Kerala's women have been Christians. Western missionaries and enlightened Church leaders, as well as the already high-level of literacy and the patronage of British rulers before Independence in 1947, contributed to the progress and social advancement of the Christian community in Kerala.

The increase in the age at marriage is partly due to the social reform movements and the conscious efforts of the Communist Party. The major castes of Hindu society, like Namboodiris and Ezhavas, launched their own community-specific reform movements in the first half of the 20th century. Educational measures taken by enlightened rulers of the erstwhile princely state also contributed to this. Even early in the 20th century, women's education was being emphasized by the then princely state of Travancore and Cochin. Kerala's matrilineal traditions among some castes may also have helped. Malappuram, then a part of the Madras Presidency, was not touched by the waves of these changes sweeping the rest of Kerala.

The reform movements always focussed on education, particularly female education, which naturally led to more freedom for women. The struggle for Independence from colonial British rulers brought women to the social mainstream. Later, the Communist movement in Kerala, which lasted several decades, had an extensive impact on grassroots level social life and a positive impact on the status of women.

But the general reform movements, which mainly took place in Kerala's central and southern regions administered by the Maharajah of Tavancore and Cochin, overlooked the Muslims who were concentrated in the Malabar district in the north, which was under direct British rule. At the same time, unlike among the Namboodiri, Ezhava and Christian societies, there was no major community-specific internal reform movement among the Muslims. "There was no capable leadership to guide the Muslim community and no progressive organization to lead them to reform and advancement," notes Professor Siddique Hassan, State chief of the Jamaat-e-Islami-e-Hind.

Education, particularly English education, was the watchword for the social reform movements of the 20th century. Muslims, however, were generally hostile to English education as the language for them was the "Devil's tongue" because of their traditional animosity to British rule. This was no doubt also strengthened by the severe British repression unleashed after the Mapilla Rebellion of peasants in 1921.

It is thus not surprising that when Kerala state was formed in 1956, the Malabar region lagged behind the other regions of Kerala in terms of education, health as well as socio-economic development. Since then there have been changes, though slow, but the Malabar region is yet to catch up with the rest of the state. According to Professor Hameed Chennamangalloor, a leading Muslim intellectual and writer, while all other communities in Kerala progressed educationally, economically and socially in the 20th century, the Muslims stood where they were till the 1970s. "One of the main reasons was that they had been hostile to changes, while other communities adapted themselves to changes in the 20th century".

He indicates that in recent times Muslims have made strides in education and female literacy chiefly because of the influx of money from the Keralites employed in the Arabian Gulf. According to Chennamangalloor, this inflow started three decades ago with the massive migration of labour from Malappuram and other districts in the state to support economic activity resulting from the oil boom in the Gulf countries. This migration has been mostly to United Arab Emirates, Kuwait, Saudi Arabia, Bahrain, Iran, Iraq and Libya. It is estimated that during the three decades of the 1970s-2000, several hundred thousand men from Kerala migrated to the Gulf countries alone. While other areas of the state also contributed women to this migratory stream, mainly nurses, those migrating from Malappuram were unskilled men.

Declining Age at Marriage

Ironically, instead of raising the age at marriage of Muslim women in Malappuram, the Gulf phenomenon seems to have had a reverse impact. "The mean age has marginally declined over the past decade," observes Professor Abubacker who feels that the mean age could be well below 16 years.

According to the Rapid Household Survey (RHS), the mean age at marriage for women was 18.7 and for men 24.7 in Malappuram—the lowest among the 14 districts. The survey carried out in seven districts found the mean age at marriage of women who married after 1995 in Kerala was 23.5, while for men it was 29.6. If it is assumed that the Hindu and Christian women, who formed one-third of the female population of the district, had married at the state-level mean age of 23.5, then the mean age of the Muslim women, who constituted two-thirds, would be a little over 16.

However, it is possible that the two studies, which have for the first time thrown light on the extent and nature of teenage marriage in the district, may have underreported age. This could be due to two reasons: first, uneducated people tend to give a random figure for age; and second, many people might have falsely stated the age of marriage as 18 for fear of prosecution. In sum, it would be safe to say that the mean age is below 16, says Abubacker.

The decrease in the mean age of marriage among the Muslim women of Malappuram is particularly worrisome when the Muslim community on the whole has made strides in the education, health and economic sectors in recent years. According to government statistics, the community has achieved 90 per cent literacy (in an otherwise fully literate state). Female education has improved vastly even though those going to universities and professional colleges are only a handful.

The Gulf boom has helped sharply reduce poverty in the community. It has also created a significant middle class. According to Dr. T.V. Sekher, the boom has helped women's empowerment and raised their social status in a significant way.

Practices like polygamy, the husband divorcing his wife by a simple pronouncement of the word *talaq* thrice over and taking on new wives in quick succession, have declined significantly.

The community has, of late, jumped on to the small family bandwagon. The Rapid Household Survey found that the mean number of children ever born to Muslim women was three and that use of contraceptive methods and female sterilization were picking up in a big way. Thus the decline in the birth rate here has been quite significant. For a socially conservative community, these are remarkable advancements, which have not been highlighted enough. But the practice of teenage marriage continues.

Skewed Gender Equations + Gulf Money = Younger Brides

"Gulf money is the best thing that ever happened to the community in a long time," says Kunhali Musliyar, a former clergyman who made it good in the Gulf. He is an avid reformer and supports charities in his neighbourhood community. The flow of Gulf money for a quarter of a century has changed the face of the district. "Gulf" has a palpable presence. From "Gulf Travel Agency", "Gulf Motors", "Gulf Textiles" "Hotel Dubai", "Saudi Restaurant" to "Kuwait Hair Saloon", there is not a single village that does not display links with the Gulf.

Estimates of the number of Gulf workers and the money they remit are hard to come by, but there is hardly any Muslim family in the 135 village administrative units in the district which has no Gulf connection, either through a son, a cousin, a nephew or a distant relative. There are a number of reasons contributing to this. Lack of employment opportunities in the industrially-backward district, uneconomic agriculture, largely due to a collapse of prices of primary commodities in the global market, relatively low governmental investment in economic development, lack of education to find work in government or the private-sector companies have all forced tens of thousands of unskilled Malappuram men to seek low-paid menial jobs in the Gulf. A huge majority of them earn less than Rs 10,000 a month after working 10 to 14 hours a day. Although severely exploited, this is unimaginable wealth for them.

Like any other conservative Indian community inured to shelling out massive dowries, Malappuram Muslims see their daughters as huge burdens on the family to be disposed off as early as possible. A girl of "marriageable age" (this begins from menarche) causes loss of sleep to all the adult members of the family, particularly the father and the elder brothers. The top priority of any family is thus the marriage of the daughter.

As soon as a father or brother finds a job in the Gulf, he focuses on saving for his daughter's/sister's wedding. In the case of a Gulf man who has no daughter or sister to marry off, his priority would be to build a house, the more garish the better, back in his village. However, if he has a daughter or sister, his top priority invariably would be her marriage. Young men have gone to the Gulf to make money exclusively for meeting the wedding expenses of their sisters. Like Kunhu Mohammed of Pandikkad, who says he was virtually driven to the Gulf by his parents to find money to marry off his two teenage sisters.

As soon as money for the dowry and wedding expenses is ready, the marriage is arranged, no matter what the girl's age or her academic potential. Thousands of fathers and brothers in the Gulf skip their two-yearly paid vacation back home to continue to work for another couple of years to earn enough for the wedding expenses. On the first visit home, they ensure the girls are married off and the "huge burdens on the families lifted". Says Abdur Rahman of Karuvarakund, "Now that I have married off my daughter, I can even think of not going back to my Gulf job".

In the case of families with two or more girls, the eldest is married off at the first available opportunity, even if she is only 14. Had there been no Gulf boom and not enough money available to these families to "shed the burden", these girls would probably have been allowed to finish school and delay marriage. The Gulf families set the standards for the rest of society. What a Gulf family does is invariably copied by the neighbours. If the neighbour's daughter is married off at 15, it is considered a shame for the other families not to "get rid of their daughters" after they have crossed 15. The demand for teenage brides mostly comes from two sources—unemployed young men aspiring to go to the Gulf but unable to do so because of the heavy financial cost and young men already employed in the Gulf.

In the first case, marriage is a passport to the Gulf. Young boys look for a girl whose parents are ready to foot the bill for their Gulf dream. These marriages are called "visa marriages" as the dowry package includes the airline ticket to the chosen Gulf country, the cost of securing a labour visa and a work permit.

Until the recent waning of the Gulf boom, parents of girls used to grab such prospective Gulf men as financial security for their daughters. The visa marriage works out cheap for the families of the girls because the visa and work permit are arranged by the father or a brother or relative already employed there. Again, had there been no Gulf boom, this section of young men would have delayed their marriages for a few more years till they were settled economically.

Most of the young Gulf men marry on their first trip home, normally after two to four years' work. Because of peer pressure, they prefer a bride seven to ten years younger. The age gap between a husband and wife in Kerala is widest among the Malabar Muslims, observes psychiatrist P M Syed Mohammed of Guruvayur, most of whose clients are from Malappuram.

The men seeking wives are, in the first place, relatively young—roughly around 25—and they look out for much younger brides. Since the Gulf men set the norms for other young men, the preference for a wide age gap extends to all sections. The preference for young brides has resulted in pushing up dowries for the older ones. To avoid the payment of a bigger dowry, parents marry off their daughters as early as possible.

A 15-year-old girl who would go with a "fifty and fifty" (meaning a dowry of Rs 50,000 and 50 sovereigns worth of gold ornaments) may require "one and 100" (Rs 1,00,000 and 100 sovereigns) three years later. Small wonder, a father or brother who has saved "fifty and fifty" from two to four years' toil in the Gulf hates to wait until the girl turns 18. Dowry and wedding expenses have skyrocketed in the recent decades. In the past, dowry had been a nominal sum of money. However, the Gulf boom and the spread of consumerism jacked up dowry. The educated middle-class practice of paying heavy dowry to the grooms, particularly prevalent among the Christians, and upper-caste Hindus, was blindly aped by the working-classes and lower-middle-class Muslims.

Professor M N Karassery points out, "It should be underlined that Gulf money does this only because of the objective realities of socio-cultural conditions of the Muslim community which are loaded against gender equality and women's rights."

One other factor has also contributed significantly: the growth of communal identities since the late eighties. Many believed this was a phenomenon particular to the north of the country and that the south was immune. However since the nineties, the RSS has made particular efforts to spread its organization in the southern states, including Kerala, hitherto considered a bastion of the Left. It is thus not surprising that communal violence has been on the rise.

The spread of the Hindutva ideology, viewing Muslims as "the Other", seeking to set up a Hindu nation, has added to the woes of Muslim women. In the wake of the 1992 demolition of the Babri Majid in Ayodhya, and the large scale communal violence that it engendered in several places throughout the country, the shocked Malappuram Muslim community responded with an attempt to "go back to the Muslim roots and traditions." Strengthening the communal and cultural identity, by strictly following the "Muslim way of life", was a direct reaction of a community feeling increasingly beleaguered. While more and more men began attending the Friday group prayers at the masjid, and more and more young men now took to sporting beards and caps, women were pressured to wear the purdha. Purdha has since been regarded as "the Muslim woman's dress" though rarely had Keralan Muslim women worn it before. The chador, too came to be worn by young women. And, since the Sharia'th (Muslim jurisprudence) allowed marriage of women after menarche, this too was considered a "Muslim tradition" and hence the strengthening of the practice of teenage marriage.

Seeking Refuge in the Psychiatrists' Couch

Psychiatrists, psychologists, gynaecologists and general medical practitioners report that the psychiatrist's couch is becoming the refuge of an increasingly large number of teenage wives in the district. "Fortunately, consulting a psychiatrist or psychologist is no big taboo in this region," says psychiatrist P M Syed Mohammed. But, for every girl who seeks and finds solace in psychotherapy, there are scores of others who suffer in silence. "What we mental health professionals see is only the tip of the iceberg," according to Mohammed, director of the Ansar Hospital at Perumbilavu, and president of the Indian Association of Clinical Psychologists. Unable to share their problems with others, and unaware of their psychiatric problems, these young women spend their lives in silent agony, says Mohammed.

What makes these young women susceptible to mental illness? "Bewildered by the total change in their life situations overnight and the heavy demands made on them after marriage, it is not surprising that teenage wives start showing signs of mental stress," says Dr Anil Kumar, a clinical psychologist from Guruvayur. Added to this situation is the emotional and physical turbulence of adolescence, lack of sex education, skewed married life and a husband who is generally ten years older. Mohammed points out that a majority of Muslim girls are married off between the age of 15 and 18, when they are still growing and in most cases attending schools and colleges. Since the girls have no say in the decisions concerning their marriage, they meekly accept what their parents decide for them.

"Marriage came as a shock to me," recalls Zuhra of Edavnnappara, who recently recovered from mental depression with a psychiatrist's help. It was just two months before her SSLC exam that she was married off. She could not take her exam and that, according to her, made her desperate and triggered off her depression.

Pointing to her six-months pregnant belly she remarks wryly: "This is my SSLC certificate." Her mother-in-law complains that Zuhra has no love for her husband and no respect for her in-laws.

Sixteen-year-old Sahla of Tuvvur was referred to a clinical psychologist by a general practitioner in Perinthalmanna after she complained of frequent chest pain. In just 20 minutes, the psychologist realized that the ninth-class dropout was expressing her psychological distress at having to cope with the pressures of life at her in-laws' home. Her in-laws (her husband was away in Saudi Arabia working for a construction company) were advised to send Sahla to her parents' home for a month. Not even once did Sahla complain of chest pain during the 27 days she was with her parents. "But, the day after she returned to her in-laws, she was at it again," he recalled.

Adjustment Disorders

"Adjustment disorders are the main problems of teenage wives," says Dr Manoj Kumar Therayil. The psychological problems of these women are now increasingly referred to as the "Gulf Syndrome". Because these girls are very young, adjusting with husbands, mothers-in-law and even with their own children is very difficult.

"You must understand that these wives are still not out of their teens—just because they are married they do not cease to be adolescents and become mature and responsible overnight," Mohammed says.

Sulekha Begum, a young lawyer who argues divorced Muslim women's cases in the Family Court at Manjeri, the main city in the district, says problems can even begin with the order in which food is served at home. "The girl who, as a school-going child, used to be served the meal first in her own home, will perhaps be the last to be served in her in-laws' home," she says. She now has to wait until all the children and male adults are served. The daughter-in-law is at the bottom of the heap in her in-laws' home. For a girl of 15, this shift in priority is baffling, says Begum. "Adolescence is a period of confusion and bewilderment," says Dr C J John, chief psychiatrist at Medical Trust Hospital, Kochi. "Sandwiched between childhood and adulthood, the children are often unable to cope with the changes in their bodies and minds."

•

Extended Families Aggravate Tensions

Though nuclear families are increasingly becoming the norm in modern India, extended families are common in Malappuram, especially among the low-income groups. Sons continue to stay with their parents long after marriage. They branch out only when they have the means to set up their own homes. Three or four sons, along with their wives and children, living in the parental home is not uncommon. Community traditions and rampant unemployment force men to stay on in extended families. The extended family makes adjustment even more difficult for the teenage bride.

Everyone in the family, especially the mother-in-law, expects the girl to behave like an adult, be polite to every member of the family and carry out household chores. "Harassment by the mother-in-law is a major cause for these teenagers' mental illness," Dr Syed Mohammed says. The mothers-in-law, in most cases in their thirties or forties, have themselves gone through teenage marriages and have suffered similarly. Psychologically, Dr Syed Mohammed notes, they want to see their daughters-in-law suffer, as some sort of perverse solace to mitigate their own past sufferings.

Psychosomatic Symptoms

The "Gulf Syndrome" is not however restricted to young girls alone. Even slightly older women, who run their homes single-handedly with little community or social support, while their husbands are away toiling in the Gulf, are its victims. "These women are a greedy doctor's delight" says a doctor who has treated such women. They present themselves regularly as Out Patients with a host of vague symptoms, are depressed and anxious. "What they need is friendship and support. Instead they are prescribed a range of medicines, regularly given injections as placebos, even as doctors run all the way to the bank", he adds.

This is also apparently part of a more general trend among women in Kerala which sees a rising incidence of suicides. Kerala also has the highest incidence of consumption of psychotropic drugs, such as tranquilisers and anti-depressants, in the country. The social and economic changes over the last two decades have also triggered what is referred to as the medicalization of Keralan society.

It is when psychiatric problems take the form of physical illness that the girls are taken to doctors. Constant headache, chest pain, stomach ache and sleeplessness are common complaints. "In many cases, these are 'imagined' sicknesses," Dr Anil Kumar says. General practitioners often fail to identify the causes and prescribe expensive drugs and order a computerised tomography (CT) scan or even magnetic resonance imaging (MRI) scan. When everything fails, the patient is referred to a psychologist or psychiatrist. Most of these girls express their mental distress through physical illness.

"We call this somatization," explains Dr John. "Somatization is the unconscious expression of mental distress in physical terms. As the Muslim teenage wives are unable to express the 'idioms of distress' like other individuals do, because of socio-cultural factors, they tend to express them physically." In a patriarchal, conservative Malappuram Muslim social milieu, the girl is culturally programmed not to express her distress and frustrations. Instead, she unconsciously masks it with headache or chest pain.

The conflicts arising out of the disparity between her actual age (teenage) and the expected role as an adult worsens the situation. Since she is not expected to have friends, she cannot share her frustrations. In the case of Gulf wives, even the limited possibility of sharing their sorrows with the husbands is denied as they get to see the husbands once in two years or so.

Lack of Sex Education

A major factor that triggers psychosomatic conditions in teenage wives is sex. A 15- or 16-year-old girl, raised in a regimented environment, is normally scared of sex. "Honeymoon horror stories" are part of folklore in Malappuram. Stories of wives running out of the bedroom screaming on the wedding night are aplenty. Since any discussion on sex is taboo and there is no sex education, sex is both a mystery and threat.

Sixteen-year-old Zeenath of Pandikkad, married for a year, would start vomiting as bedtime neared. But, she vomited only on nights when the husband was around. Her psychologist started treatment with a few fundamental tips on sex. The husband was counselled too. After a few sessions, Zeenath's vomiting ceased. Now pregnant, she says mischievously: "Now I have a different kind of vomiting."

Syed Mohammed says many of his patients narrate instances of marital rape and forced sex. He recalls the case of a 14-year-old wife who was raped by her husband on the wedding night with her legs tied. Initial violent sexual behaviour by the husband sometimes results in lifelong scars on the girl's psyche. Shabna Hydrose, a counsellor at the Family Counselling Centre, Malappuram, says many teenage wives seeking her help express an aversion to sex. These aversions are unconsciously translated into physical sickness. Hydrose feels that every bride and bridegroom should undergo a compulsory pre-marital counselling course.

The Catholic Church in Kerala made premarital sex counselling mandatory a decade ago. Couples have to take a three-day course together and get a certificate for the marriage to be solemnized in a church. Such courses can go a long way in checking sex-induced mental illnesses, she adds.

One direct fall-out of the lack of sex education and awareness of contraceptive techniques is the alarmingly high rate of adolescent pregnancy. The UNFPA's sample of 2,918 women in the reproductive age, showed that 53 per cent of them had married between the ages 15 and 17. And, most of them had become pregnant in the first year of marriage. Explains, Dr A. Mohammed, former District Medical Officer, many "Gulf husbands" who leave for work a few months after marriage are keen to make their teenage wives pregnant, as a precautionary measure against wives "straying".

"Pregnancy at that tender age can unsettle a girl's mind," says Dr Anil Kumar. The physical change and the fact that another human body is growing inside her are often quite terrifying for the girl. Many girls who consult psychiatrists are pregnant. The majority of young mothers say they do not want to bear children at such an early age and would prefer to wait till they are 20 or 25 years old.

Says Sabira of Perinthalmanna, a 19-year-old mother of two and the wife of a clergyman, "If I had the right to decide I would not have become pregnant at all; it's such a bother to look after these two kids." But in a society that puts pressure on the women to prove their fertility, that option is almost non-existent.

Post-delivery depression is also common among young mothers. Psychotherapy is useful for a majority of young Muslim wives, but only a miniscule percentage have the means to access it. A few others, in villages, go to faith healers, to get only temporary relief. Unfortunately, no community leader or government agency has grasped the extent of psychiatric illness in teenage wives.

Dr Mohammed, meanwhile, offers a one-point remedy to the Gulf Syndrome. "Please delay your daughter's marriage until she becomes physically and mentally mature." Though the legal age is 18, he says, 21 would be the ideal age. "By marrying off your daughter at 14 or 15, you could possibly be pushing her into mental illness."

But it is not just mental balance at stake here, but in a sense, life and its possibilities. As the Zuhras, Zeenaths and Shubnas testify, they have been robbed of their adolescence, their growing-up years, their dreams, their hopes and aspirations.

Safe Motherhood, Unsafe Deliveries

ANNU ANAND

Hard Labour

In a small, dark hut in Laxmani village in Jhabua district of Madhya Pradesh, a woman in her twenties writhes in pain. She is in labour, attended to by her relatives. Laxmani is typical of the hamlets inhabited by adivasis in this area, one of the country's least developed, in the BIMARU state of Madhya Pradesh. The nearest town is eight kilometres away. Laxmani village is desolate, has scattered hutments around a meandering semi pucca road. It has a health sub-centre which opens occasionally.

With the labour not progressing, elderly women with more experience are called in. A breech delivery is diagnosed and they suggest calling in a *budua*. They huddle around, comforting the woman, waiting for the budua who is not only a traditional healer, but also doubles as an exorcist. He has been summoned from a nearby village. After a few hours, he arrives and gets to work.

He puts his bare hands into the woman's uterus and straightens the position of the baby, just as any qualified and experienced obstetrician would do. Then he kicks the woman's womb and the baby comes out. Mission successful, he is paid fifty one rupees. "Most of the deliveries in Laxmani take place in homes. All the treatment is given by elderly women. The most common method is to hit the belly with the ankle and take the baby out. After the delivery, we cut the umbilical chord with a *hansia* (grass-cutter) or *bilkhi* (arrow)," says 45 year old Sundari Bai, a trained midwife. "To remove the placenta, we normally use a *tumadi* (rough-hewn utensil used to drink country liquor). After the delivery, we give the woman a bath and a glass of country liquor. It cleans up the woman's digestive system. The next day the mother goes to the fields, as usual", she adds.

The Bhil and Bilala adivasi groups comprise up to 85 per cent of the 11.2 lakhs population in Jhabua, a thickly forested area of the state known for its mahua flowers, and liquor. This is one of the areas with the largest concentration of adivasis in the country. Poverty and lack of development mark the district. One reason for this is that the 1300-odd villages in the district are scattered. Many government sponsored development schemes have been started here over the past few years, with little visible impact. The 19 per cent literacy rate is one of the lowest in the country. The infant mortality rate is an appalling 141 per thousand.

The chief occupation in the district is agriculture. This also determines the family size, which is large because more hands are needed to work on the fields. Given the IMR, it is not surprising that the birth rate here is 42.65 as opposed to the national average of 28.6. The children are not sent to schools either because the schools are too far away, completely dysfunctional or because they are needed to tend animals at home. Women look after homes, take care of children, work in the fields and also contribute equally in all income generating activity, collecting forest produce and selling vegetables. Women also work as agricultural labourers in the sowing season.

Chandpur, Kathiwada, Jobat, Bhabra, Aamkoot and other hamlets like Laxmani, reveal that buduas reign supreme, despite government-run health and family welfare programmes and the publicity given to them. Most of the families believe in buduas and not ANMs from health centres or trained mid-wives, chiefly because they have hardly seen the latter.

Same Story, Different Characters

Several hundred kilometres from the plains of Jhabua is village Divli in Tehri Garhwal district of Uttaranchal, a hill state newly carved out of Uttar Pradesh. The story is the same here, only the names are different. "All our deliveries take place in homes. Older women of the village perform them, or sometimes we call the dai. We make the woman in labour sit and apply force by pressing both hands on the ground, as a result of which the baby comes out. We cut the umbilical chord with a *daitri* (grass-cutter). After that a warm water bath is given to the new born. No injections are given either to the child or mother after that," says Kundana Devi, 67, of Divli village pointing to her five grand children, aged between two and eight years. "They were all born like this."

The natural birth method of delivering in a squatting position is common in the hilly areas, says Anuradha Joshi, an activist from the Society for Integrated Development of Himalayas (SIDH), operating in the region. While doctors may frown at the position adopted here for birthing, studies reveal that squatting is in fact a better option. It is thus clear that not everything the dais do is either irrational or superstitious as doctors would have us believe.

Divli is located in a valley 25 kilometres from the famous tourist attraction, Mussourie, a quaint hill resort established during British colonial rule. The road connection is up to Dhanolti, another upcoming tourist resort. From Dhanolti, one has to trek for about three kilometres to reach Divli. It is not a village but a settlement, the residents belong to a village called Dande ki beli which is another five kilometres into the valley. There are several such settlements in the valley—Chindokhi, Khaniri, Ganna, Doonda and Nargaichi—where clusters of 10 to 15 families live. There are no health facilities whatsoever. The only means of access to these villages is a narrow, dirt track. In Tehri, the hilly terrain and cold climate make living conditions difficult. The overall literacy rate in the district is over 48 per cent, and agriculture and tourism are the main sources of employment.

At least 50 kilometres from Mussourie, in the same district, is village Uniyal, where Madhu has delivered a baby girl just three days ago. She is feeding the baby in the corner of a dark room that looks like a kitchen. Firewood burns in an earthen hearth on one side; the room is so full of smoke that Madhu's eyes water incessantly. When asked who performed the delivery, Madhu's mother-in-law laughs, "Who else? I did it along with other women of the village. We made her sit on the floor and apply force on the ground with her palms, and then we dragged the baby out'. But this time she is apprehensive about the newborn's survival, because two of Madhu's earlier children did not survive beyond a month. She does not know the reason. "For taking injections (vaccines), we have to go to Satyon village, 7 km from here, so we don't go. And no nurse comes here," she says.

Faulty Health Care Delivery Systems

Jhabua and Tehri are symptomatic of the faulty health care delivery systems in the country, particularly for the more difficult, lesser-developed and inaccessible tribal and hilly regions. One measure of the success of any health care system would be that it reaches even the most marginalized sections of society. By that measure, the health care system in India seems to fall quite short.

According to government plans India is supposed to have an elaborate primary health care delivery system for rural areas. It is a three-tier system—Sub-centres, Primary Health Centres (PHCs) and Community Health Centres (CHCs). Sub-centres, catering to populations of up to 5000, are the most peripheral contact points between the health care system and the community. These centres are to be staffed by one male multi-purpose worker and one female worker or Auxiliary Nurse-Midwife (ANM). PHCs are headed by a medical officer and are to act as a referral system for six Sub-centres. They are to have up to six beds for patients. CHCs are to act as referral centres for four PHCs and are to be staffed by four medical specialists—a surgeon, a physician, a gynaecologist and a paediatrician—supported by over 20 paramedical and other staff. CHCs are supposed to have up to 30 beds, in addition to facilities like operation theatres, X-ray machines, labour rooms and pathological laboratories. All government programmes and schemes are to be implemented through this health care delivery system. But, this system exists mostly on paper.

By the government's own admission, the infrastructure is inadequate. As per the population norms of the 1991 census, the nation-wide shortfall in 1998 of Sub-centres was 7,727 (projected to be 22, 987 by 2002), the shortfall in PHCs was 1,966 (to be 4,780 in 2002) and the shortfall in CHCs was 3,834 in 2002.[1] The fact that health budgets have been inadequate, and subjected to further cuts under SAPs does not help matters. Not only is the physical infrastructure weak, there are severe shortfalls in humanpower and equipment. Since often even basic medicines are not available, people choose not to go to public services if they can avoid it, often borrowing money to access medical care in the private sector. It is not surprising that medical expenditure is emerging as a leading cause of poverty in the country. The "Safe Motherhood" programme in villages such as Jhabua and Tehri exists mainly on government files. Women in the villages of Jhabua say almost all their children were delivered at home, either by untrained midwives or buduas.

The stated objectives of the government's Safe Motherhood and Child Survival Programme, launched in the early nineties, was to prevent deaths during pregnancy by promoting institutional deliveries and management of obstetric emergencies. Its other components were immunization, prevention and treatment of anaemia, ante-natal care, early identification of maternal complications, promoting deliveries by trained personnel and birth spacing.

The Reproductive and Child Health Programme (RCH), launched in 1997, incorporates all the components covered under the Safe Motherhood and Child Survival Programme, besides two additional ones relating to sexually transmitted diseases and reproductive tract infections. The RCH programme is now being implemented throughout the country.

---

[1]Government of India, Ministry of Health and Family Welfare (1999), *Annual Report 1997–1998*, New Delhi.

According to government statistics, Jhabua district has five CHCs, 20 PHCs and 276 Sub-centres. The sanctioned posts of ANMs are 222, but as many as 120 are lying vacant. At least 50 posts of doctors are vacant in the district. Some PHCs like Amkoot and Bakhtagarh don't have even a single doctor. In village Bhabra with a population of 10,000, four doctors' posts are vacant. One doctor was appointed only recently. "Doctors who are trained in cities and live there don't want to come and work in tribal areas like Jhabua. This leads to lot of vacancies in Primary Health Centres and Sub-centres. Whoever gets a posting here, tries and gets a transfer through ministers' and others' recommendations," says the district's Additional Collector (Development), Sanjay Shukla. This place is considered a punishment posting.

"Yet another problem is the geographical situation of the areas. Most villages are inaccessible. There are no roads and if there are roads, they are dirt tracks. None of the 25 PHCs have any vehicle or ambulance, whereas there is a provision for one ambulance and one jeep for every PHC. Even if the vehicles are there, there is no budget for fuel. Some of the Sub-centres don't have a building. If you post a surgeon to such places, he will forget surgery," says Dr K P Sadoriya, Chief Medical and Health Officer, Jhabua.

For a population of every 3,000 to 4,000, there is supposed to be one ANM in Jhabua. And these ANMs are the only form of government health intervention in most of the villages of the district. The ANMs are in charge of three to five villages, located several kilometres from each other. As we have seen, even a single village comprises clusters of settlements sometimes located several kilometres apart. "Women health workers are helpless. Sometimes they have to cover up to eight villages. They can't cover even one village in a day as clusters of houses are located miles apart even in a single village. And they can't stay in the village after 5 p.m. as they want to be back home before it is dark due to the fear of criminals," says Sangeeta Soni, an assistant coordinator in the Rajiv Gandhi Mission in Alirajpur, the town nearest to Laxmani. Health workers also have the responsibility of executing a number of government schemes. Villagers complain that health workers come to the village, sit with the Sarpanch, fill up all the columns in their registers and go back. Meanwhile, health workers complain that they are overworked and can't cover more villages. "There are only two ANMs here. And they have a lot of work—the Vatsalya scheme (a scheme run by the Madhya Pradesh government for post-natal care, significantly only for the first two births), sterilization, copper-T, maternity forms, they have to do everything. Sometimes they have to travel 30 to 35 kilometres in a day. This is why villages depend on untrained midwives or buduas," Says Kusum Waghpude, supervisor in charge of the health sub-centre at village Chandpur. Chandpur has a population of 19,000. The Sub-centre has two ANMs, one doctor and one Lady Health Supervisor.

The job of the ANMs is to dispense iron fortification tablets, tell people about contraceptive methods and give medicines for sundry ailments like headaches and stomachaches. Their main job is when sterilization camps are to be organized, to "motivate" women for sterilization. Despite India's commitment at Cairo, every ANM has targets for sterilization. In fact, Madhya Pradesh's State Population Policy seeks to assess the performance of ANMs—and other public health staff—by their success in bringing down the birth rate. "Otherwise, most of the time health workers and doctors are busy filling up registers and records," says Dr Avasya of one of the health centres. "There are so many administrative jobs in the centre that doctors forget their medical practice."

The health centres are poorly equipped and so can, at best, handle only normal deliveries. If there is any complication or if surgery is needed, villagers have to go to any of the hospitals at Jhabua, Alirajpur, Jobat, Dahod or Chhota Udaipur. To reach any of the hospitals, sometimes they have to travel up to 60 kilometres. The normal mode of transport is a bullock cart or bus, if available. For those who can afford it, jeeps are also available at times.

It is not as if no change is taking place in the tribal belt of Jhabua, but it is slow. "The change is more visible in the past two to three years. In 1993, when I came here, people used to run away on seeing any health workers. Now we even go to the fields to register pregnant women," says Suman Chowdhary, an ANM in village Bhabra. Dr Tejlo is an indigenous woman posted at the Jobat Charitable Hospital in Jobat tehsil of Jhabua district. She says the number of hospital deliveries is definitely going up. "Now they are coming forward to take advantage of the health care system. But they come here only when a home delivery is not possible. And they just leave the hospital after delivery, without waiting for discharge, afraid of what they will have to pay," she says. Going by figures, the health status of adivasi women has improved—immunization spread has increased and fewer women die during pregnancy and childbirth.

The district administration adopts a typical blame-the-victim attitude. '"Infrastructure is there, motivation is there, but the main problem is the attitude of tribals. They are illiterate and ignorant. They are not able to accept a modern health care system," says District Collector Waseem Akhtar, completely ignoring the lack of access to services as well as the administration's inability to reach out to the people in the area.

Tehri's Woes

The situation in Tehri is no different from Jhabua. In fact, it is worse due to the difficult terrain. Most of the villages can only be accessed through narrow dirt tracks that sometimes disappear midway. If a patient, be it a pregnant woman or an old man, has to be taken to the hospital, four men have to carry the person on a charpoy. The other mode of transport is ponies and mules, which are not readily available and have to be arranged in cases of emergency. It may take anywhere between eight to 12 hours for people from Dande ki beli to reach medical help. Hospitalization means travelling even further. And the means of communication are virtually non-existent. Even an upcoming resort like Dhanolti does not have a public telephone as yet.

One health Sub-centre is located at Dhanolti, which is about 10 kilometres from Dandi ki beli village. There is no road connection, not even a dirt track. There are several villages and settlements on the way to Dandi ki beli. For all of them, the Dhanolti sub-centre is the nearest. From some of the villages, it can take up to six hours to reach Dhanolti, and even there, the available services are very limited. For complicated delivery cases, women have to be brought up to Dhanolti on a charpoy or a pony, and then they must take a bus (its frequency is once a day) to Mussourie, about 25 kilometres away, for hospitalization.

In the Saklana belt, of which Dandi ki beli is a part, there are over 40 villages with a total population of over 20,000. But the health infrastructure is quite inadequate. For residents of Uniyal and the surrounding settlements in a radius of five to six kilometres, the only health facility available is the additional PHC at Satyon village. Although the village is connected by bus, the service is irregular. So, the only other way to reach Satyon is to trek four kilometres, which takes as long as two hours. "In such a situation, how do you expect either a pregnant woman to go the Centre, or a nurse to come to the village? So the only alternative is to do deliveries at home," points out Meera Uniyal of Uniyal village.

"Saklana has only one additional PHC and one ayurvedic dispensary. The nearest hospital is 60 to 70 kilometres away. There are no diagnostic facilities available anywhere. That is why so many women and new-borns die here. They don't figure in any government statistics," says B S Negi, a retired government employee and a village elder at Mazhgaon, four kilometres from Uniyal. "In the past two years, seven to eight women must have died like this," he says. B S Nakoti, a pharmacist at the Satyon additional PHC, says the major problem is lack of diagnostic facilities and essential drugs in the entire region. "So how does it matter, if an MD doctor is sitting in the health centre or a ward boy? Both are shooting in the dark."

"Of late," he continues "there is an improvement as deliveries at home are not conducted in unhygienic conditions. This has happened due to the awareness created by television. Mortality rates have also come down, and so have communicable disease cases." The government-owned television channel Doordarshan is received in villages far and wide. Satellite television has also made inroads in some villages. "We don't have sufficient staff here, in hilly areas we need more staff than we do in the plains," says Dr O S Sharma, Chief Medical Officer, Tehri district. Currently, he says, 46 posts of ANMs, 11 for lady doctors and 29 posts of general physicians are lying vacant . And at the administrative level, four out of six posts of deputy Chief Medical Officers (CMOs) are vacant. The deputy CMOs on duty does not have a vehicle to travel in and so the question of supervision and support does not arise.

Access and Quality of Care

The RCH programme envisages upgrading of facilities for maternal and child health, for reproductive morbidity and for improving the quality of care. The programme advocates the setting up of First Referral Centres at sub-district levels to provide comprehensive emergency obstetric and neo-natal care. Similarly, it calls for upgrading RCH facilities substantially in PHCs. But, so far, there is no observable change in delivery mechanisms or at the point of delivery in Sub-centres and PHCs in these two districts. If anything, the existing machinery is understaffed, under-equipped and inaccessible to the needy.

In Jhabua, as many as 93 per cent of deliveries take place at home and a large proportion of them are managed by untrained attendants and family members.[2] In Tehri too, 94 per cent of the deliveries in rural areas take place at home.[3] Keep-

[2]Government of Madhya Pradesh (1995), *Action Plan for Women and Children in Jhabua*, Bhopal.

[3]Population Council, Centre for Development Research and Training (1995),*Tehri Garhwal –District Level Baseline Survey of Family Planning Programme in Uttar Pradesh,* New Delhi..

ing these realities in view, the government has launched various schemes to train dais and equip them with skills of antenatal, natal and post-natal care. In Jhabua, the trained dai is given a kit consisting of soap, sterile razor and sterilized thread and an incentive of Rs 15 for every delivery. The dais are supposed to be extension workers attached to the ANM. But the scheme seems to be facing problems. Sundari Bai was given a month's training in midwifery. She says she was given a delivery kit at the time of training but "now that is finished and the second one has not yet been given". Sundari, herself an adivasi woman, lives in Laxmani village. She finds it hard to convince villagers that using a scythe to cut the umbilical chord is not hygienic. She always uses a sterile razor. Since she has already run out of the kit that the government gave her, Sundari has to buy a blade every time she gets a call from any village for a delivery. Normally a village night watchman should inform her about such emergency calls. But since her village has none, Sundari's husband is entrusted with this job.

Admission into hospital is the last resort for these women. In the maternity ward of the government hospital at Jhabua, all the women had complicated pregnancies. Gendi of Macchlya village was admitted to the Civil Hospital at Alirajpur. A mother of two, she had just undergone a miscarriage at home after a three-month pregnancy. Then she got malaria and was brought to the hospital in a serious condition. Nayaki of Rodada village had her fourth delivery at home using the method of "kicking" the belly. But the placenta was not completely removed, resulting in an infection. She was brought to the hospital in a bullock cart. Both the women were anaemic. Laxmi of Naka village was also brought in a serious condition after prolonged labour for a Caesarean section. This was her fourth child.

"Here 70 per cent of women are brought in a serious condition and all cases are complicated," says Dr Anushree Gawli, Chief Medical Officer and gynaecologist of the hospital. Dr Tejlo, at the Jobat Charitable Hospital, says, "Most of the cases are of uterine rupture and prolapse. This happens because they get checked up or delivered by untrained dais." Also, anaemia is a common problem. Of the 536 deliveries conducted between June 1997 and 1998 at the Alirajpur Hospital, 132 women were severely anaemic. The Alirajpur Civil Hospital is a referral hospital for five PHCs. It has ten doctors, and ten nurses, but only ten beds in the maternity ward. If there are more cases, women have to be shifted to the children's ward. The hospital does not have any ultrasound facility.

Perceptions About Family Planning

Poverty, unemployment and illiteracy are rampant in Jhabua. Landholdings are small, but people say they need children to till the fields and tend the animals. This is also a place where child survival is precarious. Other than sterilization, there is no awareness of family planning methods. And sterilization is feared. There is widespread belief that sterilization will lead to ill health, leaving men incapable of working in the fields and women weak and anaemic.

When asked how many children she has, Kamli, 35, of village Juna Kathiwada, turns to her husband. "Three girls and two boys," he says. Asked if they use any protective methods or would like to limit their family by going in for sterilization, he retorts, "How can I have myself operated? I have to carry loads (of wood)."

Health workers say that the pills that they distribute among the women are not used, and condoms are given to children to play with as balloons. "Whenever we go, women ask for condoms, but they give them to the children to play, because their husbands do not want to use them. Women sometimes take pills. Other methods like the loop (Inter Uterine Device) don't suit them because they have to depend on doctors for insertion and for removal," says Sundari Bai.

Among the indigenous people of Jhabua, the average family comprises between four and seven children. But unlike other areas, there is no marked preference for boys. Boys are seen as additional hands to work in fields, while girls are seen as a "source of income". In the adivasi tradition called *bhagoriya*, a girl's family is given money by the boy's family, something akin to bride price. The amount could range from a few hundred rupees to as much as Rs 20,000. It is also called *dapa* in the local language. So the birth of both a boy and a girl are welcomed with equal enthusiasm.

This is not the case in the villages of Tehri. In the hills there is a marked preference for the male child. "There are no family planning methods prevalent in this area, except operations (sterilization). And till one or two boys are born, nobody goes in for operations," says Jagdai Belva, a woman member of Dandi ki beli village panchayat. "You can't think of an operation, till a boy is born," says 70-year old Kundana Devi of village Divli. Her son has three daughters and one son, and her daughter-in-law is pregnant again. This time also, Kundana Devi wants her to deliver a boy. Kundana's daughter, Bindara, was married at 18. After two years, Bindara delivered a boy, but he died within a month. The following year she delivered a girl, who also could not survive for long. Both babies were delivered at home by a dai. After that Bindara could not conceive. A doctor in the nearest town in the plains, Dehradun, told her that her uterus had got pushed out of position because of mishandling during delivery.

Bindara, now 26, says, "If you are born in the hills, you have to face all these problems. If there is no treatment, children will die like this. We leave them to God's mercy. If he wants, they will live; otherwise they will die." While this could be viewed as fatalism, it may also reflect the inability to access medical services. Bindara says even if she wants to get treated, she cannot afford frequent trips to Dehradun to consult doctors and specialists. Jagdai Belva says women in the hills do a lot of hard labour like carrying loads of fuel wood and water over long distances. So they avoid sterilization, fearing they will become weak.

Adivasi women in Jhabua also feel the same way. But, it is still women who undergo sterilization most of the time because men say that they work more than women. Government statistics corroborate the relatively high number of female sterilizations—between October 1997 and October 1998 only 14 men were sterilized, whereas the figure for women was 762 in the whole district.

Adivasi men, like men in the rest of the country, who work in the fields on daily wages or cultivate their own small holdings, feel they won't be able to make both ends meet if they get operated upon and become weak. According to Dr Awasthy of Kathiwada PHC, men don't want to use any protection. "For two acres of land, they don't mind producing ten children."

When health workers try to "motivate" indigenous women for sterilizations, the women often ask: "Will you come to work in the fields in my place, if you want me to have an operation?". Suman Chowdhary, an ANM at the PHC at Bhabhra village, says, "We do try to tell them about spacing methods, but they don't listen. They feel it is a waste of time." Interestingly, they have full faith in any injection and want a birth control vaccine, instead of using condoms or copper-Ts that are not acceptable to their husbands, she adds.

Sterilization Camps

Sterilization camps are held frequently in the villages, but the response is lukewarm. The financial incentive offered for sterilization at these camps has been reduced from Rs 130 to a mere Rs 40. According to Sumitra, a teacher at the Rajendra Ashram at Kathiwada, sterilization camps are organized from time to time, as people don't go to hospitals on their own. "Once in a month on a Wednesday, a sterilization camp is organized," says Sumitra. ANMs and field workers give a lot of importance to "motivate" couples for sterilization because three or four such cases fulfil their quota of work, says Nakoti, a pharmacist at Satyon PHC.

Operations also sometimes take place without the knowledge of women when they are admitted to hospitals for complicated deliveries. Dr Gawli, says "It's all right to talk of no coercion for conducting operations in programmes and policies. But it is not practical. Recently, a woman, who already had a dozen children, came after an unsuccessful abortion at home. She was bleeding profusely as the foetus had not been aborted properly. I conducted a laparoscopy without telling her. After one week when she came, I told her that I had shut down her child producing machine."

"Actually all the policies and programmes are based on certain principles, which are not practical. In reality, we have to do whatever is necessary. In the name of principles we can't do an injustice to the patient," says Dr Gawli. She is not alone. Other doctors in hospitals express similar views. It is clear then that the Cairo commitments—and indeed those in the National Population Policy—have not reached the level of the district.

Sterilization camps are held in Tehri district also. Normally these camps are held from November to February, just before the financial year ends. It is mainly women who come to them, "motivated" by ANMs and other health workers, says Rajendra Uniyal, an alternate health practitioner in Satyon village. He says people do not, as a rule, believe in spacing methods.

RCH: Old Wine in New Bottles

The family planning programme was launched in 1951 with the sole objective of reducing the size of the family. It was purely a demographic programme. In the mid-seventies, during the period of internal emergency, the target-led government family planning programme went into overdrive, conducting forcible sterilizations. Popular hatred for these violations of reproductive rights was so extreme that the ruling Congress party was defeated in the elections in 1977 and subsequent governments were afraid to touch the issue of population control focusing on men.

In the post-emergency period, the programme took a new shape and was renamed the family welfare programme. It was made broad-based by including the health of children and women in the reproductive age group. During the eighties, particularly in the seventh five-year plan, programmes aimed at improving the health of mothers and young children were introduced. The focus was also on providing facilities for prevention and treatment of major diseases. But a separate identity for each programme led to problems in effective management, something that was reflected in unsatisfactory results.

In the nineties, these programmes were integrated under a single umbrella and called the Child Survival and Safe Motherhood (CSSM) programme. The process of integration received a further boost with the International Conference on Population and Development (ICPD) in 1994, which recommended that all countries implement programmes for reproductive and child health (RCH). Elements of the already running CSSM programme have been incorporated in the new RCH programmes. Included now were reproductive tract morbidities and infections.

Following the Cairo summit, the Indian government took the initiative to change its basic approach to its family welfare programme and decided to remove demographic family planning targets to adopt a broader reproductive health approach. The RCH programme was launched in the country from October 1997.

According to the programme of action of the ICPD:

> Reproductive health is a state of complete physical, mental and social well being and not merely absence of disease or infirmity, in all matters relating to the reproductive system and to its functions and processes. Reproductive health, therefore, implies that people are able to enjoy a satisfying and safe sex life and that they have the capability to reproduce and the freedom to decide, if, when and how often to do so. Implicit in the last condition are the rights of men and women to be informed and to have access to safe, effective, affordable and acceptable methods of family planning of their choice, as well as other methods of their choice for regulation of fertility which are not against the law, and the right of access to appropriate health care services that will enable women to go safely through pregnancy and child-

birth and provide couples with the best chance of having a healthy infant.[4]

But the government machinery, so used to the family planning approach, still holds population control to be the ultimate objective of the programme. In a booklet to explain the programme to state and district level officials, the Ministry of Health and Family Welfare says:

> It is the legitimate right of the citizens to be able to experience sound reproductive and child health and, therefore, the RCH programme will seek to provide relevant services for assuring reproductive and child health to all citizens. *However, RCH is even more relevant for obtaining the objective of stable population for the country.* The overall objective since the beginning has been that the population of the country should be stabilized at a level consistent with the requirement of national development. It is now well established that parents keep the family size small if they are assured about the health and longevity of the children and there is no better assurance of good health and longevity of the children than health care for the mother and for young children" (emphasis mine).[5]

Clearly, then, the underlying philosophy of the Indian government is that the RCH programme should be geared to containing family size. It is apparently not understood that parents will restrict their family size if they are assured of health and longevity for their children, and that this can be achieved through health care for mothers and young children. Had there been this realization of course, health would have received higher allocations in the budget than the pittance it does.

Health workers, ANMs, nurses and some doctors reveal that they are not aware of the change in the family planning approach from safe motherhood to RCH. "We are implementing the RCH programme. There is no problem because all the com-

[4]United Nations, International Conference on Population and Development (1996), *Programme of Action*, New York.

[5]Government of India, Ministry of Health and Family Welfare (1997), *Reproductive and Child Health Programme: Schemes for Implementation*, New Delhi.

ponents of safe motherhood are in RCH also. It is only a change in name. The only problem in implementation is that of funds and manpower," says Dr Sadoriya, chief medical and health officer, Jhabua.

The shift away from targets is perhaps the only change being talked about at the district level. "We have moved from the target approach to the target-free approach," says Akhtar. He adds that in most parts of the district, it is the old safe motherhood programme being implemented. "Maybe it is old wine in a new bottle, but with a new label." But as we heard from the ANMs, targets are still in place.

Significantly, studies in other parts of the country have also exposed a low awareness about the "paradigm shift" in government policy. Research by the Academy of Nursing Studies to review RCH implementation in Andhra Pradesh reveals that targets are still present and are chased with greater intensity. Along with targets, a number of incentives and punitive disincentives are also in place. Targets are set at the local level and monitoring and review mechanisms still focus on sterilization achievements. Most of the staff is aware of the concept of RCH, but there is a mixed response to implementation at the field level.[6]

The ground situation in Tehri villages is no different. When basic infrastructure like PHCs and Sub-centres are not easily accessible, it makes little difference if the programme is called Safe Motherhood or RCH. The only difference is felt by health workers who do not have to coerce people to go to sterilization camps to achieve their targets.

Studies by the NGO Health Watch in Uttar Pradesh concluded: "Across the board, the impression that has been received is that there has been very little or no change in the mindset. While ANMs feel they are providing better services, the community perception of the same is not evident. An RCH camp is supposed to bring a wide range of services closer to

---

[6]Academy of Nursing Studies (1999), *Ground-Level Perceptions of TFA and RCH*, Hyderabad.

the client, but its full potential has not been exploited. The community still perceives it as a sterilization camp and they distinctly feel that they are better treated if they are 'sterilization cases' rather than when they are mere patients."[7] Says Dr Sharma, District Health Officer, Tehri, "The target-free approach means self-generated targets because you fix the target in an undeclared way. Nothing happens if you change the name of a programme."

Need for Barefoot Doctors?

"For all health related schemes, only the broad policy framework should be made in Delhi. The rest—implementation details—should be finalized at the district level according to local needs and environment," says Jhabua Additional Collector, Sanjay Shukla. Actually, what the official says is the crux of the new approach—decentralized participatory planning based on the needs of the community. But in practice, it is not happening.

Despite the change in approach to women's health in terms of policy, the understanding at the ground level about the changes is low. Not only are health workers unaware of the underlying philosophy of the new RCH programme, they are also not aware of its different components. Clearly, there is a communication gap between the policy makers and implementation machinery. The RCH programme not only provides for local level planning, but also for involvement of NGOs and village self-governing bodies. But concrete steps need to be taken to implement these intentions.

Despite half a century of family planning and welfare programmes, it is important to note that over 90 per cent of deliveries in rural areas still take place in homes. This is not necessarily a bad thing, say doctors and health workers. If a major proportion of these deliveries start taking place in hospitals,

[7] Health Watch UP-Bihar (1999), *Voices from the Ground*, Lucknow.

the health infrastructure might just collapse because it is not equipped to handle such large numbers.

Buduas and dais might not be trained in modern medicine, but are a vast storehouse of traditional knowledge. They have a thorough understanding of the traditional methods of healing as well as medicinal plants found in their region. They are available at all times and enjoy the unflinching faith of the local people. The government has sought to include them in the present day health schemes. They are being trained to carry out their work under hygienic conditions. It has brought some results, but here again there are problems like lack of kits and inadequate incentives. If properly nurtured, these schemes could make dais or buduas a central healthcare delivery point in a village.

"There is a need to understand the thinking and customs of indigenous people, to understand them and to treat them with respect." Pavnendra Singh, 63, a traditional mango grower from Kathiwada, says: "Health workers and nurses from the Centre do come to villages whenever somebody is ill or having some problem. But they give medicines for two to three days together. The people here either eat them all in one go or don't eat them at all. Health workers should understand the thinking of the people and give medicines in different packets."

Some efforts are being made by NGOs to understand and nurture traditional methods. For instance, the Society for Integrated Development of Himalayas (SIDH) in Mussourie has compiled the myths, legends and folksongs relating to reproductive health in Jaunpur in the Garhwal hills. There are a number of songs about the pain experienced by women—both physical and mental. One of the songs describes in detail the changes in a woman's body during nine months of pregnancy. A content analysis of this compilation proved to be a rich source of ideas and material in designing training modules for male participation in reproductive health. "Men's involvement is being tried as a new population strategy as nothing else has worked so far, including the so-called paradigm shift. But our approach is different. For us, male involvement and the issue of happiness is not a strategy, but a goal," says Anuradha Joshi, SIDH 's executive secretary.

But NGOs cannot obviously take on the role of providing health care all over these two districts; there is, in fact, no alternative to the State. However, the health of the poor is not, apparently, a matter of priority concern to the State. One fundamental problem seems to be viewing RCH in isolation from the general health needs of the population and the socio-economic fabric of society. The lack of adequate food, basic development infrastructure and education naturally has serious health consequences. Unless these are addressed in a holistic fashion and RCH seen as being directly linked to them, not much progress can be made in adopting the new paradigm.

For a Few Dollars More
Women in Export Processing Zones

T. K. RAJALAKSHMI

"There is a register that marks the number of times we can go to the toilet. If we exceed a total of five minutes put together, we are scolded and threatened."

"She was six months pregnant. Do you know what happened? Her baby died in her stomach. It was blue, we learnt later. She was like any other worker here who works standing for eight or more hours."

"I lied about my marital status at the time of recruitment. I have a three-month baby as well who has been sent off to Kerala to my parents as we cannot afford a private creche and manage the Delhi winter. We may get him back in the summer."

These are the voices of women workers in two of the six Export Processing Zones (EPZ) in the country—the Noida EPZ in Uttar Pradesh, only 24 kilometres from the capital, New Delhi, and the Santacruz Electronics EPZ (SEEPZ) in Mumbai. The NEPZ was established in 1985, while the SEEPZ came into being much earlier. The EP Zones are now rather central to the export-led growth strategy adopted by the government as a consequence of India's adherence to the World Bank-IMF led reforms for liberalization of the economy. But even before the formal initiation of the stabilization-structural adjustment programme, elements of some of these policies had already been inaugurated in the country as exemplified by the NEPZ of Noida and the SEEPZ in Mumbai.

These policies have meant a complete break with patterns of import-substitution led growth which had characterized post-Independence efforts at development of the economy, and the country. Incentives for the private sector, privatization of government owned units, delicensing, deregulation, and disciplining labour are some of the concomitants of the policy as is increasing production to meet export targets. In the 90s, the EPZs in India pursued an aggressive growth strategy contributing to higher foreign exchange earnings. This is meant to pay for the increased imports of commodities, primarily to cater to the consumption needs of the upper classes in the country.

For a visitor, the NEPZ is forbidding—and indeed forbidden. The entrance, called the Customs Gate, has elaborate checking. The zone is referred to as the "boundary" by the workers. Beyond that lies a picture of deceptive calm and undisturbed production for export—clean, beautiful buildings and lawns which do not reflect the misery within.

Electronics, garments, gems and jewellery account for over two thirds of the exports from the zones. Engineering goods, chemicals and pharmaceuticals, leather and latex products account for the rest. The NEPZ offers special incentives to entrepreneurs to set up businesses. A corporate tax holiday for five years, public utility status, duty-free imports of capital goods, raw material and components, exemption from Central Excise Duties and other levies on products manufactured within the zone as well as unrestricted remittance of profits and dividends, are some of the very liberal sops offered.

What is significant is that in contrast to the benefits given to the entrepreneurs, the benefits to the workers are minimal or non-existent. Minimum wage rules remain unenforced, especially in the case of women workers. Units often avoid making Provident Fund and Gratuity contributions and bonus payments to ordinary workers. Senior executives, however, earn five figure salaries with perks like house rent allowance, medical and retirement benefits. Some of the ordinary workers do not even have cards that entitle them to the Employees State Insurance (ESI) scheme. Overtime work is compulsory in most cases.

The women workers are worse off because of the double burden of work—productive and reproductive, in the EPZ and at home. Compelled to earn their living, health, and especially reproductive health and rights, are given low priority in the overall context of their lives. Sexual and reproductive (or any other) rights, understood as private "liberties" or "choices" are meaningless, especially for the poorest and the most disenfranchised, without enabling conditions though which they can be realized. These conditions constitute social rights and involve social welfare, personal security and political freedom.[1] For the women EPZ workers, these rights are honoured more in the breach than in their observance.

Union activity is strongly discouraged. Workers are neither allowed to hold meetings within the barbed enclosure of the zone, nor are they allowed to assemble at the boundary where there is an elaborate system of security. Every worker has to bring his or her pass every day for entry and exit and get their belongings and person frisked before entering or leaving the premises. The public utility status accorded to units in the NEPZ curbs the workers' rights to strike as they statutorily have to first go through a process of conciliation.[2] Grievances are handled through joint consultative councils, whose employee representatives are in fact selected by the management. Trade unions are not allowed to enter the compounds and their work is actively discouraged.

Baliram Verma, President of a unit of the Communist Party of India (Marxist) affiliated Centre for Indian Trade Unions (CITU) located near the NEPZ, says slogans can, however, be raised in factories located outside the boundary. The news of workers getting retrenched or that of industrial lockouts always spreads fast and neighbouring units join in agitations. At lunch hours workers come out of the premises and interact with others. This enables them to find out about the presence of unions, labour laws and workers' rights. Verma says there

---

[1]Correa, Sonia and Rosalind Petchesky (1994), "Reproductive and Sexual Rights: A Feminist Perspective," in Sen, Gita, Adreienne Germain and Lincoln C. Chen (eds), *Population Policies Reconsidered: Health, Empowerment and Rights*, Harvard Series on Population and International Health, Boston.

[2]Government of India, Ministry of Commerce, Information Pack (undated), *Noida Export Processing Zone*, New Delhi.

are two kinds of bonded labour in Uttar Pradesh—one at the NEPZ and the other at brick kilns.

According to a former Labour Inspector, a government appointee whose jurisdiction had been the NEPZ, he was never able to meet the workers at the premises. In one shoe factory, called the Taj-Rhein, the Labour Inspector said he had to negotiate for three months before the employers agreed to pay the statutory minimum wages. "Even we, government officials, are not allowed free entry into the zone," he says. "It is okay to earn foreign exchange, but it is evident this is being done at the cost of the workers."

Preference for Young Single Women

The 143 units within the NEPZ employ roughly 17,000 workers, with nearly 4,000 of these being women. The proportion of women in the workforce has been steadily increasing. Between 1994 and 1998, the number of women workers nearly tripled while their male counterparts just about doubled. The majority of these women are semi-skilled and unskilled, says an official. Among women too, there is a preference for unmarried ones under 30. Rarely does one come across a woman who has crossed 35 years. At the other extreme, in a surgical gloves factory, a study found girls as young as 11 to 15 years working for more than 10 hours a day.[3] The workers come either from Nepal or the states of Uttar Pradesh, Bihar, Kerala, West Bengal, Orissa and Tamil Nadu. Landlessness and very little education leaves them with virtually no bargaining power.

The NEPZ, according to figures furnished by the Development Commissioner's office, has sustained high export growth for the past many years. Exports have increased from Rs 720

[3]Ranadive, Joy and Indrani Mazumdar (1998), "The Effect of an Urban Environment Upon the Lives of Women: A Case Study of Women Industrial Workers in NOIDA", New Delhi, Centre for Women's Development Studies.

million in 1990-91 to Rs 6,041 million during 1997-98. The net foreign exchange earnings also went up from Rs 825.40 million in 1993-94 to Rs 2,329 million in 1997-98. But this has brought little cheer to the lives of the workers in general and to the increasing female component in particular.

Women are preferred as workers in most of these factory jobs, ostensibly because they are hard-working, easy to control, willing to accept tediousness and monotony and have nimble fingers—in short, their productivity is higher than that of men. They are also easy to lay off when there is no work or their health begins to deteriorate. Above all, they are less inclined to join unions. In other words, the perception that they can be exploited more and more easily lies at the root of the preference for women workers.[4]

Garmex India, a ready-made garment exporting unit inside the NEPZ boundary, has 600 women and at least 100 men on their rolls. One of the management representatives, Dhiraj Singh says, "There are so many benefits with women employees. They have a mental frame of doing hard, tough work. They do not get involved in fights and arguments with employers. Administratively it is easy to control women. We do not need to have too much security. Among male workers, there is always some problem or the other." He says the only problem with employing women is that they cannot work beyond 8 p.m. "We prefer the 18 to 30 age group, preferably single," says Singh. At least 98 per cent of the women employees in Garmex fall under that category. Clearly, married women are discriminated against. Says Singh, "If you employ a newly married woman, after some time she will ask for maternity leave. She will go on leave under some pretext or the other. We ask the women their marriage plans at the time of recruitment. They do not lie as they are caught off-guard by our cross-questioning. We defi-

[4]Edgren, Gus (1982), "Spearheads of Industrialization or Sweatshops in the Sun?: A Critical Appraisal of Labour Conditions in Asian Export Processing Zones", Asian Employment Programme Working Paper, Bangkok, ILO-ARTEP.

nitely prefer single women who are not engaged to be married. If they say they can delay their marriage for two three years, then we agree."

Savitri, a woman supervisor in the factory, reiterated the same reasons for the preference for unmarried women. If they got married, they were thrown out, she said. Married women like her were accepted if they had enough experience and slightly grown-up children. She said women had to undergo pregnancy tests at the time of recruitment. They are obviously not given the job if found pregnant. India's Labour Acts do not sanction pregnancy tests prior to employment. Shashi, 21, who works with a lamp exporting unit in the zone, says, "All the women workers are below 30 in my company. After marriage, they leave. If they delay their marriage beyond 25, they do not get proper grooms. We have some women who are 30 and still unmarried. Nobody comes forward to marry them."

Low Wages, Harsh Working Conditions

Most women workers at the NEPZ work very long hours. At times these can go up to 70 hours a week, including Sundays with no payment for double overtime. According to the Factories Act and the Shops and Establishment Act, a worker is expected to put in a maximum of 48 hours a week, or eight hours in a day, with one or one and a half days off a week. He or she has the right to refuse overtime work—although this is not a right frequently recognized by employers. Overtime wage rates are double that of the minimum wage—again not something recognized by the employers. These rules apply equally to men and women, although they are more easily broken, with impunity, in the case of women workers.

Singh says Garmex has set up a crèche for the women, but the designated area only stocks bulky cartons. There is no sign of any children, nor does there seem any likelihood of the store room ever functioning as a creche. Singh also stresses that there is no "casual" labour in the company. "Workers do not get sick in our company. We have air conditioners all over.

The plant is also air cooled, but in the summer months we have workers fainting primarily because they do not take care of themselves."

Casual workers, both male and female, appear as stark official figures in the logs of Garmex in a document given out inadvertently by the NOIDA authorities. The workers say there is no cooling facility and the plant feels like a furnace in the summer.

Savitri says women work standing for at least eight hours daily and that an additional three hours "compulsory overtime" is a regular feature. A twelve or thirteen hour day is quite usual for these women workers. They are paid single overtime rates although they are entitled to double overtime. No bonus is given, although Provident Fund contributions are made. She says, on many occasions, women fall seriously ill within the premises. If they have their Employees State Insurance (ESI)) cards, they are taken to the ESI hospital, otherwise they are taken to a private nursing home, where they have to pay. Meena, a Nepali worker complained of chronic pain in the lower abdomen and a burning sensation while urinating. She had been to a private doctor in her locality and been prescribed what appeared to be antibiotics. "I don't know what it is he gives me, but it relieves the pain," she said. "The ESI hospital (in Sector 24, Noida) is too far away," she said, adding that she could not have taken time off from work to go there.

On one occasion, when a Labour Inspector came to the factory, all the women were instructed to say that none of them was paid below Rs 1,800 a month. According to the NEPZ information pack, an eight-hour day costs only Rs 50 for an unskilled worker and Rs 64 for a skilled worker. The management asked Savitri to tell the workers to fudge their salaries. "Please do not mention my name in your report or I will be thrown out of the company," pleads Savitri (not her real name) repeatedly.

Shashi says her work is to check finished lamps. Chairs are allotted, but work can only be done standing up. There are shift duties since work continues for all 24 hours and many women end up doing double shifts. A lot of them work even on Sundays. If the women feel unwell, they are not allowed to take breaks. The supervisor always says sarcastically, "You don't look unwell". If one of the workers argues or disagrees with the supervisor, she is either shifted to another section or sacked. A register is maintained to mark the number of times a woman can go to the toilet. A total of five minutes are permitted in the day, preferably once before and once immediately after lunch. Women in an advanced stage of pregnancy work standing for long hours.

Dr Pratibha Sharma, a former Air Force doctor, runs a private clinic in Bhangel, one of the two to three localities in which most of the workers reside. She says, "The level of exploitation is unimaginable." If workers going home to their villages overstay even for a day, they are sacked. People do not go home for years as a result. Unions are shut down as soon as they are formed. Wages are much better outside the zone, she says, adding that the last decade had seen prices skyrocket and the living conditions of the workers worsen.

Living in Squalor

Most of the workers reside in nearby villages or urban shanties, while some come from as far as 50 kilometres away. Bhangel and Silarpur are two such shanty towns, situated ten kilometres away from the NEPZ. The roads are not metalled, nor are they lit. Haphazard construction, pools of stagnant water, as well as open drains and garbage heaps mark the area. There is no municipal water supply, so people rely on underground water sources, often contaminated, through shallow tubewells. There are of course no facilities for toilets. Given the high levels of unemployment and underemployment, these localities are also fertile breeding grounds for anti-social elements.

Morbidity among women can be traced not only to their working environment, but also to their living conditions. According to a study in Mumbai, the morbidity rates of slum dwellers of all age groups are more than double those of their counterparts in non-slum households. Married cohabiting women with children in the reproductive age who live in the slum environment are most vulnerable to ill health. Slum dwellers come into contact with toxins in the air, water and soil due to open sewers, unpaved lanes, impermanent house structures and the use of common toilets and taps.[5] They not only live in industrially polluted areas, they frequently carry the industrial toxins they work with back to their homes.

In 1977, an expert committee set up by the NOIDA authority to suggest a development strategy for the area had stated that emphasis should be on housing for the economically weaker sections. In 1987, a review of this draft plan pointed out that only 17.5 per cent of the existing residential units were within this category, while on the other end the higher income groups constituted 37.3 per cent.[6] According to a very recent study of women industrial workers both inside and outside the zone, only 40.7 per cent of the women had access to safe drinking water and 11 per cent had access to lavatories. A majority of them stayed in rented accommodation that had a bearing on their household economy. In addition, most of the income was spent on food. The government's Public Distribution System was not much help because more than half of the women surveyed did not have ration cards that would give them access to fair price shops. Those who had the cards complained of lack of availability of rations at these shops. Others could not avail of the facility because of the timings. Education and health were additional expenditures, with most workers sending their children to expensive, unrecognized private schools due both to the absence of government schools and their desire to invest in their children's education.

Sita, a Nepali woman, lives in Bhangel. Her husband is back home in Nepal, but her two daughters, one of whom is

[5]Madhiwala, N and A Jessani (1997), "Morbidity among Women in Mumbai City: Impact of Work and Environment", *Economic and Political Weekly*, Vol. XXXII, No. 43, October.

[6]Ranadive and Mazumdar (1998), *op cit.*

married with a three-month old child, live with her and work in different units in the zone. She says there are many workers from Nepal living in Bhangel and Silarpur. Sita works in a surgical gloves factory. "We thought life would be easier for us here but it is a struggle every day. My daughters have to work as my income alone will not sustain the family." Her home is one room in a row of similar "homes" in what are essentially "coolie lines". Nepali families mostly live together. Most rented accommodation follows the same pattern. A family of five could be housed in a 10 feet by 10 feet room with a shared toilet. Seven families, including the landlord's, could be sharing the same toilet. That would mean 35 or more people having one toilet between them. The males are sent out and the women shut the doors and bathe inside their rooms. Cooking, bathing, sleeping and cohabiting all take place within the same cramped quarters. Sita's is a female-headed household. Her married daughter sends her child to a creche where she pays five hundred rupees a month out of her monthly earning of Rs 1,800.

Impact on the Health of Women Workers

The working and living conditions of the women have a direct bearing on their health. The hard toil in the factories, compounded by the work at home, and also childcare takes a heavy toll on the women. The limited access to good medical care at affordable rates only adds to their problems. In Savitri's factory, thread cutting is done standing because more work can be done this way. Swelling in the legs is a common complaint as is burning and itching in the eyes due to the cotton fluff. She says girls feel hesitant to ask if they can sit when their feet hurt. The pregnant women are worse off. There was one who lost her baby at six and a half months. "The child died in her stomach. I was told that the nurse brought it in a tray. It was blue," she says. Savitri herself has only two children though she got pregnant seven times. "I lost five, one of them after getting this job." She is only 27. "I look like an old woman now. I suffer from a lot of weakness. Maybe it is because of the white discharge I have," she says.

Gita from Ilam in Nepal, says that she suffers from constant pain in the lower abdomen. She says she has developed a lot of pain ever since she rejoined work after a tubectomy. "Maybe it is to do with sitting and working 12 hours continuously," she adds. None of the women spoken to went to the ESI hospital for major illnesses though deductions were made from their salaries. The distance, long queues, unfriendly doctors and the need for repeated visits were some of the reasons cited. They preferred going to a nearby private clinic, the quality of which they know little about.

At the glove factory, the women inhaled a lot of dust while separating the good gloves from the bad. This gave many of them a permanent cough. "I could feel the dust going into my lungs before, but now it is slightly better with a mask," says one of them. In the summer, many of the women faint because of the suffocating heat and dust. Sita says she knows of a number of women who have been diagnosed with tuberculosis. Because cotton is no longer cheap, the women wear synthetic and nylon sarees, which add to the heat. "In the summer, we feel that if it were not for our helplessness, we would have left our jobs," says Sita.

Shashi says her periods have become irregular and painful ever since she started work at the NEPZ. Acute backaches and irregular and painful bowels are other symptoms. A specific complaint against supervisors, heard several times over, was that they insisted that the same target levels should be maintained even when the women were menstruating. They were punished if the targets were not met. Menstrual periods are regarded as dirty and unclean in most parts of the country and women are supposed to keep away from social activity during this time. Since a large number of women are anaemic, they tend to feel weak and ill during this period.

Sita's and Geeta's family are in debt throughout the year. Expensive food rations at open market rates, creche expenses, rent, electricity, water and medical bills ensure that the family does not save anything at all. Electricity is almost non-existent in Bhangel. "One always has to keep a dozen candles and a litre of kerosene at hand, otherwise our children's studies will also suffer," says Gita. So intent are they on educating their children to move out of poverty that they send them to an English medium private school that they can ill-afford. In fact, this is one reason they continue with their jobs.

At the ESI Dispensary Outside the NEPZ

Dr Sudhir Bhushan runs the ESI dispensary outside the NEPZ. The dispensary hours are from 11 a.m. to 2 p.m., though most of the workers come between 1 p.m. and 1.30 p.m., their designated lunch hour. Amoebiases, anaemia and respiratory illnesses are the major diseases that afflict the workers, the doctor says. The underground water in the area is not potable as tubewells are not deep enough to prevent sewage from seeping through. The deeper the tubewell, the more expensive it is. Severe and frequent episodes of diarrhoea are widely prevalent among the workers. "We treat them, they go back to live in terrible conditions and so keep coming back every now and then with the same problem," said Dr.Bhushan, adding, "It's very frustrating to be a doctor under such circumstances." He gets an average of 100 patients a day; the number goes up to 125 or even 200 during the summer. The dispensary has had only one doctor for the past six years. Dr Bhushan admitted that he did not have the time to deal with every patient properly because of the rush. He says repeated amoebiases weakened the immune system and the children of workers were found to be most vulnerable. Upper respiratory tract infections, pharyngitis, tonsilitis and bronchitis were very common among the workers and their children.

As for the women, he said a majority of them were malnourished and anaemic, had urinary tract infections and complained of leucorrhoea (heavy white discharge) and dysmenorrhoea (painful and irregular periods). At least 10 cases of miscarriages, or women with similar symptoms come to him in a month. "They might not suffer from any particular ailment but because their immune and nutrition status is low, they are constantly complaining of some pain and discomfort," he says. There is no woman doctor in the dispensary and Dr Bhushan scathingly dismisses women workers who resort to indigenous medicines as doing so "because their IQs are low".

Private Medical Services

A number of private clinics and nursing homes flourish in and around Bhangel and Silarpur. One such clinic is run by a doctor with a degree in the indigenous medical system of Ayurveda. "These women work for 12 hours a day and get Rs 1200 a month. They are all very anaemic as they hardly eat proper meals," says Dr Banodia. Urinary tract infections, leucorrhoea and repeated miscarriages are common, she adds. She says the women go through a lot of stress because of the male child preference in the area and this sometimes leads to miscarriages. She also reveals that a number of women abort foetuses after finding out the sex of the child. Another clinic is run by a husband-wife team, of whom the husband has an MBBS degree. The wife is simply a housewife turned "doctor". She confidently announces that her clinic does hysterectomies and abortions.

Dr Pratibha Sharma is a rare, committed, qualified private doctor in Bhangel. Though a sterility expert by qualification, she handles all manner of patients in the area. Breathing problems, anaemia and pelvic inflammatory diseases are common among the women workers, she says. "They get abortions done frequently for fear of losing their jobs. They will have one baby but delay the other out of job considerations," she adds. Constant abdominal pain, loss of appetite and leucorrhoea are some of the other problems they complain of. She says, "Women have double the load of work . . . husbands do not help with the housework and children." Women say that they are forced to do overtime at the NEPZ, she adds. Miscarriages are common because of stress and the extra workload. Women also come to her with prolapsed uterus which happens often when untrained midwives carry out deliveries.

Mental tension and improper diets contribute to gastric problems, high blood pressure, irregular and scanty periods, says Dr Sharma. "Until the husband says go to the doctor, or unless they become bedridden, the women workers never come on their own," she adds. Contraceptive usage is low among both men and women. The children of the workers are malnourished and anaemic. "Children here keep getting seriously hurt in frequent accidents as there is virtually no one to look after them once the parents are away for 10 to 12 hours," she says. Dr Sharma feels that since medical practice is completely unregulated, quacks proliferate in the area and many of them are there only to perform abortions. "I get many horror cases. There was a five-month pregnant woman whose rectum and vagina had got perforated, and faeces were coming out of the vagina as a result of a faulty abortion."

As for the government hospitals, the doctors are often rude, and tell patients to bring everything right down to the bandages although they are supposed to have supplies, she said. Government doctors are also busy with their private practices. and have no time for the patients, She added that things had become particularly bad with the government system over the last ten years. "Who can blame people for not wanting to go there?"

At the ESI Hospital

At the ESI hospital, a long queue snakes to the door of the gynaecologist's chamber. Inside, Dr Usha sits and chats with two more women doctors while examining patients. The medical attendant abuses a patient for allegedly jumping the queue. When her husband intervenes, he too is roundly abused. Says Dr Usha of her patients, "They are illiterate, they refuse sterilization and they just cannot comprehend what we say. We have to repeat everything 10 times before they finally understand. They want the government to go on feeding them."

Typical of the middle-classes, she holds the workers themselves responsible for the conditions of their lives, for their poverty, for their illiteracy, and what she terms their ignorance. According to her, repeated pregnancies lead to calcium deficiencies and women develop osteoporosis very early. The rate of miscarriages among the women workers is 10 to 15 per cent higher than the rest of the population because they are severely anaemic. Their malnourished status affects both their physical and mental well-being, She goes on to say that private doctors cash in on the fears of the women workers. If they are suffering from leucorrhoea, not all forms of which are abnormal, they suggest that the uterus is cancerous and charge to remove it. She said the women went in for abortions because there were no child care services available. and they worried about losing their jobs.

For many women, their babies were born malnourished and many were delivered prematurely. Both child morbidity and mortality were high among the infants of women workers, she said, although there are no data. Children suffer from diarrhoea, dysentery and repeated chest infections because of nutritional anaemia. The anaemia is because women belong to low income groups, and go through repeated pregnancies, no spacing, abortions, miscarriages and continued lactation of children even while the next is on its way. This also led to preterm babies and spontaneous abortions. Overall there was intrauterine growth retardation which led to infant and neo natal deaths, she said. Though she had an excellent understanding of the reproductive health problems of the women workers, she was less than sympathetic towards them and did not treat them with any kindness or concern.

She said the hospital was attempting to set up an HIV centre as the rate of sexually transmitted diseases (STDs) as well as tuberculosis among women patients was going up. Some doctors, requesting anonymity, said promiscuity was quite rampant in Bhangel where men were known to sell their wives to supplement incomes. They said their patients had told them about this state of affairs.

SEEPZ—The Same Story

In the Santa Cruz Electronics Export Processing Zone in Mumbai, the story was much the same. Gautam Bora, an active union member from Nepal, said the male-female employment ratio in the units was 60:40 although there was now an increasing preference for women workers. Women were, as a rule, employed in the semi-skilled category. His factory manufactured gems and though conditions were better than other units, there was still a fair amount of exploitation. If workers took more than three days leave, they were charge-sheeted by the employers. No one could refuse overtime work. If diamonds were broken by mistake, the worker was thrown out. In the absence of exhaust fans or masks, breathing problems were very common among the workers who frequently inhaled dust during the process of filing jewels.

Bora said he knew of a pregnant woman who was sacked for spoiling a diamond. She had fainted while working. He was able to help her retain her job. But there were cases where he couldn't help, when women were sacked if they took a little over three months of maternity leave because of weakness. He also spoke of a notorious electronics unit which found mention in the 1984 study of the Tata Institute of Social Sciences.[7] He said 99 per cent of the staff comprised young girls, mostly between the ages of 18 and 22. Conversation on the shop floor was completely prohibited. The women worked in shifts and the last shift got over after 10 p.m. When they went home late at night, they were looked at with suspicion and harassed. Commuting to and from work was not only time consuming but also harrowing. Mumbai once used to be safe

[7]Sharma, R.N. and Chandan Sengupta (1984), "Women Employment at SEEPZ, Bombay", Tata Institute for Social Sciences, Report Prepared for Indian Council for Research on International Economic Relations, Mumbai.

for women to travel—at whatever time—in buses and trains, but this is no longer the case. Recently there was a case of rape in a train, in the presence of five other male passengers who refused to intervene.

Says Bora, "SEEPZ girls are not regarded as good girls. They face harassment in the locality. On the one hand these girls are forced to work, on the other they are looked down upon by society for working."

Nobody in the area surrounding the EPZ shows any respect for the working girls even though their presence and the money they bring in are key factors which have improved the economic situation of the whole area tremendously. The working girls are jeered at in buses and other public places and are spoken of in derisive terms. Becoming a working girl in the Free Trade Zone is regarded as the most degrading future prospect any girl can envisage. When teenage girls neglect their studies, parents often threaten them saying they will be sent off to the EPZ to work.

In one jewellery unit, there were 100 women out of a total of 300 workers. A woman who had joined recently had a three-month baby that she had to leave with a sitter, paying a huge chunk of her salary for the service. There was no creche service. Most of the women were unmarried. As chemicals like rhodium and acetone were involved, the women's fingers would get scarred and mutilated. Gloves were given, but they proved to be a hindrance in work. Coughing and irritation in the throat were regular ailments because of the chemical fumes inhaled by women. Like the NEPZ workers, the workers in Mumbai were also reluctant to go to the ESI hospital. They go to private doctors who are very expensive. They look tired, unenthusiastic and wary because they were speaking within the company precincts.

K L Bajaj, General Secretary of the Maharashtra unit of CITU said, "The workers cannot come out without the permission of the management and the security officials. The minimum rights of a trade union are not given and so people cannot take advantage of labour laws. Barring one or two units where unions existed, minimum wage laws were not complied with." It is difficult to organize the workers because they come from different directions, assemble at bus stations and then disperse in the SEEPZ bus. Their timings are either very early or very late and they couldn't be approached within the factory premises.

Many of the jewellery workers did filing, waxing and rhodium dripping. Their day started at 5 a.m. and ended at 11.30 p.m. "We get so tired by the end of the day. I work in the rhodium section. I cough every day because of the fumes," said one. "They ask us to show our dirty menstrual cloth to check if we are hiding any diamonds there. On those days we get so tired, but we can't rest. We cannot even change our pad during the day because we have to leave our bags at the reception. We can change maybe once during lunchtime. When we protested, we were told we could leave if we didn't like the current arrangement," she added. "Our eyes hurt and we get backaches.... We are also called in on Sundays. We do not like to do overtime, but have to do it." The girls are paid a paltry Rs 1,200 to Rs 2,000 a month, though in some cases the wage could also be as low as Rs 900. "We are shouted at even if we are five minutes late. Even after we finish work, they shout at us."

In addition to factory work, the girls also do labour-intensive household chores. They say they never get to eat properly in the morning. Lunch is hurriedly gulped down, though many of them don't feel like eating. Headaches are common because of the light they are exposed to while working with gems. A study by the Tata Institute of Social Sciences (TISS) in 1984 found that a good number of women workers admitted their health had deteriorated due to their working in the unit. They complained of weakening eyesight, back and headaches, loss of weight, discomfort during the menstrual cycle that sometimes led to headaches and fever. One pregnant woman said the management objected to her wanting to take small breaks of two or three minutes during the work day. The work norms were set so high that women often developed a variety of mental and physical disorders trying to live up to them. There are frequent reports of women developing urinary infections because they are not allowed to use toilets except during the tea and meal breaks.[8]

According to Dr Amar Jessani, who was with CEHAT, a health-based organization in Bombay, the intensity of work at SEEPZ is very high although the salary is very low. He said that between the reproductive age of 12 and 45, the causes of morbidity were traced to reproduction and working and living conditions. "We normally assume that working women would be more independent and able to look after their health needs, but this is not so. They often cannot and do not want to give up a day of wages to look after their health requirements. Not that there is any guarantee about the type or quality of medical care they will receive. Nor indeed of their ability to maintain a treatment regime, given treatment costs. So we have the phenomenon of them going to dubious private practitioners, who give them dubious medicines, not all of which they can purchase, and all of which they stop as soon as they start feeling better." The amazing thing is that so many of these young women have internalized the fact that it is normal for them to be exploited both at work and by their families.

Sexual Harassment

Some of the women said that when women workers are berated at work, their male supervisors often resort to sexual innuendo. At the NEEPZ, one young female worker conceived after a relationship with a supervisor in a latex glove factory. She was shunned by her colleagues and no one believed her side of the story. The supervisor was a married man. The girl had an abortion and went back to her village. The incident is talked of in hushed tones in the factory. Baliram Verma of CITU said, "Powerlessness, worsened by illiteracy, is a big factor here. It is mainly the younger girls who fall victim and we find that

[8]Edgren (1982), *op cit*

the trend of sexual exploitation is increasing." The women also faced harassment in buses and on the roads when they returned home late from work. Their working hours made them suspect in the eyes of their neighbours, who looked on them as women of easy virtue. They felt safer going out shopping or elsewhere in groups.

This is not helped by the fact that the media routinely refers to cases of sexual harassment as "eve teasing". This trivializes and diminishes—as if to say boys will be boys and this is just a normal part of growing-up—what is a deeply harrowing everyday experience for millions of working women in the country. From verbal assaults, to physical ones, working women have to negotiate this dehumanization and learn not to complain about it. Says Lata, a CITU worker, some women workers approach the union with complaints of sexual exploitation, but are unwilling to see their complaints through since they fear they will lose their jobs, aware that there are others waiting to replace them.

Similar Global Trends

The trend of employing young, single and educated women in the EPZs started in the Philippines in the 1970s, developed in Indonesia in the '80s and Bangladesh and India in the '90s. Marginalization of married women in the labour market is a trend revealed in the newly developed industrial zones in both South and Southeast Asia. In Indonesia, for instance, companies do not give maternity leave. Pregnant women are asked to leave their jobs and come back only after delivery. No wages are paid in the interim period.[9]

The situation in the Maquiladoras or the EPZs on the Mexico-U.S. border is no different. A journalistic report on the area says the workforce is mainly female, with more than 60 per cent in the reproductive age. Quoting a researcher, it says nearly 14 per cent of children born to workers in the area are under-

[9] *ibid.*

weight, in comparison to only five per cent among women in other industries. The report also says the high stress levels in the area are associated with symptoms such as gastritis, menstrual problems and depression.[10] These workers, however, have begun to organize and protest for better conditions. The policies of structural adjustment have been known to induce what has been described as the feminization of poverty. The EPZs are one prime example of how this manifests itself.

Deliberate Non-intervention by the Government

Vivek Montero of CITU, Mumbai, says SEEPZ workers "are removed from work quite arbitrarily" the moment the employers think they are beginning to get organized. "The main problem is job insecurity and a deliberate policy of non-intervention by the State machinery," he says. Maternity benefits, creche and other welfare measures are not implemented, he adds.

The Indian Labour Commission had expressed concern over "non-cooperation from the government of UP (Uttar Pradesh) with regard to inspection of EPZ units in Noida". [11] The inspection team found during one round of inspections that there were 1,148 workers whose names were not in the list of employees and 970 cases where payments were less than what the workers were entitled to. The team could not get more information due to "non-cooperation". The anxiety of the State to maintain a stable environment for investors often means the State no longer attempts to maintain a semblance of control over working conditions and the implementation of labour laws. This makes the workers more vulnerable than those

---

[10]Vidales, Susana (1997),"Women in Maquilardoras: A History of Contrasts", in Adriana Gomez and Deborah Meacham (Eds), *Women at Risk: Revealing the Hidden Health Burden of Women Workers,* Women's Health Collection 2, Latin American and Caribbean Women's Health Network.

[11]Government of India, Ministry of Labour (1999), Agenda Paper of the Thirty Fifth Session of the Standing Committee on Labour, New Delhi.

outside the zone who have experienced unionionised employment in factories.[12]

A senior government official at the Development Commissioner's office in NOIDA said they were there to "facilitate the entrepreneurs and not to obstruct them". He said the Labour Inspectors did not do their jobs properly but instead came to the zone to harass the entrepreneurs. "We do not let any union or any government officer barge in. Union activities are forbidden inside the zone. In any case there is no exploitation of the workers," he added. He reluctantly admitted that wages were low and in some places even the minimum wage was not given, but he argued that the entrepreneurs were not to blame if "people were ready to work for less". With "overpopulation, poverty and unemployment" these problems were bound to arise, he said.

Conclusion

Trade Union Members and leaders at both the NEPZ and the SEEPZ said they wanted the implementation of minimum wages. They also wanted parity in wages for men and women for the same kind of work, besides ESI, Provident Fund and maternity benefits. The setting up of creches has also been another consistent demand.[13] They want that labour laws should be implemented within the EPZs—an aspect that has been compromised by both the employers and the government. They also want the right to form trade unions within the premises and the modification of the Public Utility Status ac-

[12]Rosa, Kumudhini (1994), "The Conditions and Organizational Activities of Women in Free Trade Zones, Malaysia, Philippines and Sri Lanka, 1970-1990", in Sheila Rowbotham, and Swasti Mitter (Eds.), *Dignity and Daily Bread: New Forms of Economic Organizing Among Poor Women in the Third World and the First*, London, Routledge.

[13]Section 39 of the Indian Factories Act (1948) makes it mandatory for any employer having more than 30 women employed on their premises to set up a creche.

corded to the EPZ units that they feel interferes with the workers' right to go on strike.

Wage employment for women does not offer a way out of subordination or automatically guarantee emancipation. It has the potential to do this if the repetitive and monotonous tasks in the assembly line of production represent the beginning of a longer industrial career of skill formation and promotion. But this is not so. This has also to be seen in the context of the State gradually withdrawing from social welfare and labour law commitments, thereby exposing the working class to the harsh vagaries of the marketplace.

The women often leave the industry after a few years of taxing work, either to go back to traditional family life or to seek an even less secure future in the informal urban sector.[14]

In the Indian context, the employers are content to retain casual workers and go on increasing the probation period so that they do not have to pay benefits that would accrue to them if they were permanent. Workers are also thrown out when units close or they leave because of lack of promotions. For women, a lifelong commitment to employment is contingent upon the whims of an employer, who in any case prefers younger and more nimble hands.

It is true that newer industries in the initial labour-intensive phase of development might still continue to use women labour of Asian and other lesser developed countries and employment in these zones may not totally disappear. But what seems to emerge is a depressing picture of multinational corporations dropping in on women from developing countries, using them till they are no longer required—usually till they develop their process of production and then disappearing only to return with newer products, newer waves of technological revolution and newer women.[15]

This kind of work is neither empowering nor emancipatory. It is emancipatory to the extent that perhaps some women

---

[14]Edgren (1982), *op. cit.*

[15]Gothoskar, Sujata (1986), "Free Trade Zones: Pitting Women against Women", *Economic and Political Weekly*, Vol. XXI, No. 34, Aug .

escape domestic violence and some acquire the confidence to face adverse situations. [16] But there is no doubt that only by finding a collective voice can women face exploitative circumstances, organize for change, and then find a voice of their own.

[16]Ranadive and Mazumdar (1998), *op cit.*

The Politics of Silence
Introducing Sex Education in India

Swati Bhattacharjee

An adolescent's ignorance of her body was not seen as a matter of consequence to public policy till very recently. At the end of the eighties, as the AIDS epidemic spread in India, and as family planning took on the new avatar of RCH, this ignorance emerged as a threat to the State. Where there was a wall of silence, one now sees carefully engineered channels of information. Is India ready to talk sexuality?

The immediate and ostensible reason is, of course, AIDS. Worldwide, half of the 16,000 new infections that occur daily are among 15-24 year olds. Eighty five per cent of the world's youth is in Asia; India alone has an adolescent population (10–19 years) of 190 million, constituting one-fifth of its population.[1] The rapid spread of AIDS in the subcontinent is fast becoming a major problem. The National AIDS Control policy of 2001 may still shy away from using the word "adolescent" and only refer to students and youth, but in each major Indian city, there are today at least a hundred voluntary organizations addressing school students or school drop outs—primarily teenagers—on the dangers of premarital sex in general and unprotected sex in particular. At the same time, various government agencies have come up with modules for adolescent programmes on health.

The National Population Education Programme (NPEP) that develops curricula for schools has, in 1998, introduced an

[1]Jejeebhoy, Shireen J. (1996), "Adolescent Sexual and Reproductive Behaviour: A Review of the Evidence from India", *ICRW Working Paper No. 3*, December.

"adolescent education" component in its population education curriculum. It includes HIV/AIDS.

Years of advocacy and efforts by some women's groups too have finally brought adolescents in to the visibility zone, albeit at the periphery. For 50 years, women's health in India meant the health of the pregnant and lactating women and of course family planning. The drive to curb maternal mortality on the one hand and infant mortality on the other had totally left out the teen years of a girl's life, years important in terms of physical growth, behavioural patterns and attitudes. The demand of researchers and activists working on reproductive health to provide a special focus on adolescents found strong expression at the International Conference on Population and Development, Cairo, in 1994 and once again at the World Conference on Women in Beijing in 1995.

The view was endorsed not only in the Reproductive and Child Health (RCH) policy of the health and family welfare ministry, officially adopted in 1997, but also in the Integrated Child Development Scheme (ICDS) and other government policies and programmes. UN agencies now talk of the right of the adolescent girl with the same fervour—and ease—with which they spoke of the rights of the girl child a decade ago. With funds from international agencies and government sources flowing in, "raising awareness among adolescents" is a worthwhile venture. NGOs working on women's health, nutrition, child labour and literacy have added an adolescent component to their existing projects. A few, like the international organization CARE, Madhya Pradesh, have even started projects exclusively on "adolescent reproductive health." So is adolescent reproductive health yet another "cause of the year"?

Not enough has happened yet to answer this question. But one thing is apparent. The most contentious part of the adolescent health issue—giving information to adolescents, especially girls, on their bodies—has shed some of its explosiveness over the last five years. From blunt denial to grudging acceptance, the attitude in society towards sex education of adolescents has shifted to what is described by a counsellor as "passive welcome".

Sex Education For Adolescents

Says Nalini, resource person, Family Planning Association of India (FPAI), Chennai, "When we started the adolescent education programme in schools in 1994, many schools would say: 'This is not a school where discussion of such a topic is needed'. Today, there is a greater openness among principals and teachers. The schools where I have held sex education programmes one year happily welcome me the next year. But they are still not coming forward to request such programmes." Such passive willingness, says Nalini, is much the same in the four slum areas of Chennai where FPAI is conducting a sexual health project among 54 adolescent boys and girls.

It is rare to see initiative from the community on such issues. In Dakshinbagi, a village in South 24 Paraganas, West Bengal, 80 per cent families are ready to send their adolescent girls and boys to sex education training camps conducted by the Child in Need Institute (CINI), an NGO. In one year, CINI has held 55 three-day camps on adolescent health in 50 villages. Quite often, say field workers, a village demands a camp when they hear that one is being held at the adjacent village. The ongoing CINI project was initiated in 1997.

Such initiatives on the part of the community to address adolescents on sexual matters are not surprising. With decline in the age of menarche and rise in the age of marriage (in India, early marriage has decreased by one quarter in the nineties),[2] management of adolescent sexuality is emerging as a major challenge.

Withholding information increasingly appears to be an inadequate strategy. A campaign upholding the utility of absti-

---

[2]Mehta, Suman (1998), "Responsible Sexual and Reproductive Health Behaviour Among Adolescents", Theme Paper, UNFPA South Asia Conference on the Adolescent, 21-23 July, New Delhi.

nence before marriage, and faithful monogamy after it, reinforces traditional norms while maintaining a show of liberalism. Thus the Adolescence Education module developed by National Council of Education Research and Training (NCERT) puts down its objectives under the Unit on Process of Growing Up as: "To enable students to appreciate the importance of socio-cultural norms of sexual behaviour." The "socio-cultural norms" are elaborated as: "abstinence, general social disapproval to pre-marital and extra-marital sexual relations, respect for members of the opposite sex".[3]

Researchers point out that "adolescence" itself is a new concept in South Asia, in many places not more than 20 years old. The community is struggling to contain and control the sexuality of 190 million adolescents, who constitute one-fifth of the population, on the face of what is widely perceived as "onslaught of Western culture" through cable TV channels and films.

There are distinct signs of enthusiasm among women on the issue of sex education. In a slum in Jabalpur, Madhya Pradesh, a middle-aged housewife points at a group of adolescent girls attending the CARE training programme and says, "They must not make the same mistakes we made." In Dakshinbagi, women praise CINI's attempts. A group of about eight women, meeting at the school building say: "When girls know about their bodies, they are more careful. They can now take better care of themselves." At Khadibedia, a village adjacent to Dakshinbagi, Mita Naskar, a panchayat member, says that mothers are both delighted and embarrassed. "Their daughters are teaching them menstrual hygiene. They are asking questions like, 'Why do you have so many children? Didn't you know what to do?'" It is the mothers, say CINI field workers, who attend the parents' meetings and voice their support and demand for adolescent health camps.

---

[3]National Council of Educational Research and Training, NPEP (1998), "Adolescent Education in Schools", Part I, General Framework of Adolescent Education, New Delhi.

Field workers training adolescents on sexual health issues say that after an initial hesitation, mothers support their adolescent daughters getting sex education, which is usually catered as "family life education", "health education" or "adolescent education". Sometimes, especially in slums and rural areas, mothers even brave the ire of the fathers while sending the daughter to training centres. In most cases, fathers remain indifferent. This is not to say that there is no resistance to sex education. Every programme officer, field worker, teacher and counsellor has a tale to narrate about opposition from village elders, religious leaders, school/college principals, parents and, perhaps more importantly, from local units of the Rashtriya Swayamsevak Sangh (RSS). But the mood has undoubtedly changed.

An exemplary case would be the Tamil Nadu government's initiative to introduce AIDS education in schools. According to Dr Veenaytheerthan, who heads the Directorate of Teacher Education, Research and Training (DTERT), Chennai, when the idea of AIDS education in schools was mooted in 1990, there was strong resistance from parents and religious leaders. But the impact of HIV, which emerged in India in 1987, was felt by the mid-nineties and there has been a perceptible shift in opinion since then. Two surveys conducted by the DTERT in three districts among 400 people—policy makers, teachers, students and parents—in 1995 and 1997 showed that those in favour of AIDS education were about 50 per cent and 65 per cent respectively.

Among students, the number was higher: 70 per cent in the second survey. But then, there has hardly ever been any doubt that adolescents have a thirst for knowledge, particularly about their bodies.

While states like Tamil Nadu woke up to the need for sex education early, others are still to catch up. The West Bengal government is considering the introduction of "life skill education," for class VIII from 2004. The recommendation came from a committee appointed for revamping school education, headed by Professor Ranju Gopal Mukherjee.

Mukherjee says, "There are many quarters of society, including teachers, who still have reservations. But we cannot avoid the issue any longer. We need to inculcate a healthy attitude towards sexuality among our adolescents, not just AIDS awareness."

Exploring Limits

"Sexuality is a limiting factor in girls' lives," writes Margaret E. Greene, summing up what patriarchy does to girls.[4] As soon as a girl in India reaches puberty, older women, especially the mother, takes on the task of moulding her life by "honour" and "shame" (izzat and sharam), the two concepts "which form the core of gender ideology". She is typically asked not to go out, not to talk to boys, not to laugh loudly, not to look at men, not to hold her head up, to cover her head and so on. Cutting across class, caste, religion and region, this cultural construction of womanhood demonstrates that "the reference point for determining how a woman ought to behave towards men is her husband, not the woman herself."

The onset of menarche often signals the time to drop out of school. In rural India, while 44.6 per cent of girls between 10 and 14 attend school, only 18 per cent of girls between 15 and 19 do so. Even in relatively advanced states like Andhra Pradesh and Tamil Nadu, where enrolment figures are high, the discontinuation of education for girls occurs in the age group of 12-14 years. Marriage becomes the prime focus of a girl's life—in 1996, about 38 per cent of girls in India—45.6 in rural India and 21.8 in urban India in the 15-19 age group were married. The fact that their nutritional status is low (a 1993 study reveals that in rural Rajasthan 93.3 per cent of all girls suffered from first to third degree chronic energy deficiencies and vastly more girls in the country suffer from anaemia than boys) in-

---

[4]Green, Margaret E. (1997), "Watering the Neighbour's Garden: Investing in Adolescent Girls in India", *South and East Asia Regional Paper No 7*, Population Council, New Delhi.

creases the risks associated with childbirth. About 17 per cent of India's fertility is attributed to adolescents.[5]

On matters of decisions regarding sexuality and fertility, however, an educated woman may be no better equipped than her illiterate/semiliterate counterparts. As an unpublished document by the NPEP acknowledges, "[the] school curriculum does not include the critical elements of reproductive health such as sexual development during adolescence, HIV/AIDS and drug abuse." It notes that schools do not provide adolescents with the "education" or the "opportunity" to make "responsible decisions."[6]

The threat of AIDS has perhaps, of late, fractured some traditional bulwarks, and knowledge about her body is finally trickling down to the Indian adolescent girl. And she finds, slowly, hesitantly, that she can perhaps cross the boundaries that she believed to be "inviolable".

It has been observed that information about the body leads not only to better hygienic and nutritional practices by teenagers, but also to a radical change in their concepts of dignity, relationships and aspirations. Sex education is thus said to act as a catalyst for profound changes in the outlook and behaviour of adolescents. Indeed that this could be so is evident from the words of barely literate teenage girls in a Jaipur slum. These girls had attended a two-day course on health education. "Earlier I was afraid to go out on my own. Today, I don't hesitate to do so," said one.

"I always felt I was up to no good. Now I feel I can do what others can. *Ladki bhi ladka ban sakti hai* (even a girl can be a boy)."

"I used to cover my face with my chunni before strangers. Now I don't. *Odni se ijjat thodi aayegi* (can a scarf ensure your dignity?)," says a third.

---

[5]Government of India, Ministry of Health and Family Welfare (1998), *India: Country Paper for South Asia Conference on Adolescence*, New Delhi.

[6]NCERT, Population Education Unit (1998), "Adolescence Education as an Integral Part of Population Education", New Delhi.

The experience of health workers shows that while boys and girls are equally keen to obtain information about body changes, diseases and contraceptives, girls tend to link sex education with lifting the veil of abuse, freedom of movement and career aspirations. For them, talking about the body creates a platform where they can talk about the repression, deprivation, shame and fear that they have grown up with.

A number of girls took part in a two-year action research project in the mid-nineties, "Empowering girls through health education," conducted by Preetam Pal in five Jaipur slums. Pal, an employee of the Women's Development Project, Rajasthan, says, "We all know that patriarchal codes are perpetuated through women's bodies. But the conflict between gender perception and self-evaluation is most acute among adolescents. Girls accept family values and attach them to their bodies. Hence a whole range of issues emerges such as health: marriage and choice, mobility, abuse, alcoholism in the family and so on." Pal asserts that unless these diverse issues are tackled, providing adolescents with information on nutrition or menstrual health will have little effect. "As long as a girl's self-worth is low, she will not think it necessary to take care of her health," she adds.

Echoes Vinitha Nathani of Prerna, an organization in Delhi working for adolescent girls for more than a decade: "Unless a girl has confidence in herself, she cannot make use of the information given to her on her sexual health." How else does one explain why, after a course on reproductive health, a teenage girl should say: "Like others of my slum, I too used to run away when I saw the police. Now when they come, I offer them tea."

Common Sex Education Strategies

This realization cuts across practically every sex education module, each developed independently. From CINI's two-day training camps to CARE MP's six-month modules, a short course on self-awareness (boosting self-worth, expressing aspirations, examining family relationships) is used as the ice-breaking session by practically every module on sexual health. This, of course, points to the unarguably low status of the growing girl in the family across the country. "Who am I? What do I want to be?" are questions natural to adolescence, but the repressive social and familial setup thwarts even the natural process of self-examination in girls. As Pal puts it, "Their natural tendency is to grow independent but culture dictates that shyness is equal to goodness." Adolescent girls, even from educated middle class families, need strong and sustained intervention to realize that their bodies are not shameful, menstrual blood is not dirty and taking good care of their health is not a useless activity.

The first changes in health practices, not surprisingly, are almost everywhere in the least controversial spheres: menstrual hygiene and nutrition. Say the mothers of Khadibedia, "Even a year ago, nobody would hang the cloth used during menses out to dry. Now every girl does so." But, at variance, and with the same pride, in a Jaipur slum, a mother beams, "I don't even know these days when my child gets periods: she never stains her clothes."

In Tamil Nadu, in four blocks of Madurai district, the Indian Council of Child Welfare is working among women to curb female infanticide. The project was extended to adolescents four years ago. Today, young girls no longer dry out the cloth used during periods in hidden nooks and corners. Says Elizabeth F. Negi, an independent consultant assessing the project: "Girls have collectively got over their shyness about hanging out used cloth." Girls attending various projects also mention the need to wash the genitals.

The awareness on nutrition has also improved. "On the way to school or work, girls now pick up the nutritious greens they would have trampled on before," says Negi. Krishna Naskar, 18, of Khariberia says, "I no longer throw away the skin of peanuts." In Jabalpur slums, girls chorus that vegetables must be washed before they are peeled.

An elementary knowledge of female anatomy, explaining the functions of the different parts of the reproductive system in males and females, is also a common factor in most programmes. Visuals are used for these; many trainers take care to use materials that would be accessible even to illiterates. Apart from illustrated books, charts in the shape of an apron are being used to give an idea of the position of the genital organs.

Organizations, such as the Family Planning Association of India (FPAI) and Ekalavya in Madhya Pradesh have brought out books containing frequently asked questions and answers. Pregnancy, childcare, Reproductive Tract Infections (RTIs) and Sexually Transmitted Diseases (STDs), including AIDS, are regular features of most programmes.

Women and Adolescent Girls: Differing Needs and Concerns

NGOs that have extended their programmes from women to adolescents have picked up another important message: designing a reproductive health package for women is very different from designing one for teenage girls. "With women, one can start off straightaway with health problems," says Andal Damodaran of Indian Council of Child Welfare (ICCW), Chennai. "They have so many immediate complaints and are so desperately in need of services that they have no time for the future. One can conduct sessions focusing only on health with women. For girls, on the other hand, health is not the prime focus. What they stress on is practical information, coupled with vocational training."

Skill development, in fact, is the prime demand of the adolescents, especially among school dropouts. Many organizations, like CARE Madhya Pradesh, started out with a module focusing on reproductive health alone, but had to add a vocational training component to sustain the programmes. Ironically, but not surprisingly, beautician courses are particularly in demand.

On a typical day in one of the training centres in Jabalpur, girls tried out their skills on each other in the first half of the day's session. The health education part came next. They sat in a large hall, intricate designs made of henna on their palms, hair arranged in elaborate styles, faces glowing with bridal make up, listening to a peer educator explaining how to prevent STDs. "What should you do if you find your vaginal discharge has a foul smell?" Several henna-stained hands shot up. "Go to the doctor," the reply came in chorus.

It could be argued that with the spectacular growth of the beauty business in India in the years since liberalization, a market is being created for beauty products. It could also be argued that these projects reflect the middle-class concerns of the programme designers. Whatever be the merits of these arguments, it is nevertheless true that these courses are in demand. And indeed, at that age it might well be better to create a market for beauty products than one for contraceptives. It is, however, true that these courses, however "empowering" they actually are, are no substitute to formal schooling.

Field workers report a drop in attendance after the vocational courses are over. At present, CARE is offering courses in commercial art, painting, embroidery and beauty care. Dr Jaya Sharma, programme officer, says that she plans to tie up with a state agency to be able to arrange regular vocational training programmes along with reproductive health programmes. Says Vinitha Nathani of Prerna, "For adolescents, reproductive health can only be a part of a comprehensive package. Otherwise, adolescents will not be able to accept it. Besides, boys and girls coming together to learn stitching or painting create a forum, where one can start talking of health issues."

With service-providers now widening the scope of health programmes for adolescents to include skill development and general awareness, organizations are also offering programmes that incorporate elements like legal literacy. Examples include the Tamil Nadu Social Welfare Department's adolescent girls programme under ICDS; courses on savings, visits to banks, post offices, police stations in the ICCW programme for girls in Madurai; vocational training for income generation by the NGO Rural Women's Social Education Centre (RUWSEC) in

Chengalpet in Tamil Nadu and Prerna in Delhi; and cultural activities by CARE M.P. that trains girls in puppet shows. Unlike women, who have too many health complaints—and thus demand only services—with adolescent girls the ground for making a health programme a true intervention is already there. The need is to have the vision and the drive to go beyond and address the issue of gender equations through sexuality. This comprehensive view, Nathani points out, is lacking in government plans. "When talking of adolescent health, the government extends its family planning programme to adolescents. It visualizes a nexus of primary health centre-counsellors-specialists, which is typically a clinical approach."

She Knows, But Can She?

So, will sex education and awareness of her body and her rights make a girl more independent? Will a girl be able to decide the number of her children? Will she be able to resist her husband if he wants to continue having children till he has one, two or three sons? Space her children as she wants? Use the contraceptive of her choice, before or after marriage? Can she persuade her partner to use a condom to avoid STDs?

Ask such questions and what seemed like the information highway looks suspiciously like a circular dirt track. The questions take women's health from a medical issue to a social issue, from diseases to behaviour, from control to responsibility. The moot question, in other words, is whether the information being handed to a girl is designed to equip her to take decisions about her body, her sexuality and her life. Are these under the control of the individual adolescent?

The answer lies not in what is being told to the girls, but in what is not. "We cannot talk to unmarried girls about temporary contraceptives. That would be encouraging sex," says Dr Dhanikachalam, NGO advisor, Tamil Nadu AIDS Control Society. More than 250 NGOs are working in the state on AIDS intervention. Condom promotion is one of the strategies, but unmarried boys and girls are left out of it. "It is a moral and ethical question," says Dhanikachalam. "Besides, a behavioural surveillance done by our department shows that only about five per cent of adolescents have premarital sex."

Other reasons offered are still more startling. "Marriage and family size are not the immediate concerns of the adolescent," claims Ashok Kumar, Deputy Commissioner, Health and Family Welfare Department. "We must not waste our time talking to them about issues like son preference." Even motivation for later marriage, he says, is outside the purview of the adolescent component in the RCH policy. "We are concerned with the girl's physical development, healthy habits, disciplined upbringing, healthy reproductive growth and behaviour." What about sexual abuse? Adolescent girls are, after all, the prime victims of harassment. One-fourth of rape victims in the country are under 16.[7] "Abuse comes under the purview of the Social Welfare Ministry," says Ashok Kumar. Incidentally, the "model" adolescent programme being run by the Directorate of Social Welfare, Tamil Nadu, under the Integrated Child Development Scheme, does not address issues of sexual abuse. The two-day camp programme consists of health and hygiene awareness, legal literacy and nutrition.

Sexuality: A Concept Unknown to Many

Although the word "sexuality" is now freely and fashionably used, the meaning and significance of the term is yet to sink in. Even among policy makers, many have little idea what it means. Piquantly, we have a situation where some women's groups focus on issues of sexuality, while others focus on issues such as employment, equal property rights, communalism and so on. Unfortunately, the twain seem never to meet.

It is not surprising that Ashok Kumar, for example, says, "sexuality is an action like kissing, fondling, stimulating." Even where there is a technical understanding, there is a reluctance to relate sexuality to actual life. Most AIDS awareness pro-

[7]Greene, Margaret (1997), *op cit.*

grammes either leave out sexuality or refer to it obliquely. The prime example is *University Talks AIDS*, a publication of the Department of Youth Affairs and Sports. It defines sexuality as "a function of your whole personality that is lifelong beginning from birth. It includes how you feel about yourself as a person, how you feel about being a man or a woman, how you get along with members of either gender. It is the way you think, feel and behave."[8]

Heartening? But wait. The training manual then goes on to instruct the facilitators: "Finally, reminding the group that the precautions for the prevention of HIV relate mainly to sexual acts, specifically intercourse and not to other expressions of sexuality. The emphasis therefore in the remaining part of these sessions will be on 'sex'."

Shekhar Seshadri, Additional Professor, Child and Adolescent Services, Department of Psychiatry at the National Institute of Mental Health and Neuro Sciences, Bangalore, explains, "Social conditioning is such that people behave as though sexuality is some abnormal extension of their being. This ambivalence, and the construction of sexuality based on male primacy, gives rise to risky behaviour on the part of boys and places girls at risk of coercive sex and abuse. It is not surprising therefore that sexuality has been entirely relegated out of mainstream discourse."[9]

This "social conditioning" which determines the position of sexuality has been, in fact, an integral factor shaping society itself. Write JC Caldwell and P Caldwell, "The Asian family was formed in state societies where families were struggling to maintain their social class position and to control their inheritance. The chief instrument of this was the control of female premarital and extramarital sexuality. Fertility control when it comes, again as in the historic West, increases with maternal age and aims at limiting further family growth. Family plan-

[8]GOI, Department of Youth Affairs and Sports (1994), *University Talks AIDS*, Module II, Third Edition, New Delhi.

[9]Sheshadri Shekhar (1998), "Youth, Gender and Sexuality: The Role of Education", *Voices for Change*, Vol 2, No 1.

ning programs find it almost impossible to provide contraceptives to the unmarried, especially if they are adolescents. The result is that sexually active adolescents usually have no access to contraception."[10]

Realpolitik also works against adolescents. "Politicians in South Asia are reluctant to address the issue of adolescent sexuality, to go against public opinion to press for change," says Dr Nafis Sadik, executive director, UNFPA. "Across South Asia, there is no real sex education. And health services outside marriage are practically nil." It is only since the Cairo Conference that adolescent health has entered the sphere of development dialogue, she pointed out in an exclusive interview.

For the state, therefore, to go against prevalent public notions on adolescent sexuality and carry out the international mandate of providing services like "family planning information, counselling and services for sexually active adolescents", as stated in the ICPD programme of action, would be subverting its own fundamental structure—for both ideological and practical reasons.

Scholars like Padmini Swaminathan of the Madras Institute of Development Studies, therefore, feel that it is not enough to critique government policies. "There will always be a gap between the goals set down and the scheme of implementation," says Swaminathan. "Women's groups by now have enough data to know where the policies have gone wrong. The whole question is gathering enough political clout to make a change."

But a critical look at the policies seems unavoidable for an added reason: the NGO sector today has largely ceased to represent an alternative movement and is more of an extension of government agencies. The Department of Health and Family Welfare, for example, plans to entrust its newly incorporated adolescent component in the RCH policy entirely to NGOs. The international agencies funding programmes on adoles-

[10]Caldwell, J. C. and P. Caldwell, (1997), *Adolescence and Developing Global Implications for Sexuality, Reproduction and Marriage*, Washington D.C. National Research Council.

cents—notable among them UNFPA and the Swedish International Development Agency (SIDA)—also act in close collaboration with the government. So even to understand the "innovative programmes" designed at the "community level" with "cultural variables" in mind, one has to first look at government policies.

It is also clear that even as NGO activity in the area of women's rights has increased, so have biases against women in general. Increasing masculinization of the sex ratio, growing violence on women, galloping demands for dowry all point to the increasing disempowerment of women. Thus the issue of sexuality as a social construct cannot be avoided. Deprived of its social content, a medically focused Reproductive Health programme can be as coercive as the previous Family Planning Services, points out Imrana Qadeer, a public health specialist from Jawaharlal Nehru University, New Delhi. A woman's ability to take care of her health, she says, cannot be viewed in isolation from her broader socio-economic capability: to support herself, to be able to fight for her rights and resist abuse.

Since RH gained currency, empowerment has been routinely linked to health. But in reality, few are willing to take up the contentious issue of sexuality. "We have always tried to make NGOs see that sexuality is central to the concept of reproductive health," says Beulah Azariah, programme officer, Initiatives, Women in Development (IWID), a support organization that provides gender training to NGOs. "We try to reveal that the root cause of women's low status is their sexuality—patriarchy strongly controlling their body and confining them to the home. But we find that they are willing to talk about health but not sexuality. Even health NGOs totally neglect the negotiating power of women."

As Azariah notes with dismay, NGOs working with adolescents stress such issues as hygiene, and offer courses on skill improvement, but shy away from issues of sexuality, which they see as threatening power structures. "Talking about such things is not permitted in our culture," is a common excuse, she says. "The reason is a combination of the fear of alienation combined with that of being marked as someone promoting free sex."

Policy Matters

In India, the State's answer to unwanted pregnancies and STDs in adolescents thus remains two-fold: raise the age of marriage and promote abstinence before marriage. There is a consistent refusal to admit the possibility that the unmarried could be "sexually active". Sexual activity before marriage, where admitted, is clearly implied to be immoral, a deviation. The idealized family, devoid of power equations, is relentlessly advocated as the ideal institution. And no reference is made to the fact that sexual abuse occurs most often within the family.

It is almost amusing to note how persistently the word "sex" is avoided even when dealing with HIV/AIDS. *University Talks AIDS*, for example, enlists the "factors which lead youth into high risk situations". The words "sex" or "sexuality" do not occur even once among the seven points laid down, while the word "traditional" occurs three times and "parental control" twice. The summary: weakening traditional value system, lack of parental control and socio-economic deprivation lead young people to high-risk behaviour.

The stress on tradition and family values, with no questions about how traditional a tradition is, whose tradition we are talking about, and how valuable or otherwise a tradition is and to whom, totally glosses over the fact that the family never acknowledges the sexuality of the unmarried, that the daughter's sexuality is seen as a threat, that the girl is often abused by family members with impunity. The fact that the family too is an instrument of patriarchy and of control, and a site for power negotiations is also glossed over. Indeed, it is barely considered that the "tradition" of sacrifice that a family often demands of its daughters is one reason for the devaluation of women.

The crucial fact that is avoided is that providing information alone does not suffice. The crux of the problem lies not in the lack of information, but women's lack of control over their bodies, and indeed their lives.

Adolescent girls are keenly aware of this. Of 17 slum girls who participated in Pal's project in the mid-nineties in Jaipur, 12 said that they wanted to have two children even if both were daughters, while the rest felt they needed at least one son. When asked what they would do if their husbands wanted more, they shook their heads sadly. "*Mard to hamari nehi sunta*" (Men don't listen to us), they said. In Khariberia, Krishna Naskar and her friends are more hopeful: "We will reason with him," they say.

Many do not realize what enlightenment without empowerment can do to a young girl. In Katra, a slum in Jabalpur, 19-year-old Sandhya stays with her mother in spite of being married to a boy of another locality. She had attended the CARE project and knows the necessity of using a condom. Her husband sleeps around, she suspects he has a disease, but he refuses to use a condom. But she wouldn't agree to sex without a condom. "Sandhya must make up her mind soon, or she will be deserted," confides a trainer.

The health and family welfare policy has totally ignored the aspect of consensus among the couple on the use of contraceptives, relentlessly advocating sterilization after two children—even after the introduction of the "client oriented" RCH. There is also a staunch refusal to acknowledge that sex life may start before marriage. To be a good Auxiliary Nurse Midwife (ANM), says the *Manual on Community Needs Assessment Approach in Family Welfare Programme*, it is necessary that "she should motivate and counsel adolescents in the area about reproductive health so that they are not misinformed: they have to be treated as youth on the threshold of adulthood." As for the male health worker, his duty towards adolescent boys requires him only to assist, "to the extent possible", village schoolteachers in health education. He should, during his trips to the village, "educate men about RTI/STDs and assist those who need medical attention." Adolescent boys, presumably, do not need such assistance.

Surveys, however, reveal otherwise. Shireen J. Jejeeebhoy quotes studies in urban and rural hospitals to show that adolescent girls constitute 27 to 30 per cent of abortion seekers. A 1993 survey by the FPAI in 16 cities found that 28 per cent respondents had initiated sexual activity in adolescence. An all-India survey by a men's magazine found the figure to be 41 per cent—a large number of them reported relations with commercial sex workers.[11]

The AIDS control programmes, on the other hand, could not avoid the need for dialogue altogether. It had to take "negotiation skills" into account. And what are the "skills" they teach women? Says Dr Dhanikachalam, who also acts as a counsellor, "Wives often come to me asking how they can make their husbands use a condom. I tell them to tell their husbands, 'I might have got an infection, and you will get it from me if you don't use a condom'. Only then do their husbands listen to them."

The status of "women's empowerment" in national policies, clearly, ranges between jargon and a joke. Highlighting gaps in the draft youth policy of 1997, a group of participants in the workshop "Youth across Asia" (September 1997) critiqued "the use of gender justice as a separate need rather than one that should underlie all programmes and policies."[12]

This "gap" is exemplified even in programme training manuals like *University Talks AIDS*. The fact that women are unable to protect themselves finds a place in Annexure 2, at page 149: "... even if a woman knows about HIV and how to protect herself, it is not possible for her to refrain from sex with her husband if she feels he is unfaithful or convince her husband to use a condom." Unlike in other chapters, no strategies are suggested to counter this reality. Similarly, a handout designed with the chapter "Safer Sex: Condoms" offers many tips on

[11]Jeejebhoy, Shireen J (1996), "Adolescent Sexuality and Fertility", *Seminar* 447, Nov.

[12]Singh, Sagri (1997), "Adolescent Reproductive and Sexual Health Needs in India", Population Council, Asia and Near East Operations Research and Technical Assistance Project, New Delhi.

how to say no to drugs or sex, but nothing on how a girl can persuade her partner to use a condom.

"At present," sums up Saroj Pachauri, Regional Director, Population Council, New Delhi, "there is a poor fit between reproductive health programmes and the needs of youth. As a result, few young people are adequately prepared to take responsibility for protecting their health."[13]

At the Community Level

This fear, that offering adolescents counselling on sex and reproductive health may be misconstrued as promoting free sex, holds most NGOs back from providing reproductive health services to adolescents. In January 2003, the Minister of Health and Family Welfare, Sushma Swaraj castigated the National AIDS Control Organization (NACO) for devising a mass media campaign that showed condoms. This was the first mass media ad campaign by NACO, developed in association with BBC World Service Trust. One of the ads showed a father talking to his son about condoms. Swaraj argued that such ads would encourage sex.

Studies indicate that there is a huge unmet need for RH information services among adolescents. This is particularly true of adolescent girls, even when married. A 1998 report of a two-year survey by Foundation for Research in Health Systems (FRHS) among 302 married girls between the ages of 15–19 in rural Maharashtra showed that 82 per cent did not use health services for post natal care and 51 per cent did not use them for gynaecological problems like RTIs. Yet the incidence of RTIs among married adolescent girls is alarmingly high: a 1998 report of a two-year survey by the Christian Medical College (CMC), Vellore, said among 379 married girls aged 16-22 years, one in two were found to have RTIs. The FRHS study found 51 per cent adolescents reported at least one type of

---

[13]Pachauri, Saroj (1997), "Youth Across Asia: Issues and Challenges", Population Council, New Delhi.

gynaecological morbidity. Another worrying fact: 13 per cent girls in the CMC study and 14 per cent in FRHS study reported having had an abortion, mostly by unapproved practitioners, to space pregnancies.[14]

Clearly, it is necessary to have accessible public health services that can also answer to the special needs of adolescents. But in a situation of crumbling health services with cuts in health spending, this might be too much to expect of public health services. This is, however, a mantle no one is willing to take up. Even Parivar Seva Sanstha (Marie Stopes Clinic), which runs centres for reproductive health education and counselling for school students, cannot offer abortion services to adolescents because of legal restrictions.

Unfortunately, like sex education, RH services for adolescents are also seen as encouraging sexual activity among adolescents. Dr Lalita Iyer of MJ Trust Hospital, Jabalpur, works closely with CARE which uses the hospital as a referral centre. "To publicise that we offer abortion specifically for adolescents would encourage them to have sex," says Dr Iyer. "For them, it is a matter of a few rupees." According to Dr Iyer, girls are already too casual about abortion and are not bothered about its health hazards. Some even resort to repeated abortions.

Dr Jaya Sharma of CARE says, "When we started, we aimed only to provide referral linkages, but now we have realized that the linkages have to be specific." Dr Sharma is in the process of identifying hospitals and private practitioners that adolescents can approach for menstrual problems and gynaecological morbidities.

The only service most organizations are willing to offer adolescents is counselling. But here again, as with referral services for diseases, adolescents under-utilize the facility. The counsellors in the FPAI counselling centres in both Bhopal and Madras, for example, say that their service is available to adoles-

[14]"Adolescent Sexuality and Fertility in India: Preliminary Findings", *ICRW Information Bulletin*, May 1998.

cents. But practically no adolescent approaches either counselling clinic: the clientele is mainly married couples seeking contraceptive advice.

Though adolescents constitute a majority of the callers in the various hotlines offering information on sex-related matters, they do not, as a rule, seek out counselling centres for advice—for understandable reasons, among which can be counted, fear of the family and community.

Towards an Alternative

The moot question, therefore, remains: are the current programmes being run by various organizations meaningful ? Will they stop at providing information? Will they equip girls to identify the patriarchal structures that use their sexuality against them?

They can. Some programmes have brought about changes, which, however limited, can as indicators of such change. Almost everywhere girls attending sex education projects show a renewed sense of dignity, better articulation of their problems and greater mobility.

The CINI project shows another interesting offshoot: a decline in what is called, "eve teasing". At Khadibedia, both girls and boys attended the three-day health camp. Together they had learnt why changes occur during puberty, how sexual contact can spread diseases, why early pregnancy is harmful for girls, how to prevent unwanted pregnancy and STDs. They also learned about common problems like malnutrition, diarrhoea, etc.

Those three days sufficed to break down the barrier of fear and shame between the boys and girls of Khadibedia. Brought up to believe in the segregation of the sexes, and the fact that what is considered macho behaviour includes victimizing and sexually harassing women, it was evident that adolescent boys too are victims of patriarchal norms of sexuality. They now interact easily with each other, meeting periodically at the local club to chalk out their next programmes. Says Ramen

Naskar, 16, "My friends and I have stopped teasing girls. We don't need to do so now; we can talk easily to them."

His sister, Krishna, 18, says, "At first our parents used to object to our easy interaction. But we have reasoned with them. We are not doing anything bad. Our parents also no longer shut us up—they listen to us."

This need to start a dialogue is dawning upon most NGOs, who are lately adding on programmes for adolescent boys. CARE M P, for example, had recently recruited two male workers to approach adolescent boys and is trying out literature that is being developed for boys by a Delhi-based organization. RUWSEC at Chengalpet in Tamil Nadu also runs an adolescent boy's programme but recognizes, like CARE and most other organizations running ARH programmes, that boys are at the periphery of their programmes.

At Dakshinbagi, the camps have liberated girls who are school dropouts from the confines of their homes—and how! They now regularly parade in the playground of the village. Some girls, acting as volunteers, also do not hesitate to go to other villages to act as facilitators for health camps.

"Girls must realize the link between sexuality and patriarchy," says Preetam Pal. This realization—not an easy one—seems to have found expression in at least one effect of the sex education programmes: a better mother-daughter relationship.

This fallout is as surprising to many trainers themselves, as it is unexpected. Andal Damodaran tells the story of a girl in a Madurai village who had attended the ICCW adolescent programme. When asked what she had gained from it, she had replied, "I now understand why my mother gets angry with me. It is because everyone, especially father, puts pressure on her to make me behave in a certain way. I used to constantly fight with my mother before, but I don't do so any longer."

The last word, of course, is that the outcome is unpredictable. Archana Sahay, programme coordinator, Young Women's Christian Association, Bhopal, is running a package of programmes, including sex education, for street children for several years. "Mothers come and tell us that their daughters are now more disciplined and do housework better," says Sahay. However, old habits die hard—field workers in different cities say that while mothers appreciate better menstrual hygiene in daughters, they still do not let them cook or fetch water during their periods.

Measuring Behaviourial Change: Complex and Time-consuming

Despite limitations, well-planned and sustained interventions seem to be able to bring change, not only in health practices, but also in attitudes and behaviour. Of course, academics point out that measuring behavioural change is a complex, time consuming procedure. In addition, as Elizabeth Negi points out, since most adolescent programmes are part of those running in the community, ascribing behavioural changes to any particular component of an adolescent programme could also be problematic. But this also assumes that behaviours are indeed the primary problem, and that they can be changed easily through education. That both these assumptions are questionable is not something that is discussed.

This complexity of assessing behavioural changes also discourages NGOs, says Azariah. "Most NGOs operate within a three to five year' framework, and must assess the impact of their programme by the end of that time. Changes in attitude and behaviour are difficult to measure—one must access not only adolescents but their families too, which is why they attempt easily measurable tasks like distribution of iron pills, holding counselling sessions or health camps."

Unfortunately, though funding agencies today are investing huge funds to generate data on reproductive health, sexuality and its wider ramifications do not appear to be a priority even in such research.

The fact that adolescent RH programmes are in their infancy is also a stumbling block. As Azariah puts it, "There is nothing concrete to go ahead with."

Faced with a similar problem, CINI, a mother NGO which has already been entrusted by the state government to implement the adolescent component of the RCH policy, is envisaging a list of qualitative and quantitative indicators to be followed by all grassroots NGOs under it. Apart from measuring improved knowledge of adolescents on hygiene, contraception, etc, it also aims to check whether health delivery personnel treat married adolescents as a separate client group, whether the village has a recognized abortion centre and whether the age at marriage and birth of first children is rising. To attribute these, if they occur, to project intervention is, however, deeply problematic. More ambitiously, CARE MP's five-year project at Jabalpur has, among its objectives, an increase of at least 50 per cent in service seeking among unmarried and married adolescents on diseases and pregnancy-related issues and an increase of 6 per cent in use of temporary methods of contraceptives among married adolescents.

The idea of having a list of indicators is not without its critics. Says Jamil Zamir of FPAI, Bhopal, "Loading workers with indicators would be expecting them to elicit information that they are not qualified to do." The fear of arbitrary responses, therefore, cannot be ruled out. More significantly, wider social issues are collapsed into narrow service access ones. Padmini Swaminathan points out that indicators are helpful only at a primary level, as they can alert us to many factors. "Sex ratio, for example, is a macro level indicator from which it is possible to infer where things have gone wrong," she says. "But the fall in women's ratio would indicate different problems at different levels."

Indicators are the starting point of research, she argues. "An increase in service-seeking behaviour, for example, could fulfil an indicator, but the matter does not end there. This should be the starting point of an enquiry. It is precisely this kind of active intervention programme coupled with research that can shed light on the nature of a problem, but very few organizations do it," rues Swaminathan.

Azariah, on the other hand, greets the idea of indicators with enthusiasm. "If they are flexible and not time-bound, indicators will help us to see where we are. One has to have a vision, a goal. Otherwise, there will be a lot of programmes which will not get anywhere."

Conclusion

The government's belated awakening to the need to address adolescent health issues, more specifically reproductive health issues is only the beginning of a long process of change. Clearly, a great deal needs to be done to make society accept the concept of adolescent sexuality more openly and offer the right package of health counselling and services for adolescents. Equally, in a situation where the government's policy is focused on controlling numbers, when the government's commitment to providing health care is increasingly whittled down, it is important to recall the commitments made to women's health in general. It is important to keep up the pressure for change without lapsing into cynicism.

Women and AIDS in India

Doubly Discriminated

VASANT BHOSALE

"No one can escape fate. I will take care of my child till I can and then everything is up to God." Mangal, 19, is HIV positive, a widow with an infant child. She has no steady income or assets. She labours in others' fields to feed herself and her child.

It wasn't always like this. She was part of a small landholding family comprising parents, two married brothers and a widowed sister. She was the wife of the younger son, living in Sangli district, on the banks of the river Krishna in Maharashtra. Since the two acres of land were not enough to provide for the whole family, two small shops selling everyday items were set up to augment their income. The brothers also began taking up building jobs on contract. But quarrels erupted very often and the two brothers divided up the property and split.

The newly-married younger brother and his wife, Mangal, had a daughter in the second year of their marriage. Mangal went to her parent's home for her delivery, which was conducted at home. She came back to live with her husband a few months after her delivery. She managed her home, her baby and the shop and he continued contract work. Everything seemed to be going well till her husband began suffering from an intermittent cough. They consulted a visiting city doctor. Medicine would bring immediate but temporary relief. After four to six months, his appetite vanished, his weight dropped drastically and he began to suffer frequent bouts of diarrhoea. Mangal, who had only completed her primary education, could not understand what was happening and finally consulted her parents. She was advised to take up the matter with her brother-in-law.

The brother took him to the Civil Hospital in the district headquarters, Sangli, where the doctor suggested he undergo a test for HIV. The hospital did the testing free of cost. He tested positive. The two brothers decided to keep Mangal in the dark. They told her that the doctor had said that her husband had a stomach problem and should avoid spicy food.

Soon he became so ill that he could not even drag himself to work. He became bed-ridden and the doctor gave up all hope. Mangal looked after her husband with the money that came from the shop. The doctor claimed he did not know the cause of the disease, but said he should have bland food and keep away from young children. A year went by, his jobs ceased and Mangal's earnings from the shop were proving to be meagre. She turned to her brother-in-law for help. He gave money on condition that she transfer her husband's share of land to him. Her husband eventually died and a full month after his death, the brother-in-law revealed the cause. In the meantime their assets were all gone. It was the first time that Mangal had heard the name of this disease. Was it a new disease? she wondered. She knew of malaria and tuberculosis. Diarrhoeas and other childhood diseases were a fact of everyday occurrence. But AIDS? There wasn't even a word for it in her language. Her brother-in-law himself was not too clear about its cause.

When she went to the doctor who had been treating her husband, she was told that her husband "visited" other women, a euphemism for his seeing sex workers. He advised her to undergo an HIV test. She tested positive. Her parents-in-law and brother-in-law hatched a scheme to pack her off to her parents and take away her share of the house. They thought this would also liberate them from the responsibility of looking after her when she fell ill. The brother-in-law even sold her shop to make up for the shortfall of money. The family began pushing for Mangal to move out. But Mangal was adamant. She insisted she would stay in her home and earn her own living.

The HIV epidemic in the country is poised to sweep away whatever little rights women could hope to exercise. Apart from the horrendous suffering and loss of lives, the spread of the epidemic is exposing the gross inadequacies of India's public health system. It is also bringing to the fore issues in her social fabric as the disease is inextricably linked to sexuality in its many dimensions—sexuality and reproduction, sexuality and man-woman relations, sexuality and the oppression of women. Given that the sexual arena is one in which women are traditionally disempowered, the epidemic threatens several of their basic and hard won rights.

AIDS in India

The first case of HIV in India was reported in Madras (now Chennai) in 1986.[1] Though classified by the United Nations as a "low-prevalence" country, India has one of the most serious AIDS epidemics in the world. Official figures put the number of HIV-positive persons at 3.97 million,[2] the second highest national total of persons with AIDS after that of the Republic of South Africa. This figure has been widely disputed, however, with some experts asserting that the actual number of persons living with HIV/AIDS in India is more than double the official figure.[3]

The official prevalence rate of HIV/AIDS in the adult population is 0.7 per cent. Because of the size of India's population, each 0.1 per cent increase in prevalence represents about half a million persons infected. All of India's states have reported AIDS cases, and surveys show that the virus is spreading from

[1]Michael Spencer (2001) "India's Plague," *New Yorker*, December 17.

[2]Government of India, National AIDS Control Organization (2001), "Estimation of HIV infection among adult population: HIV estimates for year 2001," www.naco.nic.in/vsnaco/indianscene/update.htm (consulted April 9, 2002).

[3]S. Ramasundaram (2002), "Can India Avoid Being Devastated by HIV?" *British Medical Journal*, vol. 324, January.

higher-prevalence urban areas into rural communities.[4] The disease has spread beyond high-risk groups into the general population in a number of states and municipalities.

The five states in which it is officially acknowledged that more than 1 per cent of the adult population is infected—thus considered high-prevalence areas—are Andhra Pradesh, Karnataka, Maharashtra, Manipur, and Tamil Nadu.[5] Some districts in Goa, Gujarat and Nagaland are also high-prevalence zones. Persons in traditional high-risk groups—notably men who have sex with men, women in prostitution, and injecting drug users—face social marginalization and deep stigma in India.[6] While the epidemic has spread to the general population in some states, these high-risk persons remain crucial to the national AIDS control strategy.

Women and AIDS

The World Health Organization (WHO) and UNAIDS estimated that at the end of 1997, out of a total of 29.4 million adults living with HIV/AIDS, 12.2 million were women. It is further estimated that infection rates among women will soon equal—and then overtake—these of men. In India the HIV epidemic has continued to shift towards women with 25 per cent of all HIV positive persons now estimated to be women and an accompanying increase in vertical transmission—that is from mothers to infants—and paediatric HIV.

Women are more vulnerable to HIV not so much because of their own sexual behaviour, but because of their partners. Men are more likely to have two or more concurrent or consecutive partners and are therefore at greater risk both of contracting the virus and passing it on; women are more likely to

---

[4]World Bank (2001), "UNGASS—Regional Updates: South Asia Region (India)," June , available at www.worldbank.org/ungass/India.htm (consulted April 9, 2002).

[5]NACO (2001), *op cit.*

[6]Dube, Siddharth (2000), *Sex, Lies and AIDS* , New Delhi, Harper Collins.

be faithful to men from whom they contract HIV and less likely to pass it on.[7]

Women are denied the opportunity to protect themselves because men often refuse to use condoms or to stop relations with other partners. Women also often suffer from reproductive tract trauma either due to male sexual violence or their sexual preferences, thus making them more vulnerable to HIV. In the absence of other factors (that is in the absence of an untreated STD) a man with HIV probably has a one in 500 chance of passing the virus to his partner in a single act of unprotected vaginal intercourse; the odds of women to man transmission in the same circumstance are about one in 1000.

Moreover, every year there are an estimated 333 million new cases of STDs which cause ulcers or lesions and allow HIV to enter directly into the blood stream, multiplying the risk of infection up to seven times.[8] In women, the symptoms of STDs are often absent, with the result that they rarely know they have a disease and thus seek treatment. This again increases their vulnerability. Women under 20 are even more at risk because their relatively immature genital tract has fewer layers of mucous membrane and is thus more liable to infection.

Sexual violence and sexually transmitted diseases, including HIV/AIDS, have a devastating effect on children's health, and girls are more vulnerable than boys to the consequences of unprotected sex and premature sexual relations. Girls often face pressures to engage in sexual activity. Due to such factors as their youth, social pressure, lack of protective laws, or failure to enforce laws, girls are more vulnerable to all kinds of violence, particularly sexual violence, including rape, sexual abuse, sexual exploitation, trafficking, possibly the sale of their organs and tissues, and forced labour.[9]

[7]Foreman, Martin (Ed.) (1999), *AIDS and Men: Taking Risk or Taking Responsibility*, London, Panos/Zed Books.

[8]*Ibid.*

[9]United Nations (1995), Fourth World Conference on Women, *Platform for Action*, Beijing.

In the Indian context, there is little doubt that unprotected sexual behaviour on the part of men results in more women getting infected with HIV. Patriarchy intersects with social and economic factors to prevent women from taking control of their own lives. This has prompted many women's groups in India to take the stand that marriage might be the biggest risk factor as far as HIV in India is concerned. Homosexual men are at a greater risk for HIV transmission and that also increases the risk for their female partners; given the universality of marriage, gays are often forced to marry in India. Patterns of drug injection—men are more likely to share needles with several partners while women are more likely to share with only one man—similarly increase women's vulnerability. [10]

Interestingly, groups such as VAMP (*Veshya* AIDS *Muqabla Parishad* or Sex Workers Against AIDS), a sex workers collective in Maharashtra, have reported a high percentage of condom enforcement among paying clients. "This has brought into focus the realization that women in prostitution possess some bargaining power and have a degree of equality within the sexual act. However, married women who have no power within the family are more vulnerable and increasingly bearing the brunt of the spread of HIV," says Kashibai Jadhav, General Secretary VAMP, Solapur.

In a situation where the ailments of women—whether major or minor—do not attract an adequate response from the male-centered family, women infected by HIV are not only neglected, but even actively persecuted. In many cases like Mangal's, they are denied their share in the family property, ill-treated by colleagues in the workplace or even retrenched from jobs.

At the Opposite End of the Social Spectrum

Shalini sits in front of a doctor in a village 10 kilometres from Sangli. She is smartly turned out, bejewelled and her general

[10]Foreman, Martin (1999), *op cit.*

demeanour speaks of money. She is nine months pregnant. A commerce graduate, Shalini is quite articulate and reveals that this is her first pregnancy. She married late because she wanted to complete her studies. Her husband is a postgraduate in law, but is not in legal practice as he handles a large medical supplies agency. He travels a lot to Mumbai and Pune on work.

"I come from a good family and my father was in government service," she says. "My father ensured that all his children were educated. My elder sister is in Pune, married to an officer in the State Transport Corporation. My brother is still studying. I was married three years ago. In my seventh month, I experienced considerable discomfort. The doctor felt this was due to anaemia and advised me to have my blood tested. It was then discovered that I had HIV. How long will I live? Will my child also be infected?"

Shalini sounds quite desperate. She feels her life has come to an end. She says her husband does not believe she could have the infection. She herself feels she might have acquired it through some injections she received while undergoing treatment for typhoid some months ago. She feels her husband will take care of her because she has had a happy married life so far.

However, she had come to the clinic accompanied by her father-in- law who was sitting outside, and who had not been told anything. Nor indeed was any other family member informed. She came to a government hospital because all private practitioners refused to treat her after seeing her HIV status. Her husband refused to take an HIV test. She has since given birth to a baby girl at the Civil Hospital—and not a private nursing home as would be expected in her class. She was alone and without any family support.

Sangli as a Special Case

Sangli district lies at the foothills of the Sahayadri ranges and is fed by the rivers Krishna, Warna and Panchganga. The land is fertile with cash crops like sugarcane, tobacco and grapes growing in abundance. In 1959, a strong cooperative movement was initiated in the state, throwing up a number of local leaders. Initiatives in the field of education saw further progress in the district. Upper caste leaders from this area have dominated state politics; and industrialization and irrigation have been natural corollaries of this political domination.

The social set-up is strictly patriarchal with land and property rights vested in males. Women and the landless were consciously kept out of the process of development since they did not own land. Land ownership is a primary requirement to become a shareholder in the cooperative units. Besides, sugarcane cultivation is not labour intensive and the first retrenchments done on the fields as the area switched over to cash crops were of women workers. This has further alienated women from the land and its produce, emphasizing their total dependence on men.

Patriarchy, land ownership and caste interact in striking ways to increase the vulnerability of women. In the patriarchal value system, since land is passed on from father to son, women are perceived as dependent and economically valueless. The perception of being of less value, the socialization that ingrains voicelessness as a virtue, dominant cultural practices, all increase the vulnerability of women. This vulnerability is apparent through the different levels of social hierarchy. While upper caste and upper class women are able to negotiate some safety with respect to HIV, the survival strategies accepted by poor and lower caste women often place them at much higher risk of contracting the virus.

HIV and Sangli District

Sangli ranks high in the incidence of HIV/AIDS, second only to Mumbai. In addition, it has come into prominence on the AIDS front in Maharashtra of late because it represents the urban-rural-rural spread of the epidemic in the state. The high incidence of HIV/AIDS can be explained by the fact that the Sangli-Miraj sector has a high concentration of hospitals and clinics, which attract patients from the neighbouring towns and cities. These two cities form a central junction for North Karnataka and South Maharashtra which is easily accessible by road as well as rail. Routine testing by all doctors has become the norm for any minor ailment, especially for surgery, irrespective of the need for the HIV test.

According to the records of the Civil Hospital, in December 2002, Sangli district is said to have had an overall prevalence of an astonishing 16.5 per cent, although this is not a figure obtained by epidemiological community-based studies. At ante natal clinics, the figure is put at 5 to 6 per cent, while at STD clinics, at 46-49 per cent. The prevalence rates at blood banks is 4 per cent and in paediatric clinics, 6 per cent. Cases identified by the private sector of course do not get fed into these reports.

The AIDS cell report of Maharashtra says that up to June 1998, there were 2,939 AIDS cases in the state. Of these, 1,910 were from the state capital, Mumbai, and 714 from Sangli. Of the 714 cases in Sangli, 545 were male and 161 were female. Eighty per cent of these fall in the age group 18-40 years. At least 358 people have died of AIDS in the state, 92 of these are from Sangli district (63 men and 29 women).

These are not data from the general community. They nevertheless provide some indication of the dimensions of the problem. In infection rates, Sangli ranks second only to the country's commercial capital, Mumbai. It is also significant because it marks the urban-rural-rural spread of the epidemic in the state. Routine testing for HIV is done by almost all doctors in both private and government hospitals for all cases of surgery and even minor ailments, irrespective of whether it is necessary or not. These tests have their own problems, of false negatives and positives and thus one test cannot be relied upon. Indeed it may well blight an entire life or destroy a family if a test is a false positive. But there appear to be hardly any instances of pre- or post-test counselling despite the fact that the National AIDS Control Organization (NACO) guidelines clearly state that tests should be carried out only on a voluntary basis with appropriate counselling.

Women form 30 per cent of the people affected by AIDS in Sangli. Of them, a majority are pregnant women. Six per cent of women who come to hospitals to determine if they are pregnant, have tested positive for HIV.[11]

The number of women who come to be treated for Sexually Transmitted Diseases (STDs) and are found to be HIV positive has shot up to 20 per cent in Maharashtra, according to the state AIDS cell. The Pune-based National AIDS Research Institute has, in a recent study in Pune, found that 14 per cent of the women suffering from STDs were also infected with HIV. Very significantly, these women did not have any sexual relations outside marriage.

Women's Rights

One of the major lessons learnt is that the HIV epidemic is being fuelled by society's inequalities, said Shashikant Mane, project officer in the NGO Sangram. While poverty, caste, class and sexuality have a great impact on the spread of HIV, gender places the burden of the epidemic on women. The risk of getting HIV is a gendered risk, one that strongly depends on the actions and behaviours of individual men and women, playing out the gender roles that society has constructed for them. According to Mane, if women face a disproportionately high risk due to their social status, women also face a greater share of the HIV burden. All women—single, married, pregnant, widowed or in prostitution—face the whiplash of gender when it comes to HIV. The discrimination and stigma they face is much more than that faced by their men. The burden of care also falls squarely on their shoulders. In fact, HIV/AIDS remains yet another arena where traditional gender struggles continue to be played out at all structural levels: in the family, in the community, and in society at large.

[11]Civil Hospital (2002), "HIV Status Report", Unpublished report, Sangli.

Sangeeta decided to divorce her husband because she faced repeated domestic violence. The main reason was because she was unable to bear children. She was an upper caste woman and her husband owned 18 acres of irrigated land. Sangeeta fled for her life and went to live with her parents. After four years, she filed for alimony. To her surprise, her husband declared that he was HIV positive and claimed that since he had AIDS, he could not work and was forced to spend large sums of money on his treatment. The wealthy landowner argued that he could not pay alimony. The court rejected Sangeeta's plea.

Advocate Harish Pratap of Sangli says there are a number of such cases in court and most of them deal with the right to property, to children and to work. He narrated some of the cases—a family threw the widow of a man who died of AIDS out of the house. The family owned ten acres of land. The in-laws also took custody of the children and insisted they would take care of them. Now the woman has filed a case in Sangli: both for her share in the property, as well as the custody of her children. In another incident, a woman who works for a rural cooperative bank lost her husband to AIDS. The bank authorities put pressure on her to quit her job as they were convinced that she might have contracted the virus.

It has been a practice in all government departments to absorb all widows of employees who die in service. This is never done in the case of employees who die of AIDS. The epidemic is thus having a serious impact on all aspects of women's lives. In Mangal's case she had no knowledge of the ailment and even as the person most vulnerable and at risk, she was kept in the dark about the sero-status of her spouse. Further, there was an attempt to deprive her of all her property rights and banish her from the house.

Despite her educated middle-class background, Shalini is equally vulnerable. A routine HIV test with no pre-or post-test counselling and the refusal to treat her at private hospitals are violations of her human rights. That she has been abandoned by her family is proof enough of her secondary status.

In Sangeeta's case, the husband's HIV status is being used to deprive her of her means of support. Women have been given that right because they do not have access to the instruments of production in a large number of cases. In this case also, in all likelihood Sangeeta will be deprived of her share to the property.

Most women only hear about HIV after routine tests are performed on them for some other problems. Pre-test counselling is not available and in a number of instances, they are not even informed about their positive status afterwards. It is left to the family members to explain why doctors refuse to treat them. Rules of confidentiality rarely apply and most times family members are told of a woman's HIV status before she is. The affected women then have no recourse but to visit government hospitals that are valiantly trying to cope with the influx, says Dr Usha Udgaonkar of the Sangli Civil Hospital. The women, however, feel that the hospital staff fear the virus and refuse to provide adequate care to positive women.

Udgaonkar says some private gynaecologists would like to treat women who are positive, but are unable to do so due to pressure from the junior support staff. But this is not the only reason why AIDS has become a "government disease". Unfortunately, doctors in the private sector not only routinely refuse to treat patients with HIV/AIDS, they inform patients of their status and then refuse to treat them, referring them to the civil hospital.

Provision of routine medical care for a wide range of diseases in India is mostly in the private sector. Government health centres throughout the county have failed to provide people with basic health care. The investment made by the public sector in health care gets wasted because of improper planning, financing and organization of the health care delivery system.

Theoretically, India has a wide variety of health care services available to its population. At one extreme there are the high-technology hospitals and diagnostic centres (both private and public) in metropolitan cities, and at the other, one has village health guides, folk-healers, faith healers and quacks in remote village. Between these two extremes there are district general hospitals (civil hospitals), private hospitals, 'trust' hospitals, consulting and general private practitioner dispensaries and clinics (allopathic, ayurvedic and homeopathic) rural/cottage hospitals, primary health centres and sub-centres.[12]

The problem, however, is that they are sharply polarized economically. Thus while the rich have access to the best of medical care, the poor have to either access an indifferent, if not hostile, ineffective public health system or pay exorbitant fees to access the private sector in health care, often of a dubious nature. Since many private facilities refuse patients with HIV/AIDS, they have no recourse but the government health services where access to even opportunistic infection treatment is a nightmare.

Government Policies: A Targeted Approach

And what is the state government doing in this context? Since 1986, when AIDS was first reported in Maharashtra, the response of the government has centred on controlling HIV transmission from high risk groups—such as sex workers, truck drivers and those who attend STD clinics—to the general population. This was the stated approach of the Maharashtra AIDS control programme from 1992–1999. But it is quite apparent that the approach has not worked. To see why, it is become necessary to analyse government policy in relation to the rights of women affected by the virus.

Maharashtra has a population of 7,12,00,000 and is the third largest state in India according to its size. According to the 1991 census there were 934 women for every 1000 men and a little over half the women (52.3 per cent) were literate. The state government claims that its health infrastructure compares favourably with other Indian states. For every 100,000 persons

[12]Ravi Duggal, "The Private Health Sector in India: Nature, Trends and a Critique," www.cehat.org

in Maharashtra, there are 1,587 doctors and for every 1,000 persons, there are 1.5 hospital beds. There are 21 district hospitals, 1,699 primary health centres, 9,725 sub-centres, 309 community health centres and 34 medical colleges run by the state.

But in Maharashtra, as in the rest of the country, health has not been a priority for the government. The proportion of GDP spent on health has been declining steadily over the years—while curiously, that for family planning has been proportionately increasing. Within the budget on health, expenditure on public health has been abysmal. India is thus one of the countries with the lowest public health spending in the world. After the initiation of the structural adjustment programme, public health spending has further declined, especially marked in the programmes for the control of communicable diseases. As a result the health infrastructure is weak, if not dysfunctional. This forces people to seek the private sector, whether or not they can afford it. It is thus not surprising that in the nineties health spending has emerged as the leading cause of indebtedness in the country.

Economically, socially and educationally, the state is much better off than many other states in the country. But this neglect of public health characterizes Maharashtra also. Moreover Maharashtra is among the states with the highest incidence of HIV prevalence in the country.

Disastrous First Phase: 1992-1998

With the help of the WHO, the Maharashtra state government, launched the first phase of its AIDS control programme only in 1992, six years after the first AIDS patient was reported in Mumbai! This was to run through 1998. The foundation for the failure of the programme was laid in the delayed reaction itself. Also, the powers that be were not willing to accept that the problem was inextricably linked to wider problems of development, of poverty, of women's powerlessness and indeed of sexuality. Instead, they preferred to see it as a problem of sex workers. This understanding was reflected in policy which only focused on what it perceived as high-risk behaviour groups. The Mangals of Sangli did not stand a chance.

"If an attempt had been made to get out of the targeted high risk behaviour group approach, government programmes would have met with considerable success," says Meena Saraswati Seshu of Sangram, a Sangli-based HIV/AIDS prevention centre. Adds Medha Gadgil, Deputy Director of the Maharashtra State AIDS Control Society (MSACS): "There was no alternative to reaching out to rural women and housewives through awareness campaigns. The first phase was unsuccessful because it was confined to sex workers." The government claimed to have started its programme by farming out the work to some voluntary organizations. But this was not really done. "Voluntary Organizations that did not have the capacity were awarded several projects. Such organizations could not deliver the goods. With a view to merely completing the programme, several projects were sanctioned only on paper," says Nanasaheb Patil, the state Health Secretary.

One significant feature of the years of economic reform has been not only the withdrawal of the State, but the burgeoning of NGOs. While some NGOs have indeed remarkable achievements to their credit—in service delivery, in initiating innovative programmes, in creating alternative models and approaches, and in conscientization—the same cannot be said of a large number of organizations that have come up in the name of AIDS-prevention.

The State machinery, on its part, could not even reach the sex workers that they hoped to target. Organizations like Sangram, which have been working in Sangli for twelve years, have found that the administration is neither helpful nor one that inspires enthusiasm. Take the example of condoms. Though Sangram distributed 350,000 condoms each month (provided free by the government) very often the condoms were in short supply and, in 1995 in particular, were of such poor quality that reports of tearing and breaking were very common. Things were so bad that the matter had to be brought before the then health minister.

What was considered to be the nation's first centre for the rehabilitation of HIV-positive sex workers' was set up in Sangli in 1993. According to the Maharashtra State AIDS Control Society report, this centre failed as the apparently healthy sex workers did not find it to be an acceptable option. Also, those who ran the centre had no ideas on how to "rehabilitate" HIV positive sex workers. The women who ran away from the centre said, "the centre was like a prison and we did not need rehabilitation, much less in the last stages of our lives."

"There were many problems at the level of the state machinery while implementing programmes," says Mr Patil, the seniormost health bureaucrat in the state. "There is fear and negativism regarding HIV in government-run hospitals resulting in discrimination against HIV positive patients and not providing good medical facilities for them. The employees of government hospitals are also not sensitive to the issue and several district surgeons refused to even once visit the areas in which the sex workers operated. In such areas there was no question of the AIDS control programme being effectively implemented," he adds.

This is true of the rest of the country since the early years of anti-AIDS activities created an extraordinary fear of AIDS which translated at times into violence against the victims of the disease. Indeed Kerala, the state most advanced in health and literacy, shot into the limelight in the eighties when women with AIDS were lynched to death in several villages.

"Those who worked at the government level had very little social commitment. Such people did not appreciate the gravity of the situation. Consequently, adequate attention was not paid to the problem. Even the existing facilities were not adequately utilized.... There was pessimism with regard to providing medical services. This was a general complaint. Several doctors were not full-timers," says Patil. He reiterates that a major proportion of the blame for the failure of the first phase could be laid at the door of government officials working in the field. Not only were health services not provided, they were also not sensitive to the issue of AIDS.

But not enough was done to sensitize doctors either. This also meant that no attention was paid to the iatrogenic spread of the disease. Thus doctors were not taught that the AIDS virus could be very easily killed by routine sterilization. At the same time the medical industry stepped in with television campaigns for disposable syringes. Thus a poor country like India saw doctors pushing disposable syringes, while routine sterilization and aseptic measures were neglected. Another consequence of the vertical approach to disease control and prevention was that the funds for AIDS control did not strengthen the system as a whole. According to a MSACS report, the reason for the failure of the first phase of the programme can be attributed to the lack of basic medical infrastructure, the failure of voluntary organizations and the lack of coordination among various programmes. Among the other technical reasons cited for the failure are lack of sex education and sensitivity, failure to adequately use the media and the lack of competence of those working in the state medical services.

The Second Phase

The state government, through the MSACS, took an interest free loan of Rs 177.68 crores, from the World Bank to chalk out a second phase of the AIDS control programme for all its districts, excluding Mumbai. However, it has become increasingly evident that the second phase merely seeks to modify the earlier programme and ensure that it is implemented efficiently. Says Gadgil, "..all the measures necessary for preventing AIDS will be implemented in a coordinated manner, with provisions ranging from the treatment of the high risk behaviour group to the rehabilitation of AIDS patients through hospitals". Despite evidence that the concentration on high-risk behaviour groups has not really paid off, the government has not seen fit to change track. The situation today is critical because HIV is no longer confined to high-risk behaviour groups.

A long-term five year plan in the second phase does aim at an adequate supply of condoms, improving the quality of condoms through research, promoting research on a prophylactic for women and reaching 40 million people through publicity in the next five years. It envisages promoting awareness among 20 million women and disseminating information among schools, colleges and the youth. It also aims to set in place a mechanism to oversee the HIV/AIDS control programme and to provide medical services and treatment at home to patients. But these are not on the priority list at the moment.

Targeted interventions that are based on the assumption that sex workers, truck drivers and street children are vulnerable populations are still being given top priority. Women, the general population, antenatal mothers, blood donors, students and the youth are still considered populations at a lower risk of contacting HIV. The programme document for the period 1999–2004 still says that the spread of HIV into the latter populations can be reduced by merely "controlling HIV transmissions from high risk behaviour groups".

Collectives of women organized by Seshu's Sangram helped sex workers insist that their clients use condoms. "But now it is important to promote awareness about unsafe sex among housewives. They suffer because none of them has the right to decide about safe/unsafe sex. Unfortunately, the government is still holding on to the old approach that believes that high-risk behaviour groups are the vectors for the spread of HIV. This will prove to be another mistake," she adds.

Says Amrita, a housewife whose husband died of AIDS: "Once labelled as HIV positive, our situation is much worse. Without access to health services, with no information, no counselling services, no welfare measures or any system of social support. That is our fate." Sangram has now begun its own programme to reach out to the general public, mainly women. Of the 713 villages in Sangli district, Sangram's activists have reached 610. By conducting special programmes for the 18-28 age groups, some 800 activists have been created at the village level, says Seshu. Sexuality education is a must, but unfortunately the government is sidelining this aspect because of political reasons, she adds. Indeed, recently the Health Minister, a votary of a new right-wing morality, has not made things easier by arguing that advertisements for condoms violated Indian customs and traditions.

One element that has come to light after the first phase is that the concern regarding the perils of AIDS has not really percolated down to the district level. The government itself admits this. "People have also lost confidence in government health services", says Shashikant Mane, Project Officer, Sangram. "Most of the cases who come for counselling to our centre are those who have been turned down by the government hospital," he adds.

Nanasahib Patil says that there is a need for coordination in most government hospitals between STI specialists and gynaecologists. Because of the lack of coordination patients do not get proper advice and treatment. And with the new plan emphasis on high risk behaviour groups, prevention, care and support for ordinary women affected by the virus is a far cry, he adds.

Conclusion

The study of women's lives reflects the increasing trend in rural areas of using HIV/AIDS as an excuse to deny women their rights to property, to their children, to information, to work, to access medical treatment, to alimony. The list will continue to add up if an immediate and prompt reassessment of the needs of women affected by HIV/AIDS is not prioritized by both society and the State.

For its part, the State has failed to realize the devastating impact of HIV/AIDS on the social and economic lives of women. While it has become a "government disease" in that the main access to health care is through government-run hospitals with many private practitioners refusing to treat patients, government health workers are not sensitized to this problem. There is still stigmatization, ignorance, and the refusal of treatment, stemming perhaps from the state government's insistence on concentrating on high risk behaviour groups as vectors of the disease. Within society and the State, there is no recognition of the role of women as care-givers and no means of support for women struggling to bring up families that have lost their male providers to the disease.

On the prevention front, despite a visible policy failure, the government continues to treat HIV/ AIDS as merely a medical problem—its planning, programme and implementation all betray this mindset. It does not take into account the special vulnerability and the needs of women or the lack of information, differential access to health care and concepts of personal modesty that prevent women from seeking access to government health services.

Community based interventions are lacking as are special IEC programmes for housewives and ordinary women. In prevention, in treatment and in care, women have to combat double discrimination based on both gender and stigmatization of the disease.

The Land of Vanishing Girls

Sex Selective Abortion in Punjab

Manisha Bhalla

"Gur khain pooni kattin
Aap na aain, veere nu ghallin."
"Now don't come again yourself,
But send your brother."

In days gone by, women in Punjab would sing this ditty as they took a new-born girl for burial, having snuffed out her life by making her choke on a grain of rice, or giving her a heavy dose of opium, or drowning her in cold water.

There is considerable documentation that shows that female infanticide has existed among certain clans in Punjab since the early nineteenth century. But what we see there today is something different, something quite new: the sex selective abortion (SSA) of female foetuses, something that is prevalent among all castes.

Punjab—the land of five rivers—is known for its robust, hard-working people and its agricultural and industrial progress and prosperity. In material terms, Punjab has progressed economically and industrially, and ranks among India's more affluent states. It is the cradle of the country's Green Revolution in the 1960s that remarkably increased agricultural production and incomes through the introduction of high-yielding wheat varieties, high fertilizer application and mechanized farming.

As the state notches up its economic successes every year, it wipes out more and more baby girls from its land, considering them an economic burden. The lush green fields that are a symbol of India's Green Revolution are also the ruthless killing fields of baby girls.

"Those eyes follow me still," says a traumatized mother whose husband and in-laws forced her to abort her female foetus in an advanced stage of pregnancy. She is still haunted by the sight of the struggling, partially developed, foetus that jerked out of her prematurely and was throttled by her in-laws. To the mother, it was as if her hapless daughter was appealing to her to save her life.

Even today, as soon as a daughter is born, the family remarks, "*Patthar janm paya*" or "a stone is born." A pregnant woman is blessed with "*Rabb changi cheez deve*" or "May God give you a good thing (a son)". Old women console a mother of a newborn daughter, "*Koi na, rabb changi cheez vi devega*" or "Don't worry. God will bless you with a good thing also." If a son is born after two or more daughters, there is the relieved remark, "*Chalo, kudian dhakian gaiyan*" or "The girls have been compensated for, at last".

"*Munde Khet Vich, Kudi Ret Vich*", goes a saying in Punjab's Malwa region. It means, "A boy is meant for the fields, a girl should be buried in the sand."

The female male ratio (FMR) in the world—that is the number of females per thousand males—is 990. Western Europe has a figure of 1,064 females per thousand males and Africa, 1,015. Asia as a whole has FMRs of 953, but India shares extremely negative sex ratios with a number of her neighbours in Asia. Values of less than 950 females per thousand males are found in countries of West Asia, Pakistan, India, Bangladesh, China and the Koreas, an arc of anti-female countries, cutting across religions.

The Punjab Paradox

Punjab today presents a paradox. Compared to most Indian states, it has witnessed rapid agricultural and industrial growth. The state boasts of one of the highest per capita incomes in India.

The rural population has declined from 71 per cent in 1991 to 66 per cent in 2001, while urbanization has increased from

23 per cent in 1991 to 34 per cent in 2001. There is improvement in the overall literacy figures from 58.85 per cent in 1991 to 69.95 per cent in 2001. Female literacy has risen from 50.41 per cent in 1991 to 63.55 per cent in 2001. Health conditions have improved, with a decline in the infant and child mortality rates. The IMR is 57.1 compared to the All-India figure of 67.6 and the UFMR is 72.1 compared to the All-India figure of 94.9.[1] The percentage of children under three years of age and undernourished is 28.7 per cent compared to the All-India figure of 47 per cent. On paper, women have a reservation of 33 per cent in elected seats to municipal bodies and in village panchayats.

But the number of women has shrunk alarmingly. The trend was evident in 1991 when there were only 882 women for every 1000 men in Punjab, compared to the national FMR of 927:1000.[2] By 2001, the ratio further declined to 874 women for every 1000 men in Punjab. The Chandigarh-based Centre for Research in Rural and Industrial Development (CRID) says an estimated 90,000 cases of female SSA occur each year in the state, mostly done under family pressure. Ninety per cent of those surveyed by CRID in an ongoing survey wanted to have sons alone and sought sex determination tests to eliminate female foetuses.

In India, there has been a steady decline of the sex ratio over the 20th century. The 1901 census showed 972 females per thousand males. It declined steadily to 946 in 1951, 941 in 1961, and 930 in 1971. The 1981 Census threw up a happy figure of 934 females per thousand males. The optimistic thought this indicated a halt in the decline in the sex ratio. The 1991 figure however put paid to this optimism: it revealed a further decline to 927.

The 1981 figure, it is now accepted by demographers, was caused by a significant under-counting of females due to a

[1]International Institute of Population Sciences (2000), *National Family Health Survey 1998-99*, Mumbai.

[2]Premi, M.K. (2001), "The Missing Girl Child", *Economic and Political Weekly*, Vol.XXXVI, No.21, May.

decline in the quality of the 1971 census. Demographers are agreed that the 1991 and 2001 Censuses are free from this problem. This is to say that the 2001 census figures, of 933 females per thousand males, are real and indicative of an improvement in the overall survival of females. Have we then turned the corner?

The Sex Ratio could turn feminine simply because more men than women have migrated. But the Juvenile or Child Sex Ratio (CSR) is not subjected to this limitation. And it is this that is deeply worrying. Despite the slight overall improvement in the SR, the CSR in India as a whole has declined from 945 in 1991 to 927 in 2001.

This decline in the CSR has been particularly notable in Himachal Pradesh (897), Punjab (793), Chandigarh (845), Haryana (820) and Delhi (865). In all these states, referred to as the Bermuda triangle for missing females, the number of female children per thousand male children in the 0–6 years age group declined by more than 50 between 1991 and 2001. Gujarat and Maharashtra have also unfortunately joined this group of states.

A part of the declining CSR is due to continuing anti-female rates of infant and child mortality. But more significantly there has also been a marked masculinization of the Sex Ratio at Birth (SRB). In India a figure of 105 male births for 100 female births is considered the norm. However, estimates of the SRB for 1998 reveal an all-India figure of 111 males per 100 females. This is indicative of sex-selective abortion of females. Figures above this national average are seen in Gujarat (113.9), Haryana (123.3), Punjab (122.8), Rajasthan (114.8) and Uttar Pradesh (118).

A 2003 report simply titled "Missing", by the United Nations Population Fund (UNFPA), Ministry of Health and Family Welfare and the Census Commissioner, which mapped the adverse CSRs in India captures the decline in the number of girls.[3] In Punjab, all districts except Nawanshahr recorded a

[3]UNFPA (2003), *Missing: Mapping the Adverse Child Sex Ratio in India*, New Delhi.

CSR of less than 900 girls to 1000 boys in 1991; Nawanshahr was the only district to have a CSR of 900. By 2001, none of the districts recorded more than 850 girls.

Thus is 1991 the district of Gurdaspur had a CSR of 878, Hoshiarpur 884, Nawanshahr 900, Jalandhar 886, Kapurthala 879, Amritsar 861, Moga 867, Faridkot 865, Firozpur 887, Muktsar 858, Bathinda 860, Ludhiana 877, Sangrur 873, Roopnagar 884, Patiala 871 and Mansa 873.

In 2001, 10 of the 17 districts recorded a CSR of less than 800 girls for every 1000 boys. Fatehgarh Sahib has the lowest CSR—merely 754 girls to 1000 boys. In other districts it was 775 in Gurdaspur, 810 in Hoshiarpur, 783 in Amritsar, 775 in Kapurthala, 797 in Jalandhar, 810 in Nawanshahr, 805 in Faridkot, 819 in Moga, 819 in Firozpur, 807 in Muktsar, 779 in Bathinda, 814 in Ludhiana, 784 in Sangrur, 779 in Mansa, 770 in Patiala and 791 in Roopnagar. These are truly remarkable declines in CSRs within the space of just 10 years.

Rupan Deol Bajaj, Finance Commissioner and Principal Secretary to the Government of Punjab and ex-Director, Census of Punjab, says this social evil is getting worse. According to her, and bearing in mind the incomplete registration of births and deaths in Punjab, the total number of missing daughters in the 0-6 years age group is 3,52,792. As per the 2001 Census, she said, the total number of children was 30,55,492, with 17,04,142 males and 13,51,350 females.

A National Family Health Survey from 1992-93 showed that in Punjab, almost 59 per cent of women wanted their next child to be a son. Only 6 per cent wanted their next child to be a daughter.

The Land and the People

There are 3 distinct regions in Punjab—Majha, Malwa and Doaba. Majha, that lies close to the international border with Pakistan, is the hub of trade and commerce. Smuggling thrives through the porous border. Doaba, known locally as the "NRI belt" for its considerably large numbers of Non Resident Indians (NRIs) who have migrated out of the country, has a high influx of foreign earnings. Agriculture dominates the Malwa region that was the first to witness the Green Revolution and the consequent improvement in the living standards of its people in the 1960s.

Comparatively, the plight of the women is better in the NRI-dominated Doaba that has higher literacy rates. For example, in 2001, the literacy rate ranged between 74 and 81 per cent in the Doaba region, compared to 52 and 78 per cent in Malwa and from 68 to 74 per cent in Majha. But the plight of women is deplorable in the Majha and Malwa regions, especially the Majha region that is close to the international border.

Punjab has historically served as the gateway to India for invaders who came from the northwest, whether it was the Greeks or the Mughals. Women were often vulnerable targets for invading troops, leading to the custom of veiling women—a practice that is still followed in the region. Parents preferred to marry off their daughters young, to rid themselves of the responsibility of protecting them from the invaders. But this of course is only a very partial explanation.

The Emperor's Mother

The tendency to get rid of daughters continues, indeed it has spread and deepened. The history of Punjab is replete with incidents of female infanticide. The inhuman tradition of killing a baby girl and burying her with a song appealing for a son continued till Guru Nanak, the founder of Sikhism, raised his voice against the practice in the 15th century. Asked Nanak, "*So kyon manda aakhiye, jit jamme rajan*?"—"Why condemn women when they have begotten emperors?"

It is widely believed that Raj Kaur, mother of one of the most famous kings of the state, Maharaja Ranjit Singh who ruled the state in the 18th century, narrowly escaped death soon after she was born. She was put into a pitcher after her birth and buried, when a soothsayer visited the royal court and prophesized, "The girl you have just buried is destined to bear a son who will become a king and illuminate the name of the dynasty." So the pitcher was dug out and fortunately the baby girl was still alive.

But that was Raj Kaur who was allowed to live because of the prophecy that she would bear a son who would be a famous king. Other baby girls are not so fortunate.

The only difference is that the methods to eliminate them have changed over time. Where a female was once killed after her birth, she is now killed even before she is born. With advances in medical technology, the sex of a foetus is determined during a mother's pregnancy and female babies are selectively aborted.

Dr Vina Mazumdar of the Centre for Women's Development Studies, New Delhi, who was one of the key members of the path-breaking report of the Committee on the Status of Women in India *Towards Equality*, says that SSA has spread like an epidemic these last few years with increasing consumerism. She also pointed out that it has, in fact, spread to new areas and communities and has widespread social support.

Dowry: The Bane of Women

The main reason for parents not wanting to have a daughter is the new turn to the old social custom of giving a huge dowry with the bride. Despite the fact that Sikhism provides for excommunication of those who kill daughters and the Sikh code of conduct also prohibits dowry,[4] there is no stopping people who have hit upon dowry at the time of a son's marriage as the quickest way to social and economic mobility.

But the problem of dowry has taken new forms, spread to new castes and communities. What was once largely an upper caste custom has spread to other castes as they sanskritize or move upwards in the social scale. Thus, today, the greed for dowry is prevalent in all religions, castes and classes across the state, as is true elsewhere in India. The result is that parents decide to kill their daughters as a way out of paying huge

[4]Simran, Kaur (1991), *Prasidh Sikh Bibiyan*, Amritsar, Singh Brothers.

dowries that they cannot afford. The strict societal and patriarchal structures leave no room for education or economic independence of a girl, or for allowing her to marry someone of her choice without paying a dowry.

"The demand for dowry is increasing sharply lately. Punjabis no longer gift a Maruti car at their daughter's marriage. There is a race for bigger and costlier cars now. An expenditure ranging from Rs. 500,000 to Rs. 10,00,000 incurred on a single marriage is widespread now. A lower middle-class person spends up to Rs. 200,000," observes Surinder Kaur Grewal, chairperson of the Punjab Women's Commission.

Along with cars, a range of other expensive goods are demanded, from washing machines to DVDs to microwave ovens, the latest wide-screen televisions, music systems, mixies and so on. This, of course, is in addition to expensive clothing, cash and jewellery, and indeed flats or land. The expenses do not stop there. Heavy amounts are spent later, on every festive occasion, after marriage, points out Grewal. Clothes, ornaments and household goods are demanded by the daughter's in-laws on all these occasions. Even if someone dies in the daughter's married family, her parents have to pay for the food served after the cremation, or give a gold ring or chain to the parents-in-law and clothes to other in-laws. "So having a daughter means an additional life-long expenditure," says Grewal.

How deeply the dowry system has penetrated Punjab society can be gauged by the case of Harkishanpura village that was one of the earliest areas to taste the fruits of the Green Revolution. Today the entire village is mortgaged in debts amounting to more than Rs 40 million incurred due to increasing losses of its cotton crop, destroyed by the American caterpillar pest. But farmers of Harkishanpura continue to buy tractors—not for farming but to give as dowry for their daughters' marriages even if they are steeped in debt. Some have opted to commit suicide, leaving behind wives and children to cope on their own.

According to Renuka Dagar, a researcher with the an NGO called Institute for Development Communication (IDC), the

Green Revolution has only made matters worse. Higher productivity and rural incomes have led to more greed for money and flashier lifestyles. The landowners too, are keen that they have only sons who can inherit their property, thanks to the patriarchal system that prevails. Girls are discouraged from studies or taking up jobs and denied any property rights.

Rupan Deol Bajaj links the phenomenon of female SSA to property rights. She says that girls are not provided their share in ancestral property. The logic is that in order to prevent fragmentation of landholdings, daughters are provided with dowry. Although, in the Hindu Succession Act—under the personal laws of our country, Sikhs are also counted as Hindus—girls are provided full property rights, this does not apply to property that has been earned, and in Punjab, not to agricultural property either. The fact that a daughter is considered to belong to the in-law's family also adds to the idea that daughters are not equal and need not have equal property rights.

Girls who do not bring sufficient dowry are subjected to humiliation and even physical abuse. The higher the education or income of a boy, or the social status of his family, the higher is the dowry demanded. The girls do not and cannot protest. Indeed some girls see dowries as guaranteeing them respect and security in their in-law's home, despite huge evidence to the contrary.

In 2000, the Punjab unit of the Voluntary Health Association of India (VHAI) organized two meetings in Patiala and Fatehgarh Sahib districts to gather feedback from local communities on why the girl child is killed even before her birth. The participants identified dowry as the major reason for the prevailing trend. Other reasons cited were family lineage, sociocultural and economic factors, funeral rituals and the population control policy that advocates a two-child norm. One ironic finding from Punjab is that the practice is more prevalent among the better-off and the better educated.

Dagar says that for every one case of in-laws' harassment for dowry that is registered, 299 go unregistered. An IDC survey in Punjab in 2000 showed that for every one registered dowry death, 27 are unregistered. Further, the survey revealed that one out every two households harassed their daughters-in-law for dowry and every fourth household reported wife beating for dowry.

A report by the Punjab Women's Commission which surveyed crimes against women from March 2002 to March 2003 showed 232 registered cases of dowry, 241 cases of domestic violence, 66 cases of property-related denial of rights, 44 cases of extra marital affairs and 35 cases of sexual harassment at the workplace. This is, of course, a gross underestimation but nevertheless a pointer to the low dignity and status accorded to women in society.

Festivities for a Son, Mourning for a Daughter

In Punjab, women who bear sons command more respect. Wedding-like festivities running into hundreds of thousands of rupees are arranged on the occasion of a son's birth. The parents of the daughter-in-law have to purchase clothes for her, her in-laws and the newborn. Gifts are showered on the married daughter for an entire year after the birth of a son. The mother of the newborn son is allowed to rest for three months after delivery and served delicacies and nutritious food. The in-laws are ready to serve her day and night.

Contrast this with the scene when a daughter is born. There is an air of gloom and mourning in the family. Visitors come to the family to console the mother, "Do not get disheartened. There may be some delay in the abode of the Almighty, but there is never an injustice." The mother is not given a proper diet and she starts doing the household chores a few days after delivery, with an air of one atoning for her sins. The baby girl, too, is not fed properly. There is a rising trend of women being divorced for not bearing a son.

The Jats, the traditional landowning community, are the predominant community in Punjab. A daughter among Jats is considered *begana dhan* or "another's wealth". She is to be guarded by the parents as a liability and "disposed" off as quickly as possible. If two or three girl children are born in a Jat family, they are given names such as *Rajji* indicating "we are satisfied with daughters now", or *Akki* indicating "we are fed up with the girls" or *Kauri* meaning "bitter". Women are blessed by the elders in the family only when they give birth to a son.

Popular sayings mirror social attitudes towards girls. These include "*Dheeyan walean da sir neewan*" or "Those who have daughters cannot hold up their needs"; "*Kudian tan apne ghar chalian jangian munde nal nishani the jandi hai*" or "Girls leave everything and go to their own (married) homes. With boys, the seed of the family tree is maintained."; "*Putte chahe nanga phire, dhee nu tan jammdi nu tinn kappde chahide ne*" or "Boys may roam unclad in the streets, but a girl requires three clothes immediately after birth." Girls are often referred to as stones or heaps of garbage. Given this attitude, killing a baby girl is considered the done thing—and there is no remorse.

For Punjabis, a daughter is not counted as a child. A woman from Bhatinda, when asked how many children she had, replied, "Two children and a daughter"

Sex Determination to Pre-empt the Birth of Girls

Modern medical technology has added a further twist to the saga of vanishing girls in Punjab. Earlier a family waited for the birth of the baby to see whether it was a son or a daughter. Modern medical technology now makes it possible to detect the sex of the unborn child. Unscrupulous doctors have cashed in, offering their medical expertise to get rid of baby girls even before they are born, giving rise to increasing incidence of SSA.

SSA was first documented in India in the 1970s with the advent of amniocentesis. In this technique, a bit of the amniotic fluid surrounding the foetus in the womb is taken out and its chromosomes—coiled structures within a cell's nucleus which contain the genetic material—analysed. Chromosomal analysis of amniotic fluid was developed originally for the diagnosis of genetic disorders, but in India it almost immediately began to be used in genetic clinics for determining the sex of the unborn child. Private foetal sex determination clinics were first established in the north-western and western states of India and the practice of selective abortions of female foetuses became popular in the 1970s and early 1980s.

One of the earliest studies on the subject found 430 of 450 women in an urban clinic who, when told that the sex of the baby was female, wanted to have an abortion. In contrast, all 250 cases where the baby was male continued with the pregnancy, even with the risk of genetic disorders.[5]

The use of amniocentesis remained largely confined to urban areas. It was only with the increasing availability of ultrasound machines in the mid-1980s that sex-determination became widespread. Here an ultrasound image helps find out the genital formation and determine the sex of the baby. But unlike amniocentesis which is done at around 13-14 weeks, ultrasound imaging for foetal sex determination is done much later at around 18-20 weeks, which makes abortion riskier. Also, ultrasound imaging is less reliable.

Chorionic villi biopsy is relatively expensive and can be conducted at eight weeks of pregnancy, with 90-95 per cent accuracy.

Newer technologies now allow sex selection prior to conception. These use methods to separate the X-and Y-chromosome bearing sperms and use the preferred sperm for In-Vitro Fertilization (IVF) (that is, fertilization of the egg or sperm outside the body in a laboratory) or artificial insemination. Methods to determine the sex of the embryo prior to implantation, followed by IVF are becoming a more accurate, though an expensive, alternative.

Sabu M. George, a health activist who has worked extensively on SSA and was one of the petitioners to the Supreme Court, says that the law would work if there was ethical medical practice. According to George, SSA is still going on though

[5]Oomman, Nandini and Bela R. Ganatra, (2002), "Sex Selection: The Systematic Elimination of Girls", *Reproductive Health Matters,* Vol.10, No.19.

not so blatantly. The only difference is that after Supreme Court attention this has become expensive. In Delhi, he added, 30 per cent of the ultrasound centres are not even registered. One of the weaknesses has been the failure to regulate the private sector, and the inability of the IMA (Indian Medical Association) to inculcate ethical practice.

The PNDT Act—and its Loopholes

In an attempt to prevent SSA, India enacted the Pre-Natal Diagnostic Techniques (Regulation and Prevention of Misuse) Act in1994, which came into force in 1996. This was one of the major successes of the women's and health movements in the country. The Act bans determination and disclosure of the sex of the foetus, as well as advertisements on pre-natal sex determination, and prescribes punishment for its contravention.

The Act provides for three years imprisonment or a fine of Rs. 10,000 or both for first time violators, and five years imprisonment and a fine of Rs. 50,000 for those who violate the law more than once. The law specifically stipulates that a woman can undergo a pre-natal diagnostic test under the following conditions:

i. the age of the pregnant woman is above 35 years;
ii. the pregnant woman has undergone two or more spontaneous abortions or foetal loss;
iii. the pregnant woman has been exposed to potentially teratogenic agents such as drugs, radiation, infection or chemicals;
iv. the pregnant woman or her spouse has a family history of mental retardation or physical deformities such as spasticity or any other genetic disease;
v. any other condition as may be specified by the Board.

Once the government became stricter with amniocentesis tests, doctors started misusing ultrasound tests to detect the sex of the foetus. When the Indian Government included ultrasound tests in the purview of the PNDT in 2000 and made it mandatory for all doctors owning ultrasound machines for gynaecological purposes to register themselves formally, the tests went underground and became much more costly.

Couples are willing to pay four to five times more for the clandestine tests. A test that cost Rs. 500 earlier now costs between Rs1,500 and Rs. 2,000, while Medical Termination of Pregnancy (MTP) costs Rs 5,000. But couples are willing to pay more money rather than change their attitude.

Under section 3 of the PNDT Act, only a person who possesses a medical qualification recognized under the Indian Medical Council Act, 1956, or who has a post-graduate qualification in ultarsonography or imaging technology or radiology can conduct ultrasound tests.

Similarly MTP can only be done by a qualified doctor or gynaecologist who should also be registered in the state medical register and who should have conducted at least 25 MTPs during training.

A clause under this section specifically states, "no person including a relative or husband of a woman shall seek or encourage the conduct of any sex-selection technique on her or him or both."

Section 5 of the Act says "no person including the person conducting prenatal diagnostic procedures shall communicate to the pregnant woman concerned or her relatives or any other person the sex of the foetus by words, signs or in any other manner."

Religious authorities in the state too have pitched in to raise their voice against female SSA. Sikh religious authorities issued an order, known locally as *hukumnama*, on April 18, 2001 against the practice of female foeticide.

But the ground reality is different. Even illiterate midwives handle ultrasound machines, disclose the sex of the unborn child and conduct sex-selective abortions, says Grewal.

Earlier clinical laboratories advertised in newspapers "Invest Rs 500 and Save Rs 500,000", meaning an ultrasound test costing Rs 500 will help one know the sex of the unborn child and aborting a female foetus will help save Rs 500,000 on the wedding expenses later. The Punjab Health Department has now banned such advertisements under the PNDT Act and violators can be sentenced to three years imprisonment. But the advertisements continue to appear in Punjab-based dailies, couched in different words.

The law against disclosing the sex of the foetus is not followed in most parts of the state. Doctors may not use the words "boy" or "girl" explicitly, but the phrases they use are revealing. Phrases such as "No problem, try again next time. God will definitely shower His grace on you," or "Lakshmi has come. Don't worry or lose heart. A huge expenditure is in store for you," imply a girl, while sentences like "Sweeten our mouths (for the good news we will give)", "Go and be merry. Keep fit", "Everything is okay", "Take care of your wife", "Well, you have saved Rs 500,000" indicate a boy.

Rise in incomes has led to almost every household owning a television set and gaining access to more medical information. This has helped increase knowledge on medical facilities like ultrasound devices that can help detect the sex of an unborn child. So the business of ultrasound machines for sex determination continues to flourish, even if on the sly. So high is the demand for such services that mobile vans fitted with ultrasound machines do the rounds of villages, points out D P S Sandhu, Director of Punjab Health Services.

Couples also take advantage of loopholes in the Medical Termination of Pregnancy Act, 1971, which allows abortion in case of pregnancy due to contraceptive failure. Once they realize a daughter is to be born, couples pretend there has been a contraceptive failure and seek abortion. The Punjab Health Department recently suggested making the procedure more stringent by making it mandatory for all ultrasound machine owners to record names and contact details of those seeking ultrasound tests and tracking them.

Midwives, traditional birth attendants and ANMs have played a key role in popularizing the ultrasound tests for sex detection, according to Dr Rameshwar, former Director of Health Services in Punjab. Satwant Kaur, a midwife in a village for the past 30 years, says: "The (ultrasound) clinic people approach us offering us a commission. If a test costs Rs. 650, our commission is Rs. 250." Lured by such commissions, midwives have spread awareness among villagers on the ultrasound machines and even campaigned for specific doctors to grab their commissions. They take the pregnant women to ultrasound clinics and once the sex of the foetus is known, some midwives themselves conduct the abortion. Others take the woman to a nursing home for an abortion, pocketing some more commission.

The PNDT has failed to break the nexus between midwives, ultrasound clinics and nursing homes in most areas. Some midwives say they are under immense pressure by powerful local politicians to take their daughters-in-law for sex determination tests.

Most women in rural Punjab prefer the services of midwives as the state of the government health services is unsatisfactory. The primary health centres in the state are in none too good a condition, points out Manmohan Sharma, Executive Director of the Voluntary Health Association of Punjab. "Where there are doctors, there are no medicines, and where there medicines there are no doctors," says Sharma. Most women consider any ailment their bad luck and prefer to stay away from government doctors. In any case, it is not the public system that provides them SSA.

Women: Mute Partners

"Several micro-studies have shown that women themselves accept and endorse sex selection. But a deeper look reveals how loaded the choices are," say Nandini Oomman and Bela Ganatra, two independent researchers, in *Reproductive Health Matters.*[6] The decision is often a response to intense pressure to produce male heirs, often through implicit threats of violence or the husband's remarriage. Most women make their

[6]Oomman, Nandini and Bela R. Ganatra, (2002), *op. cit.*

choices in the context of their families and the patriarchal system that does not favour the birth of a female child.

Some feminists refer to the issue in terms of reproductive rights and choice, ironically justifying SSA. The argument goes that people have no use for abstract concepts as sex ratios. The lives of Indian women were so terrible that this technology offered them an element of choice, indeed of empowerment. Over time a decline in the supply of girls might improve the demand for girls and thus their status.

What this argument misses out is the extremely important point that women are not in fact exercising agency when they exercise this "right" to SSA.

Take the case of Surinder Kaur, a resident of Kalamajra village in Fatehgarh Sahib district of Punjab. Surinder Kaur was the first woman to be arrested last year under the Pre-Natal Diagnostics Test Act, 1994 that bans SSA. She was charged with burying her three-month-old female foetus in a small pit in her cattle shed. Initially, says Surinder, she had an abdominal pain three months after conception. The village nurse gave her an injection. "I don't know when the child was taken out of my belly," she says. She suspects the village nurse has a grudge against her and has aborted her baby.

But one visit to Surinder's home and the true story emerges. Two sisters-in-law, older than her and into menopause, flank Surinder. The three women have already borne seven daughters. The two older sisters-in-law have no hope of begetting another child. So it is up to Surinder to bear the cherished son—and certainly not another daughter. Surinder looks blank, but her sister-in-law asserts, "The girls have to leave for their in-laws' house after marriage, the sons keeps the family tree flourishing." She adds, "we are poor people, with just six *killas*[7] of land. People have become greedy and we are afraid of dowry."

A little while later, Surinder asks sadly, "We have to further our lineage. How can the Jats do without a son? Moreover,

[7]*One killa* is equivalent to one acre of land.

from where can we arrange the dowry for daughters?," She had no choice or say in her decision—it was a collective family decision and she was pressurized by her husband and in-laws.

Says Jaswant Kaur, a resident of Surinder's village. "Marrying daughters is a problem. We have only five *killas* of land. The daughters will go to their in-laws. The sons may or may not respect you, but at least there will be no problem of getting two square meals a day." Surinder and Jaswant echo the views of over 200 women I interviewed during the course of this study.

A 1995 IDC report "Life Enhancing Mechanism", too, attributes the high incidence of female SSA in Punjab to dowry.

A Ray of Hope?

In February 2000, Sabu George, and two NGOs, Centre for Enquiry into Health and Allied Themes (CEHAT) in Mumbai and Mahila Sarvangeen Utkarsh Mandal (MASUM) in Pune, filed a public interest petition in the Supreme Court against the government's non-implementation of the PNDT Act. The petition also called for inclusion of all emerging technologies that can be abused to eliminate girls under the purview of the Act.

One of these is the Pre-Implantation Genetic Diagnosis (PGD) that is also called Ericsson's technique. Here eggs are fertilized with active sperms in a laboratory petri-dish, the eight-celled embryo that forms after 72 hours is tested for sex chromosomes and only the male embryo implanted back into a woman.

The petitioners acted after seeing advertisements of clinics in leading dailies of Punjab, Haryana and Tamil Nadu, which offered sperm separation and sex selection before conception.

In an interim judgement delivered in May 2001, the Supreme Court directed state governments to implement the Act more strictly. Following the Court's directives, state governments have undertaken awareness raising campaigns on the issue.

In December 2001, the Court directed manufacturers of ultrasound machines to provide information on their customers over the last five years. In January 2002, the Court asked three professional medical associations to provide lists of all members who use these machines.

One outcome has been the awareness campaigns undertaken by the government with the help of religious leaders. The IMA, UNICEF and the NCW organized a national meeting, with religious leaders from all communities. Madhu Kishwar, a leading feminist, using the language of the World Bank, argued in the *Times of India* on July 17, 2001 that it is necessary to involve so-called religious leaders in a campaign against female foeticide since it is cost-effective.

This has its critics. Says Dr Mohan Rao of Jawaharlal Nehru University, New Delhi: "No amount of 'cost effectiveness' justifies marching along these self-appointed religious leaders, who are the struts of patriarchy and some of whom are, the proponents of worse, of appalling murderous evil. We cannot sup with the Devil, just because he quotes the scriptures." Pointing out that this meeting had been taken over by Sadhvi Rithambara, known for her leading role in Anti-Muslim pogroms, he added that leading women's groups such as the All India Democratic Women's Association (AIDWA), and health groups such as the Jan Swasthya Andolan, who had been leading a campaign against SSA boycotted this meeting.

Brinda Karat of AIDWA adds, "All religions are anti-women. None of them has gender equity on the agenda; all are equally opposed to property rights for women. This is at the root of anti-female attitudes and practices in the country."

The National Human Rights Commission (NHRC) has taken up the programme of administering oaths to doctors not to indulge in SSA. But the IMA is not, unfortunately, putting its own house in order. Neither are there discussions on ethics in medical education nor are medical students sensitized to issues of gender. What is also curious is that apparently more and more obstetricians are marrying radiologists.

A recent study on abortion in Maharashtra found that a large number of doctors were performing SSA even though they knew it had been banned.[8] Their reasons were many: that it was for the woman's sake, to save her from illegal abortions; that if they didn't do it, other doctors would; above all that it was for the good of the country since it brought down population growth. Curiously, a large number of respondents in a study on female infanticide in Salem district also explicitly stated this. The women interviewed felt that they could not use many modern contraceptives as it interfered with their ability to work in the fields. What they were doing, they argued, was "traditional" and achieved precisely what the Government of India wanted. Yet another study in Mumbai revealed that a majority of doctors performing sex-selective abortions stated that they did so in order to control population growth.[9]

What we have, then, is profit making hand-in-hand with population policies, with a dose of concern for the health of women and a bit of hypocrisy to make a deadly cocktail. What is left unsaid is the whole issue of the position of women, their lack of rights to property, to equality, to citizenship, in a country that supposedly worships women.

---

[8]Bandewar, Sunita (2003), "Abortion Services and Providers' Perceptions: Gender Dimensions", *Economic and Political Weekly*, Vol.XXXVIII, No.21, May.

[9]FRCH study cited in Jyotsna Agnihotri Gupta (2000), *New Reproductive Technologies, Women's Health and Autonomy: Freedom or Dependency?*, New Delhi, Sage.

Quick-fix Medical Ethics

Quinacrine Sterilizations and the Ethics of Contraceptive Trials

RAJASHRI DASGUPTA

Every afternoon, when people in the industrial town of Phuleswar in West Bengal are deep in siesta, women quietly squeeze into the chamber of "Doctor" Chandi Charan Pramanik, an unregistered medical practitioner. They come looking tense and embarrassed, clutching a friend or neighbour for support. They come in search of the promised miracle that will rid them of the burden of pregnancy—for life—within minutes.

Local women call the method "injection". It requires no surgery. There are no tell-tale marks on the woman's abdomen for the husband to find out. Nor can a prying mother-in-law detect anything amiss because it requires no hospitalization. Widely known as the quick-fix method, it is chemical sterilization by the anti-malarial drug, quinacrine.

It is a method that was banned by the Supreme Court of India in 1998 following intense campaigns by women's groups in several parts of the country and a public interest petition by the All India Democratic Women's Association and the public health faculty of Jawaharlal Nehru University, New Delhi.[1] Even earlier, in June 1994, the WHO Special Programme of Research Development and Research Training in Human Reproduction (WHO/HRP) had warned researchers to immediately stop quinacrine trials on women all over the world.

WHO was categorical that quinacrine sterilization (QS) was not approved by any national drug regulatory authority in the

[1]Following the advice of the Drugs Technical Advisory Board, the Supreme Court banned QS. But Section 10 of Drugs and Cosmetics Act contains loopholes, since terms are ambiguous and thus leaves scope for misuse.

world. It urged researchers to first complete laboratory and animal studies, essential steps towards the development of a new drug, and test the toxicity and carcinogenicity of quinacrine "before further studies are carried out on women". Giuseppe Benagiano, director of HRP wrote to the *Lancet*, " The high standards for safety in testing and use of contraceptives should apply whether the subjects recruited to the studies are from the developed or the developing world."[2]

Says Pramanik, a high-school pass, "QS is popular because it takes two minutes to sterilize a woman. Come see my operation theatre." The "operation theatre" adjoining his chamber is a poky dark room with a high wooden collapsible bed, a bench and an enormous tin trunk. Instruments for the "injection" and other operations (mainly abortions) are bunched together in a covered metal bucket. In one corner of the room, a much-used towel hangs limply near a plastic water tank. The pillow is dirty with hair-oil stains left by his numerous patients.

Another practitioner who enjoys a roaring practice is the affable Madhavanandan Bairagi of Julpia village. Like Pramanik, Bairagi is a friendly neighbourhood doctor with a pill for every ill. "I specialize in breast cancer. I also have medicines so that women can have a son," claims Bairagi. Women from across the international border in Bangladesh seek his expertise in QS. "I am world famous and have done more than 30,000 QS," he says. Bairagi has expanded his medical practice by teaching his younger brother QS.

Rural practitioners like Bairagi and Pramanik combine traditional medicines with a smattering of knowledge about allopathic drugs, and are part of a vast network of unregistered "doctors". In the absence of adequate public health services, their easy availability and accessibility makes the community dependent on them, and the fact they are locals, makes them trusted members of the community. The local NGO Nishtha, that works in the area surrounding Julpia, testifies to

[2]Benagiano, Giuseppe, (1994) "Sterilization by quinacrine" (Letter), *Lancet* 344 (3 Sept).

the popularity of Bairagi and the quick-fix method among agricultural workers since the late seventies. The older women who took Bairagi's "injection" now encourage their own daughters to visit him after "completing their family".

Bairagi allowed Jhumma payments in instalments because she is poor and Mohua is given the second course of QS free of cost because she became pregnant even after undergoing the procedure a few years ago. Said Ashalata, a grandmother at 40, "I got a discount fee for my daughter because I have undergone QS myself by him." Usha too, bargained about the fee, "I am an old patient and since I have undergone two abortions at his hands, he agreed." Pramanik promises commission to women who bring in patients regularly for QS or abortion. And in Tripura, PS Thakur offers each woman the equivalent of five months' family income to report any pregnancy following QS and a free abortion service.

The practitioners are enterprising and use creative methods to encourage women to opt for QS and to expand their practice. They are indebted and sing paeans to the "Dr Sir" from Kolkata who has trained them in QS and the philanthropy of a "sahib" from a distant land who provides the necessary quinacrine pellets.

Quinacrine for a Quick-fix

Quinacrine sterilization is a non-surgical, permanent sterilization by the synthetic anti-malarial chemical. It is popular among women because it does not require surgery or hospitalization. Women who have undergone QS say that they can continue with household chores without "bed rest or good diet as is needed in the case of surgical sterilization". They can get it done quickly and easily without the knowledge of family elders. This is important to the women, particularly in a society where they are valued only as mothers, and male-dictated cultural, social and religious pressures force them into repeated pregnancies.

All that is required for QS are quinacrine pellets and an intrauterine inserter that women generally mistake to be an injection syringe. Rural medical practitioners themselves promote QS as an "injection" since women are familiar with the word and are not afraid of it. "It does not arouse suspicion or cause alarm in the family and community, it is acceptable to them," says Pramanik.[3]

For QS, the clinician guides the inserter containing seven cylindrical-shaped quinacrine pellets (dosage varies between 216 to 324 mg) through the vagina and the cervix deep into the uterus. The pellets are then placed at the top of the uterus and the inserter is withdrawn. Quinacrine is a sclerosing agent. This means that as the pellets dissolve in the uterus, they cause inflammation and form scabs in the uterine lining. The scar tissues block the inner end of the fallopian tubes and prevent the sperm from reaching the ovum after sexual intercourse. To ensure complete blockage of the tubes, insertion of the pellets is repeated once or twice after a month's interval. During this period, additional contraceptives are advised till the fallopian tubes are completely blocked.

In the seventies, Dr Jaime Zipper of Chile, the scientist behind the invention of QS, had injected quinacrine solution into the uterus of Chilean women and observed whether they could still become pregnant. When they suffered severe adverse reactions, he switched to quinacrine pellets. He was following the lead of doctors in Nazi Germany who experimented with women in concentration camps. The doctors used a range of chemicals to damage their uterus and fallopian tubes in order to render them infertile.[4]

Independent studies in the US indicate that quinacrine causes cells to mutate. This is circumstantial evidence that it

[3]Sanjeev Mukherjee, a gynaecologlist maintains that the medical establishment has successfully created an "injection culture" and for the non-literate population any treatment that comes through the needle is considered "superior".

[4]Will, Annette, (1997) "Quick fix Sterilizations—Widespread Abuse of Quinacrine", Women's Global Network for Reproductive Rights, *Newsletter* 59.

may cause cancer, say some scientists. According to the WHO, between 60 and 80 per cent of known mutagens are cancer causing.[5] The risk of administering contraceptives or untested methods like QS to women who later become pregnant has to be viewed with even more caution as it can affect the progeny.

The effect can be mutagenic due to the alteration of the genetic composition of the ovum leading to chromosomal anomalies like Down's syndrome in children, says epidemiologist Dr C Sathymala who has worked extensively on hazarduous contraceptives.[6] "Drugs can also pass through breast milk and delayed effects can make their appearance decades later."

Pramanik says the failure rate of QS is around 3 per cent but among the Indian doctors interviewed, none could guatantee the physical and mental health of babies born to women who have undergone QS.[7] "We have not received any complaints," they say. But this does not indicate that all is well, say social workers, mothers may not be aware enough to link their children's problems with the QS they had undergone years ago.

Women who discontinue the QS course after receiving only one insertion can become pregnant and also face the potential danger of ectopic or tubal pregnancy. "Since the QS method is crude and imprecise, no one can control where and which way the uterine tissues will get damaged and whether the tubal blockage is complete," says Shree Mulay, Director of the Centre for Research and Teaching on Women at McGill Univer-

[5]Freedman, Alix M. (1998) "Two Americans Export Chemical Sterilization", *Wall Street Journal*, June 18.

[6]C Sathyamala is the author of, *An Epidemiological Review of the Injectable Contraceptive, Depo Provera*. Published by Medico Friends Circle, 2000.

[7]In the 1960s, congenital malformations were induced in children born to women taking an anti-emetic drug Thalodomide during pregnancy. Another powerful synthetic hormone prescribed to pregnant women was Diethystilbesterol or DES for threatened abortions led to "DES daughters". These were daughters whose mothers had taken the drug and who were exposed to it in the uterus as a result of which they developed a rare form of cancer of the vagina later in life.

sity, Canada. In the absence of adequate health infrastructure and where poor women lack resources, tubal pregnancy could prove to be life threatening.

Another area of concern is that women in the early stages of pregnancy might unwittingly seek QS that can trigger off severe bleeding and abortion of the foetus. None of the women interviewed said the practitioner enquired or advised medical investigations about health problems before the QS procedure. Yet the website promoting the method cautions that QS should not be used or should be delayed if the woman suffers from, among others, severe cervicitis, intermenstrual bleeding, pelvic inflammation, uterine fibroids, purulent discharge, problems that are common among poor women.

The International Planned Parenthood Federation, numerous scientists and women's health advocates have expressed serious reservations about the safety and efficacy of QS in low health care settings since the procedure requires at least two or three insertions to be fully effective.[8] It is difficult to ensure adequate follow-up where women may not have the time or the financial resources to return for a second or third visit.

The short-term side effects of QS are headaches, abdominal cramps, fever, yellow pungent smelling discharge, lower back pain, pain during urination, vaginal itching and irritation. "But these are transient and minor," says New Delhi based Dr J K Jain, one of the most ardent promoters of QS in the country. Jain, a former Bharatiya Janta Party (BJP) Member of Parliament, and a surgeon by profession, adroitly merges the business interest of running a media empire with his medical duties. "Within a few days, the women will be healthy," he adds.

But for 34-year-old Nafisa of Tekiapara industrial town, a mother of four who has had QS at the hands of Pramanik, the pain is neither transient nor minor. "The pain sits on my abdo-

[8]Reproductive Health Technologies Project, 2002. *The Quinacrine and Beyond – Exploring the Challenges of Reproductive Health Technology Development and Introduction.* A report from the meeting convened in April 2001.

men like a stone. I have spent a fortune, got a sonography done and taken medicines, but nothing seems to work. My whole life is a misery of pain," she says desperately.

In 1997, four women who had undergone QS at Bairagi's hands visited Dr Sanjeev Mukherjee, a gynaecologist at the Bangur Hospital, Kolkata. Their complaint was "failing health" and "drying up" of the body, says Dr Mukherjee, who has shown interest in following up QS patients. Of the women, Maya's uterus had completely dried up. "It had atrophied, something I have never seen in my 20 years of practice," he says. The four women looked frail, worn out and unwell. One suffered from continuous fever. "Her husband suspects QS to be the cause because it is only after that that she fell ill. Without scientific studies it is difficult to determine whether her failing health is the result of QS," he says.

Despite inadequate research data on the toxicity of quinacrine in humans, and the warning by the WHO, widespread QS trials on Third World women continue unabated. More than 100,000 women in 20 developing countries have been sterilized by this method. The countries include Bangladesh, Chile and China.[9] In Vietnam, the Ministry of Health and a US-based NGO, Family Health International (FHI), which sponsors QS, conducted a retrospective study of more than 1,600 women who had undergone QS in 1994. The results are yet to be published.

Illegal Trials

In India, women and health activists have opposed QS because of the illegal and unethical nature of the human trials, and its dubious history as an intrauterine agent for non-surgical female sterilization. Among the concerns raised is the widespread use of poor and non-literate women as trial subjects

---

[9]Rao, Mohan (2001) "The Rhetoric of Reproductive Rights: Quinacrine Sterilization in India", in Imrana Qadeer *et al* (Eds.), *Public Health and the Poverty of Reforms: South Asia at the Turn of the Century*, New Delhi, Sage.

without informed consent. Concerns were also raised about the lack of safety testing and the shoddy quality of existing data on the method. Activists argue that the use of QS is a "textbook example" of how, in the name of providing a wider range of reproductive choice, generations of women in developing countries are targeted for sterilization in order to meet political ends, that is to reduce the fertility of "problem populations." Said journalist and health activist Laxmi Murthy, "QS follows a trajectory fraught with inertia and controversy and we cannot divorce it from the history of abuse and attempts to control population in our country."

It was in this spirit that the faculty of the Centre for Social Medicine and Community Health, at Jawaharlal Nehru University, Delhi and the All India Democratic Women's Association (AIDWA) filed a public writ petition in the Supreme Court. In response, the Court in 1998 directed the Drug Controller of India (DCI) to ban QS but the order was limited as the court refused to prosecute the guilty and made only future violations punishable. The Supreme Court also did not address the issue of follow-up, care and compensation to those already sterilized raised in the PIL.

Rules for the conduct of research in India require the DCI's approval for any drug trials. The Indian Drugs and Cosmetics Act lays down norms to test any new drug or method before it can be launched for widespread use. Contraceptive (and other drug) trials begin with laboratory tests followed by animal studies and then controlled trials in human beings in several phases to find out the safety, efficacy and dosage of the drug. "There is no question of allowing quinacrine's routine use on women and for trials," says DCI, Partha Dasgupta.

Despite the Court ban, the use of QS continues in pockets of rural West Bengal while there is lack of information about other parts of the country. For more than two decades Indian women in slums and rural areas have been soft targets of worldwide human trials of QS. Apart from the rural practitioners, there are city-based private doctors who have been promoting and experimenting with the number of quinacrine pellets.

the strength of the quinacrine dose and the method of insertion to establish the efficacy of QS. Dr A Ghosh, former head of the department of gynaecology of a state-run hospital, conducted trials on 300 women and offered QS in his private chamber. "Its so easy even the ayah can do it," he says.

It is the rural practitioners like Pramanik and Bairagi who are pivotal to the entire operations as they have access to a large female population. Their major contributions to the trials have been that they are conduits of information and their experiences with QS women are invaluable data for advocates of QS. Among the leading advocates are the 'sahib' and the "Kolkata Sir" who visit the rural centres and have set up a system to receive the information regularly, which is then analysed and presented at international conferences to gain acceptance and legitimacy for QS method.

The "Kolkata Sir" is the towering septuagenarian, Dr Biral Mullick, who claims to have trained thousands of rural practitioners in West Bengal in QS. His chamber in crowded central Kolkata is the headquarters of the dubious Indian Rural Medical Association (IRMA), set up in the late 1970s. IRMA, according to Pramanik, has a membership of more than 40,000 practitioners "all over India", but mainly from West Bengal. Here for a fee, Mullick trains practitioners in QS and abortions. Thakur who is "grateful" to Mullick for training him in QS in 1990 later returned to Tripura to initiate trials on 611 women and kept "careful records" on each case which were later sent to IRMA[10].

Abortion is legal in the country but only qualified, registered practitioners are allowed to conduct the operation. Since government clinics are absent in many areas, rural practitioners are keen to offer abortion service and make "quick money". As abortion for women remains shrouded in social stigma and taboo, the "quick and secret" services provided by the rural practitioners make them popular. "I teach the doctors how to perform abortions because women who seek QS are not al-

[10]Thakur, *Quinacrine Sterilization in Tripura, India.* www.quinacrine.org.

ways aware they are pregnant. If QS is done during a pregnancy, it can cause heavy bleeding. As a routine we advise a woman to undergo a 'wash' if she is uncertain," says Mullick whose operation theatre is no better than Pramanik's hole.

In 1979 Dr Zipper himself visited Calcutta to propagate the QS method of birth control. It was a period in the country's history when the government was aggressively promoting its family planning programmes and viewed the rapid growth of the country's population as the primary source of all its ills from poverty to unemployment and illiteracy.

Mullick was savvy enough to understand the potential of QS in the background of the country's agenda of population control. Most of his patients were Muslim women who were relieved because of the confidentiality of the method since some interpretations of Islamic texts come down heavily on sterilization. "They breed like any poor women and there is no stopping them," says Mullick denigratingly. "What will become of the country?" He even deliberately seeks out Muslim women, assuming they will be more willing and pliable because of their social and religious circumstances.

With the women completely in the dark about its potential hazards, Mullick gained invaluable experience by trying out the new method on them. Based on his trials, Mullick says he figured out the required dosage of quinacrine pellets and the number of insertions required for complete sterilization. He also determined that pellet insertion should be deep into the uterus and if the woman bleeds during the procedure, the sterilizing effect is nullified." My own research is focused on development of a single insertion protocol so that there is no chance of women missing an insertion. There is no way to follow-up with these women because I do not have the records or the money," says he. "If the women have any problems, they will come to me."

Though exact figures are hard to determine as the practice is unregulated, according to Mullick in West Bengal alone, more than 10,000 women are estimated to have undergone QS since the seventies. Since the Supreme Court ban, QS use has gone underground, and this means that the price has shot up almost three times from Rs 500 to Rs 1,500 for the three-course insertion. But even today, women do not know that they are part of so-called drug trial or that QS has been banned and could have harmful effects on their health.

International Links

The person actively promoting QS in the international arena and reaping even bigger benefits is the "sahib" behind the quinacrine pellet supplies—Dr. Elton Kessel, the consultant behind the creation of IRMA in Kolkata. He and his partner, Dr Stephen Mumford, run a two-man institute, the evocatively named Centre for Research on Population and Security (CRPS) set up 1984 in the US. The two elderly Americans from North Carolina are ardent advocates of QS and have devoted their entire lives to fight the growing population in developing countries and the threat of increasing immigrants in developed countries.

In an interview with Alix Friedman of the *Wall Street Journal*, Dr Mumford admitted that he saw birth control as a means of reducing the potential number of immigrants from developing countries to the US. "This explosion in numbers will come entirely from immigrants and their offspring and will dominate our lives. There will be chaos and anarchy. . .it's even more serious than the nuclear threat." Kessel, speaking to me in Kolkata in November 1998 said, " The threat of immigrants invading and taking over is real, they are swarming all over and draining the resources. Look at the chaos in your eastern region with thousands coming in from Bangladesh and in the USA, Mexicans and Carribeans are pouring in. No civilized government, neither yours or mine, can allow this."

It is thus not surprising that Kessel and Mumford receive support from right-wing anti-immigration lobbies like the Federation for American Immigration Reform (FAIR). Among quinacrine's most devoted fund raisers is the Washington-based Epstein couple who are also on the board of the Federation for American Immigration Reform, a strident anti-immigrant group. "I feel like a missionary because quinacrine is something that can help Third World poor women help themselves," says Sally Epstien. Other rich anti-immigration foundations have provided thousands of dollars to the quinacrine kitty.[11]

Couched in "developmentese" and feminist jargon, well-known doctors espouse the cause of quinacrine at international conferences and scientific fora. Dr J K Jain promotes QS as a "safe" family planning method that provides "an option to women with their informed consent". Dr Pravin Kini, who sends free samples of quinacrine pellets to the medical fraternity in Bangalore, sees QS as a panacea that can "liberate" poor women of the developing world from the tyranny of repeated pregnancies and abortions. Dr C S Dawn of Kolkata argues that the method should be supported against the powerful lobby of manufacturers of surgical equipment in the West. It is this lobby, he claims, that is discrediting QS for their own profits.

The advocacy kit of QS is packaged and championed as the method that can "prevent maternal deaths" and make a dent in the very high figure of 50,000 impoverished women who die from pregnancy-related complications in India each year. "In a developing country with low contraceptive prevalence and high maternal mortality, the benefits of QS are considerable, as a new contraceptive method can raise contraceptive prevalence and thereby lower maternal deaths," says Dr Kessel. If each additional sterilization prevents two pregnancies and maternal mortality is 5 per 1,000 live births, then each 1,000 additional QS procedures prevent approximately 10 maternal deaths, he argues.

Following Kessel's logic, every woman should be sterilized to prevent risk of maternal deaths. Moreover, Kessel's argument is scientifically flawed: the fact is that women at risk of maternal death who want a baby are a much bigger group than those who do not. "The risks and benefits of a steriliza-

[11]Freedman, Alix M (1998), *Op cit.*

tion method should only be compared with those of other sterilization methods, not with the risks of maternity," said Mulay.

The QS lobby that promotes the method because it is "ideal" for developing countries, never addresses the poor quality of health care services plagued by lack of resources, lop-sided priorities, poorly trained staff and poor outreach. The primary health care levels in the rural areas where 80 per cent of the country's population reside, are grossly inadequate to deal with simple ailments like malaria or diarrhoea, and are inaccessible due to poor communication or are unaffordable to the poor.

'Their concern is not for making delivery services safer for women. Women die not because of lack of contraception, but due to lack of safe delivery systems before and during child birth," said Imrana Qadeer of the Centre for Social Medicine and Community Health, Jawaharlal Nehru University, New Delhi. Women frequently lack access to simple ante-natal and post-natal care which could save many lives, insists Qadeer.

In India, anaemia affects more than half the female population and malnutrition is rampant. Yet women are forced to continue to have children till a son is born because girls are not considered as important as boys. Says Sarojini of SAMA, a resource centre for women and health, that as long as women are treated as reproductive machines—both by society and the population controllers—and have no position in the family save as mothers, as long as they are kept out of decision-making processes, they will be in no position to plan their families.

Hidden Agenda

Women in developing countries have been targeted for generations with a range of reproductive technologies like QS which supposedly improve their reproductive health and provide contraceptive choice. But in reality, say activists, these are thinly disguised agendas to promote aggressive population control policies, not to increase women's freedom. Birth control as a woman's right has been submerged under the rhetoric of family planning as a "patriotic duty" the "national interest".

In the case of QS, as in most other contraceptive trials, the agenda can easily be traced to the international population lobby consisting of private-government-academic-corporate support that sees the "population explosion" in the developing world as a "threat" to the wealthy north. Kessel-Mumford are mere path followers advocating "population control in developing countries and immigrant control in rich countries".

The lobby with its population fixation has never questioned the impoverished lifestyles of women and the social and gender inequality that supports high fertility and leaves the majority of women with little choice in marriage, sex and reproduction. The focus on "population as a problem" is a device of national governments and the international population lobby to shift attention from the urgent issues of food security, unemployment, rising costs of education and health.

"This view (of the population lobby) ignores the historical basis of poverty and demographic change in the developing world," says economist Sushil Khanna of Indian Institute of Management, Kolkata. "Centuries of colonial rule and enforced globalization have sucked out investible resources through a process of unequal trade. In the new global order, control over natural resources remains confined within the structure of global corporations," he adds.

It is this ideology, rather than concerns for women's welfare, that has shaped family planning programmes in developing countries including India. As a consequence, population control programmes have come to reflect a combination of big business (involving millions of dollars) and political interests.

Women became the chief targets of research for contraceptives designed to be highly effective, long lasting and independent of a woman's control, says Dr Sathyamala. In other words, it was decided that birth control was too important to be dependent on a woman's remembering to take the pill or using the contraceptive improperly. Whether a woman could stop using the contraceptive when she wished, was not at all a priority. By the 80s, the ICMR joined the bandwagon and participated in trials on hormonal injectables, implants and anti-fertility vaccines for women.

For pharmaceutical companies it is big business and though exact figures are not available, the US contraceptive market in the 1980s for the oral pill was $ 520 million whereas the worldwide market was estimated at $ 700 million to $ 1 billion. For the long effecting contraceptives, the global sales for Depo Provera were about $ 250 million in 2000 and increased by 20 per cent in 2001. The Pharmacia & Upjohn company, manufacturers of injectables, spent $ 7.7 million alone on advertisements in magazines and TV spots in the first six month of starting the campaign in the US, unusual for a drug that is almost 40 years old.[12]

The Indian State has always placed the greatest responsibility for preventing pregnancy on Indian women. In the 60s, women were forced to accept IUDs. This quickly shifted to contraceptive pills once IUDs were found to be defective and caused severe side effects, says Badri Saxena.[13]. According to a report in 1993, $ 5 million worth of defective IUDs were imported into India from an American firm, after "pressure seems to have been exerted to get the ministry (Health and Family Welfare) to lower its standard and accept the consignment."[14]

"For the population lobby, the issue of the development and promotion of contraceptives is more important than women's safety and health. This bypasses the challenge of providing and building up basic health care services and equipping the population, especially women, with the skills and knowledge necessary to make rational choices," says Mohan Rao of

[12]SAMA (2003), *Unveiled Realities: A study on Women's Experiences with Depo Provera, an Injectable Contraceptive*, New Delhi.

[13]IUDs were introduced into a programme plagued by poorly trained staff and poor sanitation. Women were "motivated" to adopt IUDs in the absence of technical competence for sterile insertion.

[14]The report was refuted by the president of the firm in *Reproductive Health Matters* No.3 May 1994. Jyotsna Agnihotri Gupta, *op.cit.*

the Jawharlal Nehru University's Centre for Social Medicine and Community Health. Adds economist Navsharan Singh, "The bogey of overpopulation is a smokescreen to cover up the failures of successive governments in the social and economic fields."

Ethical Issues

The 1964 Helsinki Declaration by the World Health Assembly has been revised a number of times to ensure the safety and rights of human subjects participating as volunteers in drug trials. The Declaration clearly states that the interests of humans should take precedence over the interest of science and society. "Freely given informed consent" is one of the basic clauses of this code of ethics that should be obtained from each volunteer prior to the clinical trial. The Declaration also lays down that volunteers should be assured of treatment for any injuries resulting from the trials and have the right to withdraw from the research at any point. This is possible only if they are informed of the purpose of the research and its risk and potential benefits.

But the women who seek QS are neither informed that they are "volunteers" for a drug trial, nor are they told about the experimental nature of the method and its unknown long-term risks. Doctors simply take advantage of their desperate need for contraception and their ignorance.

Sabita who has not only undergone QS herself but taken patients to Pramanik was upset that she was not informed that the method was experimental and its long-term effects still undetermined. "I will have to live with this guilt all my life," she said. "It's only because we are illiterate, people can make fools of us." Bani of Julpia, a mother of five children, looks distinctly uncomfortable when she learns that the government "does not approve" of this method. "And I took my own daughter to Bairagi and I have had it done too. Will I get cancer?" she asks apprehensively. "I thought it was offered by the government. No one told us not to get it done. Is it harmful?" asks

Jhuma. Other Nishtha members look distressed and swear never to refer their relations to Bairagi for sterilization.

Barring a few exceptions, it is the poor, illiterate or semi-literate women of developing countries who are used as guinea pigs for trials of new contraceptives. They can be lured by offers of financial compensation as in the case of the contraceptive pill first tested on Puerto Rican women. Clinical studies have shown that poorly educated and rural women tend to complain significantly less than better-educated ones. The former are given less information than the latter and seek information less actively.[15]

The QS trials are as unethical as the trials for the contraceptives Net-en and Norplant in India. The only difference is that the latter trials were legal and conducted by scientific bodies like the ICMR. But the women who were the "volunteers" for the Net-en and Norplant trials were recruited through family planning clinics and the experimental nature of the contraceptives and the transaction was hidden from them. In 1986 three women's groups, and concerned individuals filed a PIL in the Supreme Court against the ICMR and the Ministry of Health and Family Welfare, among others. The main contentions of the PIL were concerns about Net-en's safety, the unethical manner of the trials and the potential for abuse in family planning programmes.[16]

It was members of a Hyderabad-based women's organization, Stree Shakti Sanghatna who discovered, at a family planning camp, that women were being deceived into accepting the injectable (manufactured by Schering AG of Germany) as an approved method of contraception. The incident brought into focus, for the first time in the country, the social, medical and ethical issues involved in this kind of research and the nexus between the drug companies, scientific establishment and the State.

---

[15]Jyotsna Agnihotri Gupta (2000), *New Reproductive Technologies, Women's Health and Autonomy: Freedom or Dependency?*, New Delhi, Sage.

[16]The writ was filed by the Stree Shakti Sangathana, Hyderabad, Saheli, New Delhi and Chingari, Ahmedabad. The Andhra Pradesh Civil Liberties committee was also one of the petitioners.

The Norplant trials conducted by the Indian Council of Medical Research in Kolkata also confirmed fears about contraceptive trials. The issue of informed consent was blurred, trial protocol was lax, follow up studies absent, records and data backup poor. Most of the "volunteers" were picked up from the hospital family planning department where women had gone to seek family planning services. A signature on the dotted line was what was taken for "informed consent".

Social workers at the prestigious Seth Sukhlal Karnani Memorial hospital in Calcutta say they were relieved because the women "volunteers" were poor and "never asked questions like you". They never told the women that Norplant was experimental. "No one would agree to participate (if we did)", they say. But the Research Officer, Mira Khetri, would insist on informing the patients. "Because of her we lost many of our patients," says Apurba Mukherji, the clerk in charge of the Centre.

Bano, who was only 15 years old, was given Norplant after the birth of her first child. She was never told that it was an experimental method and the doctors themselves seem unaware that a teenager was too young to be on Norplant. Putti, an ayah in the hospital, was also given Norplant and has never forgiven the doctors at the hospital for it. "My hand was very painful and because of it I could not work for years. They refused to take it out. I had to go to a private doctor and spend thousands of rupees," says she. "Norplant is the worst thing that can happen to women after men!"

Well-known gynaecologists of Kolkata admit the complete absence of stringent culture of research protocol and respect towards patients. "Where were the funds to conduct tests?" asks Dr Anil Misra, former head of gynaecology at the government National Medical College about drug trials, asks. "The government sat on research proposals for years", he adds. When drug companies "informally" approached doctors like him to conduct trials in public hospitals, most would agree. They did have access to desperately poor and ill-informed patients.

"Doctors often treated the women like goats," confesses Dr. Dawn, reflecting on the general attitude towards patients. "Most of the women thought doctors were treating them and not doing research on them," says Dr Nagen Ray Choudhury, another leading gynaecologist. "Getting numbers was never a problem in government hospitals. If the women did not come for follow up tests, sorry. They were left out", says Dr Ray Chowdhury.

Informed consent and lack of follow up are not the only issues involved here. "The implicit purpose of the drug trial should be questioned", says women's rights activist and publisher Urvashi Butalia. "Why another new contraceptive? Do the anticipated benefits justify the foreseeable risks? How does one ensure that researchers' intentions are not unduly influenced by funding agencies that have their own agendas?" she asks. Activists argue that scarce resources should not be devoted to further research and development of QS. "Funds should be for improving the dismal state of existing health services," says Navsharan Singh. Moreover, the priority should be to integrate family planning services with the need to combat sexually transmitted diseases.

The Modus Operandi

The modus operandi of the Kessel-Mumford duo in promoting QS is fascinating in its simplicity. They get invited to medical conferences like the one in Kolkata and come loaded with suitcases full of quinacrine pellets, video films and manuals on QS. They spot their target doctors and work on their twin anxieties of overpopulation and deteriorating quality of life. They convince them about the merits of this cheap method and liberally sprinkle "information" about how QS can save mothers in countries like India.

"I don't do anything illegal in your country. I don't personally conduct drug trials. I only provide technical assistance to my doctor friends and I supply them with pellets," says Kessel. "Doctors here feel the benefit of QS for women is more due to the high risk of pregnancy."

During the interview Kessel said that for 15 years he tried to convince the ICMR to accept QS in the government's national family planning programme, but had failed. In 1991 Dr JK Jain, then member of the Indian government's Central Family Welfare Council, introduced QS to I C MR and the following year its then deputy director general, Dr Badri Saxena proposed an ICMR-supervised study. Eight women were enrolled and five of them were sterilized. The three failures were attributed to "violation of the recommended protocol guideline". ICMR however terminated the study as a failure.

Kessel changed track. If the government was not willing to initiate trials and introduce QS in the public family planning programme, Kessel decided to promote the method through private doctors and NGOs. In Kolkata, he targeted Mullick's IRMA and Dawn's National Association for Voluntary Sterilization and Family Welfare of India (NAVSFWI) and in Bangalore, Dr Pravin's Contraceptive and Health Innovations Project (CHIP) that claims to be "in the forefront of a movement to disseminate and encourage the QS method throughout their region".[17] Says Dawn, "In the private health sector, Kessel is not restricted by government diktat and interference and he can utilise our vast medical contacts." According to Kini, although the earnings per patient are lower in QS, the specialists make up the difference in an increased patient volume.[18]

During his 1998 visit, Kessel addressed the NAVSFWI's (now known as NARCHI) annual general meeting in Kolkata to "personally appeal" to doctors to put pressure on the central government to rescind the quinacrine ban.[19] Following the meet-

[17] www.quinacrine.org

[18] www.quinacrine.org

[19] Dawn set up NAVSFWI in the 1970 in response to the political climate in the country that laid stress on sterilization as a means to curb population growth. It has a private "medical college" in Kolkata with over 40 'centres' in the country with hundreds as members. With the 'change in mood' in the country, the organization was renamed appropriately National Association for Reproductive and Child Health in India (NARCHI). For a hefty fee, a diploma in gynaecology and obstetrics can be got from one of the centres.

ing, as secretary general of NARCHI, Dawn appealed to the DCI to rescind the ban on quinacrine but till date they have not heard from the department.

That Kessel-Mumford are also the sole world-wide distributors of quinacrine pellets manufactured by the Swiss pharmaceutical company Sipharm also helps.[20] The quinacrine pellets come cheap at Rs 35 for one insertion and are available in plastic containers of a few hundreds. The distribution centres like IRMA, in turn, sell the pellets to their members. Kessel and Mumford target women from the developing world because drug trials in the U.S. are stringent and expensive. "No pharmaceutical company in the U.S. is willing to touch quinacrine with a bargepole," admits Kessel. "To do toxicity tests will take eight years and cost another eight million dollars. No company is interested because quinacrine cannot be patented," he adds. The Wellcome Trust showed some interest, provided they didn't have to do the toxicity tests, Kessel said.

Another problem, he pointed out, was the difficulty of getting women volunteers for the trials in the US. "We could not even get ten volunteers, even those who were to undergo hysterectomies were unwilling," he said. Since the 1970s, pharmaceutical companies have invested less and less in contraceptive research because of high development costs resulting from more stringent standards to be complied with before registration. [21] Today the pharmaceutical industry does little contraceptive research, most of which is done by NGOs, national governments and international agencies. For example, a drug company in Finland manufactures Norplant, an implantable contraceptive, but clinical trials are under the umbrella of Population Council with the support of WHO. The withdrawal of the industry from direct trials is because it fears an increase in

[20]Kessel maintains that because of the controversy and opposition by women's groups in Switzerland Sipharm has stopped making quinacrine.

[21]Richter, Judith. (1990) *Vaccination Against Pregnancy: Miracle or Mirage?*, London, Zed Books.

financial claims from women who suffer adverse effects from their contraceptives.[22] Of the $155 million spent on contraceptive research throughout the world in 1979, while 58 per cent was spent by the US government, only 9 per cent was spent by the pharmaceutical companies and the remaining by foreign governments and NGOs.

Since 1986, support for clinical trials has been limited to Kessel's International Federation of Family Health, Mumford's CRPS, individual investigators and governments of developing countries that are evaluating the method to determine if it should be included in their service programmes. Following pressure from the WHO, Indonesia and Vietnam stopped the QS programme and in 1998 the method was banned in India and in Chile where it was first pioneered.[23]

But the major setback to the Kessel-Mumford combine was when the Food and Drug Administration (FDA) issued a "warning letter" to Mumford in October 1998 to "immediately halt" all distribution of quinacrine pellets. The letter said that quinacrine should not be imported, manufactured or exported for female sterilization and that the FDA "was unaware of any scientific evidence from adequate and well-controlled studies" that quinacrine was "safe and effective" for female sterilization. FDA urged him to destroy his stock of 290,000 pellets[24]

Skirting the Ban

In a bizzare but ingenious game plan, the advocates of quinacrine are working out a strategy to influence not only

[22]AJ Robins, the firm that developed Dalkon Shield, an intra uterine device, was ordered by the US courts to pay damages to claimants for death and permanent infertility. By 1986, 320,000 claimants filed for damages and the company had to recall every device they had sold.

[23]Foro, a coalition of activist groups in Chile, raised concerns about QS on the grounds of unresolved issues of safety, need for improved informed consent and improved ethics committees.

[24]FDA letter and Mumford's reply supplied by Kessel during the interview in Kolkata,1998.

the FDA strictures, but also the Indian ban. The motive is to sway the Indian government to allow QS because the drug has a better chance of survival among the poor in India rather than among the moneyed and health-conscious women of the US. "India is where the money comes from—the sheer numbers. Donor agencies always try to pressure the government to include various contraceptives in the national family planning programme," says Badri Saxena.

The game plan is to prove QS use and popularity in the US, in the hope that the Indian authorities will assume that what is good for that country is good enough for India. "The US drug law is explicit: if a drug is permitted for one use it can be used for other ailments," says Kessel. Quinacrine is used both against malaria and giardiases. Taking recourse to this clause, Mumford-Kessel now hope to compound quinacrine in US labs under doctors' prescriptions for female sterilizations. To improve the pellet shape, they even plan to send their pharmacist to Sipharm in Switzerland to be trained. "We have consulted our lawyers. There is nothing underhand," says Kessel.

The first batch of pellets was made in Atlanta on November 19, 1998. Health insurance companies in the US are said to have shown interest, according to Kessel. Poor Carribean and Latin American women, not covered under the insurance schemes, are very interested because QS will cost them only $200 against the much costlier surgical sterilization. "My Indian friends tell me that the future of lifting the ban in India will largely depend on the acceptance and use of QS in the US," says Kessel.[25]

Women health activists in India insist that despite FDA sanction of a particular method, in this instance QS, the approval of a drug in the individual country must be based only after critically examining its use in the context of its specific socio-political scenario. "Accepted that FDA regulatory guidelines

---

[25]In 2001, to evaluate the safety and efficacy of QS, the University of Buffalo granted approval for Phase I study to be conducted. It also received FDA approval.

act as a credible standard, but it cannot be a license for a drug or a method's widespread use without taking into account a country's specific health needs and the capacity of the service delivery system," said Qadeer.

In November 1998, 26-year-old Zulekha, a mother of two, unaware of the QS ban, sought Pramanik's help. Pramanik did not tell her that the method was banned nor did he warn her of possible side effects. Instead he impressed her with his "connections" in Kolkata and worldwide. As she lay in Pramanik's room, stiff with fear, Pramanik "told me that he had treated hundreds of women with QS and that the big doctor in Kolkata had personally taught him the method. That the sahib had donated the "injection" and he belonged to a reputed international organization where the Kolkata sir and the sahib are members." Sabita, an employee in Zulekha's husband's factory had recommended Pramanik to her. She herself had undergone QS more than 12 years ago under Pramanik and was "so relieved" that she had stopped having babies that she later took several of her relatives and neighbours to him.

For Pramanik, despite the ban, it was business as usual—with a boost. He charged Zulekha Rs 1,000, of which he passed on Rs 100 to Sabita for bringing Zulekha in. Pramanik pays her every time she brings in a new patient either for QS or for abortions. When Sabita herself underwent QS, she was charged only four hundred and fifty rupees. He has raised charges because the "sahib" is unable to supply the pellets regularly, explains Sabita.

On January 3, 1999 after the third quinacrine insertion, Pramanik gave Zulekha a "prescription" on a printed letterhead embossed with his various "designations". For Zulekha, the chit of paper looks reassuringly official "like they give in a government hospital". In the slip of paper Pramanik wrote the words IUD (Inter Uterine Device), along with Q3, which he has circled.

Zulekha's husband agreed to the procedure because it did not require surgery or tampering with the body which is forbidden by some interpretations of Islam and, moreover, he did not want his mother and large family to know. This confidentiality makes QS an attractive option in developing countries, argue advocates of the method.

Farida Aktar of the NGO UBINIG, Bangladesh questions such reasoning. "In saying QS has an advantage in developing countries, because it is a method which women can hide from their families or religious heads, one does not question unequal gender relations and patriarchal oppression."

Voices of Protest

The 1980s saw the emergence of a strong demand for safer contraception from the women's rights movement in the country and in fact, the writ on Net-en marked the beginning of the health movement among Indian women. In the last two decades there have been campaigns, litigations, posters, workshops, articles and publications on these issues, including on QS. In Kolkata, the Ganatrantik Mahila Samity was instrumental in forcing Mullick to abandon his trials, and in Delhi, AIDWA, the Joint Women's Forum and other groups jointly staged a demonstration at Jain's clinic.

In 1997, Saheli, a Delhi-based group, came out with a detailed report, *Quinacrine—The Sordid Story of Chemical Sterilizations of Women* and the documentaries, *The Human Laboratory* by BBC in 1995 and *The Yellow Haze* in 1997 by Jamia Milia students did much to publicise the unethical practices of QS promoters. The petition for a ban by the Centre for Social Medicine and Community Health and AIDWA took the movement forward.

Also, for the first time in India, there has been a study conducted in West Bengal (to be released very soon) documenting the experiences of women who have undergone QS. Through in-depth interviews with women, followed by a medical exam offered to consenting women, the study probes the socio-economic context in which women are making sterilization choices, the health impact of QS and the issue of easy availibility of QS from private practitioners in the context of the existing public health services.[26]

Contraceptive research is fundamentally different from other drug research, health activist Laxmi Murthy argues, because contraceptives are used by normal, healthy women to prevent a normal physiological process of pregnancy and not for the prevention of disease. "We demand reorientation of contraceptive research so that it takes note of local health care conditions and the position of women in society", says Murthy. In short, it should recognise the need for accessible, affordable, safe and effective contraception, which is different from family planning programmes emanating from ideologies of population control.

The experience of the movement against hazarduous contraceptives has been mixed. On the one hand, while women and health activists have failed to convince scientific bodies to stop unethical trials or monitor such trials or prevent the availability of hazarduous contraceptives in the open market, on the other, they have been successful in preventing the entry of contraceptives like Depo Provera and Norplant into the family planning programme. The two litigations filed by groups in the Supreme Court, of which one was against Net–en, led to the formulations of a set of rules and regulations in drug testing[27] and to the QS ban.

Equally important, stresses Sathymala, the Net–en case set the tone for opposition to other hazarduous contraceptives like Norplant and anti fertility vaccines. "It was instrumental in politically educating an entire generation of feminists and health activists in India on informed consent and patient rights in clinical trials." In the process what has shot into prominence is the debate on the nexus between the pharmaceutical companies,

---

[26]The study has been conducted by Shree Mulay, Navsharan Singh, Rajashri Dasgupta et al. Dr Sanjeev Mukherjee conducted the medical examination of the women who consented.

[27]In September 1988, the Indian Drugs and Cosmetics Act incorporated this as Schedule 'Y'. This is a guideline and requirements for import and manufacture of a new drug.

the international population lobby, donor agencies, medical experts and the Indian State.

Silent Complicity

Untested procedures like QS would never have been possible in the country without the silent complicity of the State, scientific and professional bodies and the drug regulating authorities. Indeed deeply complicit is also the entire middle class of the country.

The open advocacy of an unapproved method like QS for more than two decades has been possible because the government wished to turn a blind eye to it and the elites don't care what happens to poor women as long as their fertility is controlled.

The role of "neutral" bodies like ICMR in the quinacrine saga is also not above board. Dr Mullick proudly shows off a letter from ICMR as "proof" of its approval for his trials. The ICMR invitation to Mullick in May 1992 "in view of your expertise in the area" to discuss possible studies on QS, shows that it was aware of Mullick's unauthorized activities and legitimizes them by giving him recognition. Though ICMR officially withdrew QS trials in 1992 following the failure of the trials, the ICMR-sponsored follow-up study by Dr Anita Sabherwal continued till as late as 1996. Even now, the ICMR has not initiated a probe into the violation of medical ethics involved in QS trials.

In West Bengal, the State Drug Controller, though aware of the continuing use of QS, says there is "nothing" he can do about it. The Central Drug Controller, West Bengal chapter, says his office has banned the drug. "What else is there to do?" he asks. The Director of Health Services of West Bengal said he was not even aware of the ban a good six months after it was imposed. Dr Gauripadda Datta, from the health think tank of the West Bengal government asks, "Where are the women and their complaints about QS?" This despite the fact that a

Marxist, former Member of Parliament led the agitation in Kolkata at Mullick's clinic.

Proponents of QS have always received a boost as they go unchallenged in medical seminars hosted by professional bodies like the Federation of Obstetrics and Gynaecological Society of India (FOGSI) and NAVSFWI (now NARCHI). In 1996 in Agra, Kessel was honoured for his "contributions" at a gynaecological conference and in 1997 he spoke about QS in a scientific conference in Patiala. In November 1998, NAVSFWI held a special session to reopen the debate on QS. No one questioned the data or asked whether ethical procedures had been followed in the human trials.

Says Vasantha Muthuswamy, Member-Secretary, Ethical Committee of Medical Research, ICMR, "Doctors are not fully aware of the issues of ethics because it is not taught seriously in the medical curriculum. Most of the review and ethical committees, essential components in a research team, were only on paper." Moreover, as Mutthuswamy underlines, "The guidelines are not mandatory..there is no legal sanction. No one can be penalized if they do not follow the rules."

Even the 1994 ICMR document on the clinical trials of contraceptives has very little to contribute in terms of ethical issues. While the mandatory steps for contraceptive approval are delineated, there is no mention of the manner in which trial participants should be recruited, consent should be obtained or long term follow up should be done.[28]

The new ICMR guidelines, on clinical trials are silent about contraceptive research. They have not addressed the concerns arising out of their specificities and ensured adequate safeguards. This is essential, firstly because the bulk of the contraceptive research is targeted towards women, a section of our society that already has lower nutritional levels and poor ac-

[28]Srinivasan, Sandhya (2001), "Discussion on Biomedical Research on Humans in India. A Short Review", Paper presented at the Workshop on "Research Ethics in South Asia", Thiruvananthapuram, Achutha Menon Centre for Health Science Studies.

cess to health facilities. Secondly, most of the emerging contraceptive technologies have multi-systemic effects, and require more careful studies in order to ensure their long- term safety vis-à-vis women's health. In addition, of course, is the fact that the impact of such technologies/devices/drugs is not limited only to the health of the research subjects but extends much further and affects the health of future generations.[29]

What is significant is that the ICMR Code, 2000 on Ethical Guidelines on Biomedical Research Involving Human Subjects has watered down the provisions for mandatory informed consent. In the section on International Collaboration/Assistance in Biomedical Research it talks about the "best possible *nationally available* care' instead of *international standards* thereby bypassing adequate safeguards against exploitation of research volunteers from developing countries.

The Code thus apparently follows the recent pressures to modify the Helsinki Declaration to make clinical research easier in developing countries. Among the significant changes sought is to permit "proxy consent" that would eliminate the need for the individual trial participant 's consent by obtaining permission from a government or non- governmental agency. The second change sought in the Declaration is regarding the standard of care to volunteers: it need not be the "best- proven care" but rather "best care available in the country".

The Guidelines and the Code are directed only at the institutions funded by the ICMR and there is no agency to monitor the research by private organizations, or NGOs such as those run by Mullick or Dawn. That is how a doctor in Assam transplanted a pig's heart into a 32-year old man in 1997 without following research protocols or obtaining any permission from any drug authority.

With the opening up of the market economy, and the effort by the drug companies to reduce costs and bypass strict drug

[29]Saheli Women's Resource Centre (1999), *The Consultative Document on Ethical Guidelines on Biomedical Research Involving Human Trials. A Critique and Some Recommendations*, September.

regulatory norms, a higher proportion of drug testing is being moved to Third World countries. According to a report in *The Economist*, India is making a mark in clinical trials and other services for pharmaceutical companies.[30] India's "not-so-healthy" people, the contract research organizations (CROs), the cheaper human power (researchers, nurses and computer staff can be hired at less than one third of western salaries) and faster trials are an advantage to the companies. According to the report, India's "billion potential guinea pigs" also suffer increasingly from ailments which trouble the rich countries such as cancer, heart disease and AIDS.

While foreign CROs have found partners for joint ventures in the country, Indian companies like Nicholas Piramal and Max India have quickly grabbed the opportunity to launch their own clinical- trials business. Piramal's revenues will be around a hundred to a hundred and twenty million rupees within three years, so much so that *The Economist* states the "advantages" look so obvious that it seems a wonder that more companies have not entered the market.

India can emerge as one of the top ten destinations for drug discovery and clinical research in a decade, feels D S Brar, CEO and Managing Director of Ranbaxy Laboratories Limited. He wanted all stakeholders involved in drug research to join together to collectively enable the country to attain this status in the near future.[31]

Another outcome of the liberalized economy has been an attempt to reduce the mandatory steps of clinical trials in the country by substituting post market surveillance for phase III trials as was the case of the sub-dermal Norplant.[32] Since one third of the total funds of $500 million for drug development goes towards clinical trials, "each day saved in testing can bring millions of dollars in extra revenues to the patent's owners";

---

[30]*The Economist* (2000), "Patient Capital: India Promises to Become the World Centre for Testing" *New Medicines*. January 29.

[31]Chronicle Pharmabiz (2003) September 25, Mumbai.

[32]Sathymala, C. (1998), "Hazardous Contraceptives and the Right to Life", *Journal of the Indian Law Institute*, vol. 8,1998.

this is because the life of a patent begins to ebb away from the moment it is filed.[33]

Activists fear that in the absence of vigorous trial guidelines, strong national regulatory agencies and increasing privatization of drug research, accountability is the first victim as corporate profit is the king. QS would then only be a small chapter in an ongoing sordid saga of human exploitation.

[33] *The Economist* (2000), *op.cit.*

Contributors

Mohan Rao teaches at the Centre of Social Medicine and Community Health, Jawaharlal Nehru University, New Delhi. He is the author of *Malthusian Arithmetic: From Population Control to Reproductive Health* (Sage, forthcoming) and has edited the volume *Disinvesting in Health: The World Bank's Prescriptions for Health* (Sage 2000).

Sreelatha Menon is principal correspondent, *Indian Express,* New Delhi. She joined the Cochin edition of *Express* in 1989, and moved to the Delhi edition in 1996. She covers the health and social sectors, as well as rural development. Her stories of sterilization camps in UP were a matter of debate in Parliament.

Sandhya Srinivasan is a freelance journalist with master's degrees in sociology and public health. She writes on health and development issues for Women's Feature Service, Inter Press Service, *The Telegraph* and other publications. She is consultant on health and population to www.infochangeindia.org, a website covering development issues. Since 1998 she has worked as executive editor of *Issues in Medical Ethics* and has received the Ashoka fellowship for writing on medical ethics.

Dhirendra K Jha is a Correspondent with the Delhi edition of *The Pioneer.* He has written extensively on development issues, with a focus on Bihar's migrant agricultural labour. He has received the National Foundation Media Fellowship and the Centre for Science and Environment/Madhya Pradesh Government Fellowship. He has now taken a year's sabbatical to spend time in the field.

GEETANJALI GANGOLI, with a Ph.D. in history from Delhi University, has worked as a freelance journalist with various newspapers and journals including the *Times of India, The Asian Age*, and *The Pioneer*. She has also published frequently in the *Economic and Political Weekly*. She is now an academic and currently works at the School for Policy Studies, University of Bristol, on domestic violence and sex work.

RUPA CHINAI was, till very recently, special correspondent, health, for the *Times of India*. She is currently a freelance journalist writing on issues of public health, development and environment. Working as a newspaper correspondent for over two decades, she has covered these issues for leading Indian newspapers including the *Times of India*, *Indian Express* and *Sunday Observer*.

LYLA BAVADAM has been with *Frontline* magazine since 1996. Prior to that, she worked with *Sunday*, *Blitz* and the *Sunday Observer* and the *Business and Political Observer*. She writes on development issues related to environment and health, and covers political issues in Maharashtra. She was the first recipient of the Bellagio Forum Fellowship for Environmental Studies and the Reuters Foundation Fellowship Programme at Oxford in 2002.

K P M BASHEER is a Cochin-based Correspondent with *The Hindu*. He has written extensively on social issues, human rights, women's rights, and the environment. He has won several awards, including the V Krishnamurthy Award instituted by the Trivandrum Press Club for the Best News Reporter in 1996, and for the best news report and the best feature from the Trivandrum Press Club in 2001 for reports emanating from the Panos fellowship. He also received the Journalist Education Trust Award in 2002.

ANNU ANAND is a senior journalist specializing in development issues. She received her early training in journalism at the Press Trust of India, Bangalore. She has worked for the last decade in New Delhi with *Chauthi Duniya* and *Jansatta*. Currently she is working for the Press Institute of India as Associate Editor for *Grassroots*, a monthly paper on development issues. She is also Associate Editor of *Vidura*, a quarterly magazine on media issues published by the Press Institute.

T K RAJALAKSHMI works as a Principal Correspondent with *Frontline*. She has been with *Frontline* for eight years, writing on critical issues concerning the social sector. Prior to becoming a full-time journalist, she worked as a researcher with the National Commission For Women.

SWATI BHATTACHARJEE is a special correspondent with *Ananda Bazar Patrika*, Kolkata. A postgraduate in philosophy, She has also done an MSc in Media Research from the University of Stirling, UK. She writes on health, with a focus on women and children. Her articles have appeared in national and international publications. She also writes books for children.

VASANT BHOSALE, based in Sangli, is currently News Editor with the Marathi daily, *Pudhari Noe*. He was earlier News Editor of *Dakshin Maharashtra Kesari*. He has reported extensively on farmer's and labour movements and on the rights of beedi workers.

MANISHA BHALLA, the youngest of the Panos fellows, was reporting for the Chandigarh edition of *Dainik Bhaskar* for the last three years; she has just moved to the Delhi edition. Her investigative reports (which form the basis of this essay) prompted the Punjab State Human Rights Commission to issue a far-reaching order that women undergoing SSA are victims and thus not to be prosecuted under the PNDT Act.

RAJASHRI DASGUPTA was till recently Features Editor at the *Telegraph*, Kolkata. She is now working as a freelance journalist, with a special interest in issues relating to gender, health, development and politics. She is active in the women's and peace movements.